THE CAPTAIN'S STEWARD
Falklands, 1982

Barrie Fieldgate

Published by

MELROSE BOOKS

An Imprint of Melrose Press Limited
St Thomas Place, Ely
Cambridgeshire
CB7 4GG, UK
www.melrosebooks.com

FIRST EDITION

Cover designed by Bryan Carpenter

ISBN 978 1905226 46 7

Typeset in XML by Kerrypress Ltd, Luton
http://www.kerrypress.co.uk

Printed and bound in Great Britain by:
CPI Antony Rowe, Bumper's Farm,
Chippenham, Wiltshire, SN14 6LH, UK

THE CAPTAIN'S STEWARD
Falklands, 1982

Barrie Fieldgate

The ship is met by the Mayor and Mayoress of Chester on arrival in Plymouth. Chester is the ship's affiliated city.

The Ship's Company.

Foreword

It is fascinating to read through the following narrative and to appreciate the private thoughts, worries and views of a respected member of HMS Broadsword's company whose main source of information was the never ending supply of lower deck 'buzzes' supplemented by periodic 'Sitreps' from me.

Therefore, the author's comments were largely uncontaminated by the unending flow of signals traffic in and out of the operations room which obviously coloured my own perception of the land, sea and air battle as it developed in the South Atlantic during the conduct of Operation Corporate.

While the author's commentary will obviously be of greatest interest to HMS Broadsword's company during the period from April to July 1982, it will also appeal to a wider readership.

Bill Canning

(Royal Navy Retd) Captain Bill Canning DSO MBE DL
Commanding Officer HMS Broadsword

HMS Broadsword rescuing survivors from HMS Coventry off Pebble Island, West Falkland, after an attack on 25th May 1982.

HMS Broadsword.

Acknowledgements

This book is solely dedicated to the memory to my foster parents, Mr John Vestey and his dear wife Winnie who sadly are no longer with us. Their daughter Pippa and son-in-law Ray Neill took over the tremendous responsibility of raising myself and Tim when we were eight years old, even though they were bringing up four of their own children. Pip and Ray so admirably held this responsibility until I joined the Royal Navy at the age of fifteen years old on the 15th of September 1969.

Further Acknowledgements

1. *Captain Bill Canning DSO, MBE, DL Royal Navy*

    Commanding Officer HMS Broadsword during the 1982 Falklands War and Captain of the Second Frigate Squadron (Captain F2)

2. *Melrose Books in Ely Cambridgeshire: The Commissioning Editors Austin Kehoe and Ross Hilton and their staff: Jill de Laat – Executive Secretary/Sales Manager; Bryan Carpenter – Production Manager and Artist for the book; Sophie Fitzjohn and Tom Brennand – Promotions Co-ordinators along with; Prudence Golding Fuller – Sales Administrator; Sarah Parkin – Sales Administrator and Advertising. A lot of hard and dedicated work has been put into this book by the publishing team to make sure this first edition is ready for publication to commemorate the 25th Anniversary of the Falklands War. I thank each and every one of the Melrose staff.*

3. *HMS Broadsword Association Committee Members for their support*

4. *Dean Webster (Spider). An ex-crewmember who set up the Broadsword website and contributed a lot of the ship's photographs*

5. *Emil Topping (Topsy) also contributed his photographs*

6.   *Lieutenant Bell-Davies for his Bridge photograph*

7.   *MOD Navy-Army-Airforce for some of the photographs*

8.   *The Daily Mail newspaper for the "Calling of Shipmates" page*

9.   *HMS Ganges Association for their photographs and support*

10. *A special thanks to Rena (Midget) Harman who prompted me to get started and kindly volunteered to type up my manuscript. Unfortunately Rena suffered a very serious car accident which consequently prevented her to continue the typing of the text. "Thanks anyway Rena".*

11. *To ex-Royal Naval Stewards, Gazz and Trish Stephenson who have given me so much encouragement and support as loyal and very good friends.*

12. *Ian Hall, my Contracts Manager in Reliance Security Services (my present employment) for his support in difficult times in the last couple of years while writing the book.*

13. *Ron and Sue Morris who have given me so much dedication and support from the start as well as being very good friends and colleagues of mine throughout.*

14. *Paul Adams (Reliance Security); colleague and friend who has supplied some invaluable photographic work for the book.*

15. *Rocky and Michelle Pheby for their suggestions, comments etc and their full support for this project*

16. *Paul, Maryann and their children Jordon, Jasmine, Jocie, Jemma and Jamie (JJ) for their enthusiasm, friendship and support throughout. Also to my mother as we often all met together to discuss the book.*

17. *Charanjit Sidhar (Chas), Kamlesh (Kam) and Kajol Jassal for their tremendous support and encouragement.*

18. *To Directors, Managers and Staff Members of Slough Estates and their Commissionaires, Steve Haylor, Stuart Yearly, Dave McCann and Kevin Hyland for their continuous support.*

19. *Not forgetting my many friends and colleagues either serving or now not serving in the Royal Navy and royal Marines. Again, I thank them all for their support.*

20. *Finally, to the families who raised me; to their children, Debbie, Simon, Caroline and Michael Neill and their children. Also, not forgetting my own family, Richard, Mandy and Mark (my cousins. Also to their children, Jessica, Freddie, Gemma and Nicky all of whom have contributed in one way or another. With the guidance of my Uncle Bob (who has sadly passed away) and to Auntie Norma (Fane) who has been so wonderful in her loyalty and support and who has, above all, given me so much encouragement and support from the time I started putting pen to paper.*

Many thanks to all concerned.

Barrie

HMS Broadsword

General and Weapons

The BROADSWORD CLASS are designed as general purpose frigates with a primary role to detect, hunt and destroy submarines. To this end there is a sophisticated sonar fit and a wide range of noise reduction measures. The main offensive weapon is a torpedo which may be delivered by helicopter or tube launched from the ship. Other weapons include Exocet (SSGW) and Seawolf (Point Defense Missile System).

Aviation

A hanger and flight deck are fitted for operation of two Lynx helicopters.

Machinery

COCOG plant is fitted consisting of twin sets of main Olympus gas turbines and cruise Tyne gas turbines driving controllable pitch propellers through non-reversable double reduction gear boxes. Control is exercised from the bridge or the Ship Control Centre.

Eletrical power is supplied by four diesel generators each of 1000 KW capacity.

Hull

The hull is of all welded construction using 'B' quality mild steel plate. The mainmast, funnel and minor areas of the superstructure are aluminium alloy.

Stabilisers

Two pairs of non-retractable stabilisers are fitted within the length of the machinery departments.

Steering

An electro-hydraulic installation is fitted which incorporates rotory vane type gear operating on two spade rudders.

Accomodation

Accomodation is provided for:-

25 Officers

5 F/CPO's

25 CPO's (1 in FCPO cabin – MAA)

39 PO's

115 Junior Ratings

A Royal Marine detachment of 1 Sergeant, 1 Corporal and 8 OR's can be carried in lieu of the same number of RN personnel.

Broadsword Class Frigates (Type 22)

From 1 January 1998, it would appear that the Royal Navy will be operating 10 x Type 22 Frigates whose primary role is anti-submarine warfare:

(Commissioned)

Boxer	1983	Batch 2
Beaver	1984	Batch 2
Brave	1986	Batch 2
London	1987	Batch 2
Sheffield	1988	Batch 2
Coventry	1988	Batch 2
Cornwall	1988	Batch 3
Cumberland	1988	Batch 3
Campbeltown	1989	Batch 3
Chatham	1989	Batch 3

The Batch 1 ships HMS Broadsword, Battleaxe, Brilliant and Brazen, all commissioned between 1979 and 1982, were sold to the Brazillian Navy between 1995 and 1997.

Major Characteristics – Speed 30 kts+ on Olympus turbines or 18 knots on Tyne turbines; Range 8,370 km at 18 knots; Displacement 4,600 full load; Engines – COGOG Type system with 2x Rolls Royce Spey SM1A gas turbines delivering 18,770 shp and 2x Rolls Royce Tyne RM1A gas turbines delivering 8,500 shp to two shafts; Length 143.6m; Beam 14.8m; Draught 6.0m; Complement 23 officers and 302 rates; Aircraft Carried – 1 or 2 Sea Lynx with Sea Sku and or Stingray torpedoes or 1x Sea King HAS.6.

At 06:15hrs on Monday 5th April I was shaken by the Bosun's Mate carrying the early morning shakes book, which is usually kept on the flight deck in harbour with the Quartermaster. This book is used for any member of the ship's company who requires an early morning call before, "Call the hands. Call the hands. Call the hands." is piped over the main broadcast system (tannoy system). This is as done by every British Naval Ship in the fleet (afloat or shore establishment) every morning to wake all the ship's company at 07:00hrs. Any member requiring the early morning call, before "call the hands" is officially piped, must be signed by the person requiring the early shake, so there can be no dispute or any excuse to say they weren't shaken. Because of the nature of my duties I was required to do this every day, whether at sea or in harbour, as the Captain's Petty Officer Steward. I shared this duty with Shaun Manuell the Captain's Steward on alternate days.

Once the shakes book had been signed my first acrobatic daily routine started. Being on the top bunk with two other bunks below me I had to reach out for the safety bar above me, grab, hold and swing out my legs, dangling horizontally to the deck (floor) still grabbing hold of the safety bar, which is attached to the deckhead (ceiling), then drop to the deck below about eight to twelve inches. Being 5 feet 5 inches, short arses like me weren't really meant for top bunks. Nine times out of ten I would make a perfect landing, depending on the previous night's "grog" run ashore with a few shipmates, but having to perform this daily exercise at sea in a force nine gale, or just even rough weather, was a completely different ball game. Often I'd go crashing against the bulkhead (wall) or the cabin door much to the annoyance of my five colleagues in the cabin who at 06:20 didn't really want an early morning wake-up call by me bouncing all over the place. When you join a ship usually you have little say in the matter of what bunk (bed) you are allocated to as it is normal procedure to take over the bunk of the person you are about to relieve. In Shaun's case, being five feet ten to six feet, he'd have no problems on the bunk to deck contact (lucky bugger). After retrieving my flip flops, towel and dhobey gear (wash gear) from my locker I proceeded along the "main drag" (two deck main passageway) to the heads and showers, returned to the cabin, dressed and was ready to start my day.

Making my way forward along two decks and up the ladder to One deck outside the Wardroom and Wardroom Galley, I proceeded up yet another ladder to 01 deck and then to the Captain's pantry, unlocked the door and put the kettle on. The time now was 06:50hrs. After pouring the Captain's tea in a bone china cup with saucer and boasting a fine gold band, at 06:59 and 30 seconds, I walked through the Captain's Day Cabin across to the sleeping cabin and knocked on the door and walked in for 07:00hrs, which, if actually executed should have exactly coincided with the ship's main tannoy system announcing "call the hands" for the rest of the ship's company.

The Captain going to his ablutions was my cue to square off (tidy up) the sleeping cabin and to lay out the uniform or dress of the day and then start preparing breakfast and the laying of the table in the day cabin. The majority of Commanding Officers in harbour prefer to be dressed and breakfasted by 07:55hrs so as to be present for the first ceremonial duty on the ship which is the hoisting of the Union Jack (forward mast at the bows) and the Naval Ensign (aft of the ship) for which the mast is situated at the end of the flight deck. The Captain and Officer of the day take the salute while both flags are being hoisted. This would undoubtedly have been witnessed by the Admiral of Gibraltar (FOG) as we had berthed alongside only a few days earlier to take part in a large naval exercise – Codename: Exercise Springtrain.

Under a very hot sun with a slight cool breeze in the air we slipped (sailed) out of Gibraltar after a very entertaining weekend with all the other naval vessels that were involved with Springtrain.

Rocky (Hudson), our Petty Officer "Club Swinger" or PTI (Physical Training Instructor) and his counterparts from the other ships had organised an Olympian Sports Competition prior to the ships arriving in Gibraltar, which

HMS Brilliant leads the ships after the exercise Operation Springtrain.

included many sports such as volleyball, soccer, tug of war and of course not forgetting the ultimate naval traditional "Gib Rock Race". Everyone who managed to complete this gruelling slog up the rock on a sweltering hot, humid day would be rewarded with a Rock Race Certificate Award, presented, at a later date, by the Club Swinger (in our case Rocky) with your name, usually superbly done in italic writing and signed by the Commanding Officer of your appropriate ship.

The Commanding Officer on our ship, HMS Broadsword, which is a type 22 frigate was Bill Canning; Captain Royal Navy of the 2nd Flotilla Frigate Squadron.

Going back to the Rock Race, I passed many of my colleagues throwing up along the route. Needless to say so was I, to the immense disapproval of the onlooking Rock Apes which are scattered all over the Rock, usually badgering tourists for food. These apes, if they take a dislike to you can become quite bad tempered and aggressive. After bringing up last night's spoils, obviously the price to be paid after a "good run ashore" (boozy night out) on the town the night before, the race was becoming to feel like something out of hell. Anyway I plodded on more at a walking pace than a run and managed finally to reach the top of the Rock, where the course ended. I think I was clocked in second from last.

"Well at least I got there".

A very good friend of mine Jerry Billinger was awaiting my final crossing over the line to have a couple of "grogs" (drinks) on the way down. I suppose it must have been ten to fifteen minutes before we started our descent down the Rock.

I'd known Jerry ever since joining HMS Broadsword and he also was a fellow Petty Officer in the S+S Department (Supply + Secretaries) as an Stores' Accountant (POSA) who not only was a very good friend and drinking oppo (opponent) but a very valued person to know, as he was in charge of Naval Stores in the Ship's Storerooms. Many a time I could go and change items of clothing, torch batteries, exchange silverware (if carried), order crockery for Captain's use etc, with no bother. So, not only a good mate but a handy person to know. Jerry is married to Maureen and has two wonderful daughters. As most married families, they live on one of the Naval Estates back at our home port in Plymouth.

Before sailing from Devonport, where Broadsword was berthed alongside at Plymouth Naval Dockyard, our duties started at 08.00 to 16.00hrs. At 16.00hrs some of us would meet up, either in the Royal Naval Fleet Club or the Avondale, which were both popular drinking venues at that time in the evening for Matelots (sailors). We'd probably stay for a couple of barrels "sorry" hours then go our separate ways home.

However if you were unlucky enough that the duty roster had suddenly caught up with you yet again, (it seemed you only did one the day before yesterday), then your duties would commence at 08:00 on the completion of Colours. It would be your responsibility to muster (check all duty personnel) all the Duty Watch Fire and Emergency Party that were on call for the next 24 hours. I would have to check that they were properly dressed and read through their individual responsibilities as regards to any emergency, for example, fire, flood, intruder attack or any out-of-the-ordinary situations that may occur during the normal day-to-day routine of the ship. After the check-off list had been established the duty watch were bought to attention for me to report and salute to the Duty Officer (Officer of the Day) that the duty watch had been mustered and were correct. In some cases they were incorrect, for instance, personnel had not turned up for some reason or another. Once all this had been established and before we could get on with our own daily routine, the response force, which were made up out of the Duty Watch, would have to go through about twenty minutes weapons training on small arms; the weapon used was the SA80 (sub machine gun).

There were usually two teams in this force, with five in each, and what was required by the DPO (Duty Petty Officer), including me, was to strip and clean these guns. The members of both teams always managed to put all the firing mechanisms back together once cleaned and checked, with the exception of one team member: usually me. I had a heck of a job mastering these weapons and many a time had to ask for assistance from the rest of the team, and thankfully for me they obliged good heartedly.

Every day, either at sea or in harbour, there was always a drill exercise for either a fire, flood or sometimes an intruder attack on the ship. The response force team for the intruder attack would be required to systematically check the whole ship from top to bottom. They had to check not only for the intruder, who somehow had managed to escape the security nets, but also for any bombs or detonators the intruder may have planted on their illegal tour. Prior to all this (it goes without saying) the whole of the ship had to be cleared and mustered on the Jetty. Only once have I known this to happen for real and that was in Mombasa. One man managed to get onboard by swimming up to the ship's ropes but it didn't take long for the culprit to be caught in one of the Messdecks (crew members' quarters) and handed over to the proper authorities.

Once we had done all our weapons checks we could get back to our normal daily routine and at 16:00hrs enviously look on as our remaining shipmates went home or just retired for the day to their Quarters, with us literally being on alert for any Emergency Call or unusual situation for the next sixteen hours (roll on 08:00hrs). Just before I leave the subject of the weapons training for the response force, I'd just like to add that on one of my many ships in the Royal Navy it was also put on the NCO I/C (non Commissioned Officer in charge) of the response force to be responsible for knowing how to fully operate a side arm (pistol) which all duty Petty Officers had to carry when the real threat arose. One CPO (Chief Petty Officer), whose name was Jan, had the misfortune of putting me through my paces. I must be quite honest with you now, I have and always will detest the use of handling and firing of any firearms: that's probably why I've always made a botch of it. Anyway there's Jan trying his best to show me how this damned pistol worked and many a time I came away with blood blisters just cocking the b—-y thing. I'm sure these guns have a personal vendetta towards me, sensing I hated them and responded by "pay back time".

One occasion which I'll never forget was when we had to do weapon firing from the Flight Deck; firing over the Stern (back of ship) out to sea at a target that was attached and trailing behind the ship. We were put in teams of about four or five and the weapon being used for practice firing drills was again the SA80. Our team was ordered to the line for our turn to have a crack at the target. I don't know why but when ordered to fire at will, I just closed my eyes and shot away hopefully at the target splashing around in the sea. As long as I kept my weapon in the sea direction there was no danger to other shipmates. Anyway once this dreaded task was done, to my disbelief (absolutely pot luck) I'd managed to get a hit on the target. Thankfully though I wasn't asked to join any Naval Gun Firing Club or Team after the event.

Even during my basic training at HMS Ganges in 1969, joining the Royal Navy at fifteen and a half on the fifteenth of September, we were taught to use the SLR (self loading rifle) and even 44 years on I still remember the apprehension whenever we had to take our turn on the firing range. Needless to say I hardly ever managed to hit the target.

However having said all that I truly did enjoy a moment on one of our warships and that happened in the mid-1970s on HMS Argonaut under the command of Captain Anthony Norman (who I believe made Admiral). I was serving as a Leading Steward (LSTWD) for the Commanding Officer and the ship was patrolling somewhere in the Atlantic at the time. We were carrying a detachment of the Royal Marines from, I think, 42 Commandos. A memo (memorandum) was passed throughout the ship and also published on the ship's DO (daily order), that there would be up to twenty places for any volunteers wishing to take a position in the ship's Lynx Helicopter for a jolly (free ride) and having a chance while airborne to fire at a splash target trailing astern (behind) (hopefully miles astern in my case) with a GPMG (general purpose machine gun). This was to take place on a Sunday afternoon and this was Monday or Tuesday. This was a first-come-first-serve-slot, and believe it or not with my history on guns, I thought this might be fun, so appended my name to the list of hopefuls. The twenty slots were soon filled within minutes of being published. A list was drawn up but unfortunately mine wasn't on it. It was while serving the Captain's lunch at around 13:00hrs on that particular Sunday that the lucky participants were going for their rightfully volunteered place in the Lynx Helicopter with the GPMG. All this was due to commence at 14:00hrs so the Captain was keen to get lunch over as were the rest of the crew; to observe either from the bridge or port (left) and starboard (right) waists (sides of ship's passageways outside). Each serial (event) would take up to fifteen minutes for the volunteers: that was from the Lynx getting airborne; flying over the positioned splash target; firing the GPMG; and returning to the flight deck to pick up volunteer number two and so on. All this would take up to four hours by the time each of the twenty people had fulfilled his jolly ride and firing.

Having served the Captain with a tasty bowl of soup, it wasn't until the next course of fresh salads and ham or pork meats, that I casually commented that it should be quite an enjoyable afternoon witnessing the GPMG firing from twenty of the ship's members and Royals (Royal Marines) on the Lynx Helicopter. The Captain replied, "Yes, it should be quite an eventful afternoon," and added, "I noticed that you, Leading Steward, had your name on the list of volunteers." My reply was, "Yes sir, but unfortunately as it was a first-come-first-served basis I just wasn't quick enough. Never mind I shall still enjoy the entertainment and good luck to the lucky people who managed to be quick enough to append their names to the list."

Anyhow after serving coffee at around 13:30hrs in the Captain's Day Cabin I stowed away (put back in proper cupboards and drawers) all the lunch utensils and wash-up in the pantry. The Captain proceeded to the Bridge at around 13:45hrs (fifteen minutes prior to the first member carrying out the first firing). Once I'd squared off the Captain's Day Cabin and washed and stowed away all the lunch gear, I was just about to lock up the pantry door (around 13:55hrs) when I was approached by the Master-At-Arms (basically the policeman on Naval Ships). I thought this to be unusual as normally the MAA's responsibility at flying stations would be the Flight Deck Officer (FDO), whose job would be to guide the Lynx Helicopter off the ship and bring it safely back on again with the aid of batons, so I presumed he must be one of the volunteers and had managed to get someone else to stand in for him, who was fully flight deck trained for this role. Well, he informed me that someone had dropped out of the afternoon flying list and that I was next in line and would I still like to take part.

"But of course, Master." was my reply, to which, he replied, "Right go and get changed into number eights (working clothes – blue trousers and blue shirt) and report to the Duty Flight Petty Officer for a safety flying brief asap." Ten minutes later I was in the back of the hanger going though all the safety brief with the PO (Petty Officer) should (heaven forbid) the aircraft need to ditch in the sea and what procedures needed to be carried out. It must have been around 15:30hrs when I finally got the order to board the Lynx Helicopter and there mounted in the back of the starboard side, hanging out of the door and bolted firmly to the Lynx's deck (floor), was this monstrosity of a gun with a belt of massive bullets. Not really knowing what a GPMG was let alone to have seen one, it was quite a shock to see this monster literally taking up half the space in the cab of the helo (helicopter). Ah well, in for a penny in for a pound and can't show face now and back out with three quarters of the ship's company looking on. Once strapped in and given a brief by OBs (Flight Observer) the FC (Flight Commander) took off. The FC flew down the starboard side of the ship from bow to stern and along the port side until we were hovering right on the port bridge wing in full view of the Captain, OOW and all duty personnel on the bridge at the time. I couldn't help but noticing the very slight smile from Captain Norman as we zoomed off a few seconds later, a mile or so ahead to the positioned target area.

After the exceptionally professional brief by the OBs it was now my turn to get into position to take up the firing practice. So donned with full flying suit, life jacket and ear defenders and with Mr Monster in front of me ready to be fired I felt like a real little action man. These guns on a standard setting can fire up to 600 rounds per minute and 750 to 1000 rounds on rapid fire or SP (not sure on SP but it's the right phrase to use apparently). To my delight I had made quite an acceptable hit on the target as observed by the ship's crew looking through their binoculars from the Argonaut. After the firing I was back on the flight deck by 15:45hrs. All this since getting airborne and returning hadn't taken any more than fifteen minutes. After thanking the flight crew and returning their flying suit, life jacket and ear defenders I had ten minutes to get below to the messdeck, get changed into white front (white sleeveless shirt with a blue band collar) and a pair of black naval trousers, return and unlock the Captain's pantry and be on the bridge to serve the Captain by 16:00hrs with a cuppa and a few biccies which was done with seconds to spare (all Naval COs love to have a cup of tea and a nibble of something around this time). Later I served the Captain with dinner, which is the main meal of the day. It is usually a full three course meal beginning with a starter (soup, pate, melon etc), main joint (usually a roast, mixed grill, steak) and a savoury to finish (usually something quite light and tasty), served with coffee to follow. At around 21:00hrs, once I'd prepared the next day uniform requirements for the CO and with the Captain's permission, I retired for the day, getting down to the messdeck at around 21:10hrs. The crew members of about 25 in my particular messdeck were all in full swing, having a good old sing-song. This was an absolutely fantastic way to finish off the Sunday evening at this time. In 1976 Naval Ships weren't yet equipped with TV, videos, CDs etc, and it was (thankfully) up to the crew to make their own entertainment and this was done by a damn good sing-song throughout the evening (sometimes going on until midnight or one o'clock in the morning). We would sing all the old sea shanties, of which the list was endless. It goes without saying about the light refreshments needed in the form of a few, a few more and then lots and lots of tinnies (beer) to keep the vocal cords well lubricated for three to four hours. Something that baffled me for weeks and weeks after this day was who had backed out of the jolly. Was I really the next in line and how was the timing so precise to get me up in the Lynx and back so as to be on time to serve the Captain with his afternoon cuppa? I, to this day, never did find out but obviously some influential forces must have been at hand. Maybe the perks of being the Captain's flunky (steward) could have had a bearing on this. I was never to find out how it all came about but I did however hear much later that no such volunteer had been taken off the list at all (says it all: who was the culprit here? The Captain perhaps!).

With the Rock Race now behind us we were making fairly good progress in our descent and desperately in need of a good jar or two. After practically disposing of all our valuable body fluids on the way up we were greatly relieved to see the first signs of an inn ready to serve and cater for the tired and weary, with their fine stocks of wines, ales and "grogs" (basically a pub). Needless to say it took us four times as long to journey down than it did to "run" up. It was our last night ashore in Gibraltar before we sailed at 09:00hrs the next morning, so we, along with, I'm sure, 90 per cent of all the ship's crew alongside, were damn well going to make the most of it. It often makes me think: the sheer sense of excitement, with any ship's company, of the prospect of entering a foreign port, or any port come to think of it, and know once alongside and tied up to the jetty or in some cases anchored out in the harbour you can, once all your duties are done, get ashore and relax. Most of us who were single would (depending if aids wasn't rife in the area) try and pick up the local talent and hopefully then have, not only a hostess to act as a guide, but also become very good friends before the ship set off again. Letters to each other on many occasions would go on for years.

I don't think anybody forgets their first experience of getting laid. I'd only just turned sixteen in the very early seventies and one of our early visits to a foreign country was Mombasa and some of the women were absolutely gorgeous and very willing as long, of course, you could pay. It was the completely normal thing to do back in the seventies (probably is now): get ashore, get laid and then get pissed. I still remember and always will, that first and many other occasions in Mombasa. Of course the more mature you got in life, charm, respect, wit and, of course, as long as the chemistry was right "Hey Presto" you've got your girl and payment wouldn't even come into the equation due to the respect for both partners and friendships formed.

Before certain members of any ship's company are allowed to proceed ashore in any port there are certain duty responsibilities to perform before leave is granted. On the entertainment front, prior to any Naval Warship entering a foreign port it is customary for all Commanding Officers and Ship's Officers to hold a reception in the form of a cocktail party; ourselves of course being the hosts of the ship. Usually the ship, once berthed alongside, will always be met by a British Official Delegate either from the British Attache, the British Embassy or in some cases the British Consulate; it all depends what country is visited and what official residence is commissioned and in operation.

A lot of preparations are done before we get alongside; sometimes thought about weeks beforehand. The British official then briefs the Captain about what has been organised for the crew in sports, tours, guides, grog runs, grippos (families wishing to take sailors on their own private tour of the country), brewery visits etc. Also the official will advise the CO what is expected of the ship to show the British Navy's friendship to a foreign port; it's what we call "showing the flag". The Captain will almost definitely be asked by the MoD high officials in Whitehall, London to hold either a dinner or lunch party for the senior official, in the capital the ship has berthed alongside, in addition to the main official CTP (cocktail party). This would normally be a President or country's High Commissioners. Additionally the other guests would probably be high ranking military officers and in turn, to support the Captain and the ship, he would more than likely invite the Executive Officer (XO) who would be second-in-command to the Captain of any Naval British Warship (the XO is better known as the First Lieutenant) to join the lunch/dinner party.

Guests normally arrive about half an hour before either of these functions. They would be met on the gangway by the Captain, the XO and OOD (Officer of the Day) and then make their way to the Bridge, where I would have had a mini bar prepared with the help of one of the ship's Stewards with hors-d'oeuvres and other tasty munchies scattered around. With close liaison with the Wardroom ship's PO Chef, in this case Stu McMillan who would prepare all the CO's functions and when everything is ready, I would announce to the host (i.e. the Captain) lunch or dinner, "Is ready to be served, Sir." On that note all persons attending the function would make their way down one flight of ladders (stairs) to the Captain's Day Cabin where the dining table would have been fully laid with silver knives, forks, spoons, trophies, flowers, candelabras with candles lit (if dinner party), menus, placecards, placemats, cruets, wine and sherry glasses, napkins and a water glass with ice cold water. The Steward and I would then serve the function. This meant getting all courses from the Wardroom Galley, which was another flight of ladders below.

Normally all these functions ran smoothly from the starters (first course on menu), to the serving of coffee and mints at the end of the other scrumptious courses served in between. Many COs much preferred to hold a lunch party rather than a late night dinner party, which is quite understandable, because once the official acts had been acknowledged everyone, including the Captain, could relax and get ashore for a good time.

The first function to be held would always be the main cocktail party, which in my case as a Petty Officer Steward I would start thinking about preparing at least two weeks beforehand. Most frigates would carry onboard only one POSTD but HMS Broadsword carried two as the Captain was the Capt "F" which means to say he was in charge of the Squadron of up to six frigates and be Captain of his ship and have the other Captains of his Squadron (usually the rank of Commander) to follow his lead in battle or exercises. So, being on F2 (2nd Frigate Squadron) one POSTD would fully manage the Officers' Mess and Quarters with the assistance of two leading Stewards and usually three Stewards. I therefore, with the assistance of one Steward, would manage the Captain's Mess and be entirely responsible for his Quarters and all entertainment of any functions.

I joined HMS Broadsword on the 8th May 1981 and took over the role as the Wardroom POSTD and it wasn't until about eight months later Scouse Bradburn and I swapped over roles, as Scouse was looking after the Captain of the time. I think at the time Scouse was a much more senior rate than me and they needed someone with more experience to run the Wardroom, as I was only Acting Petty Officer at the time (I thought I was doing ok but obviously not!). Anyway while I had the dizzy heights of running the Wardroom Mess I had to prepare for many cocktail parties, and that meant discussing with the LSTD of the Wardroom Bar and controlling all the stocks in the Wardroom Cellar for the requirements needed for the numbers attending. On average we would cater for 200 to 250. Once establishing the guest list, which would be signalled to the ship from our Supply Officer from London, we would then obtain this information along with the Captain's guest list for the lunch or dinner party to be held, usually the following day.

It was now up to Vic Frewer our Leading Steward to get all this together prior to the arrival in a foreign port. Vic, being a very professional Leading Hand, always managed to get the amount of drinks spot on and very rarely, once the function had started, had to go back to the wine cellar (three decks below) because we had run out of stock. I'd always admired Vic for this as it's better to overstock on the day than to understock in the bar areas, which would be set up in the flight deck once we were berthed alongside.

Any Naval Leading Rate, whatever the profession, is usually referred to as a Killock. A Killock will always wear the badge of the anchor on the left upper arm as a Junior NCO (Non Commissioned Officer). The word Killock derived from or means in the nautical sense, a small anchor "one made of heavy stone".

The other Wardroom Leading Steward was Johno Johnston. Johno would be in charge of all the cleanliness of the Wardroom and Officers' Cabin accommodation and also all the flats (passageways) associated in and around the Wardroom complex, as well as the cleanliness of the Heads and Bathrooms used by the ship's Officers. Both Leading Hands would each take turns in these duties and swap roles usually between six to eight months, so both have a fair crack at both jobs. Johno would have three Stewards to cover all the Wardroom Area of the daily cleaning tasks and his team at the time were Johna Jones, Dean Bonsall, Ali Barber and Shaun Manuell, who teamed up with the Captain's POSTD. It would be marvellous to meet up with the bunch again although I have seen Vic and Johno (LSTD) once and had the privilege of meeting up with Shaun on my final shore base at HMS Seahawk which is a Naval Air Station in Helston, Cornwall (Culdrose). It was a double pleasure to see Shaun had got his Killocks rate, Vic had made Chief and Johno (LSTD) had made POSTD. Since 1984, after the Falklands War, an annual event was set up called "The Pembroke Club 84". Pembroke used to be the Royal Naval Supply Training School in Chatham, Kent, then it was transferred to HMS Raleigh in Torpoint, Cornwall, where now all Naval ratings will eventually do their initial training whatever profession they decide to undertake in the Royal Navy. In March a letter is sent to all serving Senior Rate Stewards for a Reunion Dinner to be held, usually in June, at one of our shore establishments. Venues so far that I have attended have been HMS Raleigh (Torpoint, Cornwall), HMS Nelson (Portsmouth, Hampshire), HMS Drake (Devonport, Plymouth, Devon). Hopefully I might be lucky enough to meet up with a couple of the old crew Stewards, if not all of them. I know HMS Broadsword holds a reunion of some kind and I am determined to try and make the next one as for some reason or another I just haven't been able to make it.

Once the numbers had been ascertained and of course the knowledge of the port we were visiting, Vic could start to box up and put aside all the wines, beers, spirits and mixers in the Wine Cellar, prior to our arrival in the foreign port. It's essential we got feedback information from other previous visiting ships of the Royal Navy: for instance, it would be bad forward planning to, let's say, visit a port in Saudi Arabia (Abu Dhabi) and have all the bars laden with whisky, rum, gin, brandy etc and find 80 per cent of the guests are non-alcoholic drinkers and would much prefer a soft drink. This would be very embarrassing to all concerned if all the bars had to be re-stocked. Mind you, having said that there was one port of call we made in Saudi Arabia and one of the Saudi guests arrived at the start of the CTP a little worse for drink and was delighted to see the litres of Hankey's Banister whisky we had on our bars. Needless to say in less than an hour he was absolutely legless (drunk). He collapsed completely trying to get his footage on the gangway and passed out. We had to get an ambulance to take him to hospital who must have at least pumped a gallon of whisky out of his stomach. I'd hate to be nursing his hangover the next day.

Johno with the rest of the Wardroom Stewards would start to organise all the glasses needed and that meant getting them from Stores, transferring them from four decks below up to the Wardroom Pantry and cleaning them. It's good policy for any function to always allow double the amount of glasses needed so if the CTP is for 250, 500 glasses needed to be cleaned; from goblets, tumblers, wine and sherry glasses, beer mugs, half and pint, and flutes if champagne was asked for.

To make a CTP successful in every respect meant having loads and loads of ice. Before ice machines were introduced to Naval Ships, Stewards like me, back in the late sixties and seventies, had to rely on the Marine Engineers to make them in blocks or tubes in the Engine Room spaces. This was then collected on a daily basis, usually by the Duty Steward, and taken up to the Caterer's main fridges if, of course, he allowed you to do so. This had to be in process at least a couple of weeks before getting alongside. We could not afford, as in some ports we visited, to rely on the local water because of pollution or contamination risks. If anyone did go down with serious bug disorders, we could only be to blame.

My next visit would then be to probably go and liaise with the ship's PO Caterer who was Jim Goodwin and the Wardroom POCK who was "Stu" McMallan. We would all come up with a plan of when to serve the hors-d'oeuvres. The cold hors-d'oeuvres would be placed on tables on the Flight Deck where the function was to be held five minutes before the guests arrived and usually half to three-quarters of an hour later the hots were passed around by the staff.

So now I'd got the number for the CTP attendance (250), Vic and Johno with staff sorting out glasses, wines, spirits and other bar arrangements, Marine Department making ice and being collected on a daily basis to be stored in fridges prior to the function, Jim and Stu on the catering side aware of the hot and cold savouries (hors-d'oeuvres) to be served during the CTP and the times to be served, what I need to do was to see the Supply Officer, who was LTCDR (Lieutenant Commander) Bartlett, later relieved by LTCDR Johnson (both I was glad to hear later made promotion to Commander), to come up with my plan and brief before we both briefed the XO for final approval. The Supply Officer would organise all the floral and greenery needed to decorate the Flight Deck once alongside by signalling to british representatives at the embassies or consuls who would in turn contact the local traders to deliver these arrangement to the ship on arrival. Once the plan had been approved and I had the green light it was time to do a bit –

a hell of a lot – of grovelling around the ship's company to ask for volunteers to help out on the day to assist the Stewards in the serving of the drinks and hot and cold eats which would be placed on silver trays for drinks and entrées (silvers). During the function as a non-steward this would definitely not be everyone's cup of tea, but with the prospect (unofficially) of a thank you "grog" afterwards you'd be surprised how many volunteers we could get. I would do this by getting the permission from the 1st LT who was LTCDR Mowlam to be placed on daily orders, which has to be read by every crew member every day, and it would be a simple sentence like, "Any Volunteers for the official Cocktail Party to be held on such and such a date, please contact Petty Officer Steward Fieldgate in the Wardroom." No mention of grog at this stage!

I would then brief all the volunteers in the Wardroom flat and ascertain the jobs that needed to be covered and who would do them. What I needed was one glass washer-upper, one cloakroom attendant to receive coats, officers' hats etc; they in return would be given a numbered ticket. This method saved a lot of confusion when the function had finished as everyone would more or less leave at the same time and you can imagine the chaos it could cause, everyone fighting all at once to retrieve their items of head gear or coats. I also needed at least two bar assistants. Usually we would set up two main bars, using three trestle tables for each bar covered with white table clothes and the full bars were set up with the wines, spirits, glasses, mixers, water jugs, ice buckets and ice with tongs, lemons, squashes etc. The remaining volunteers would then be teamed up with the rest of the Stewards to initially serve drinks. This would entail having a full tray of assorted drinks and lining each side of the gangway on the Flight Deck ready to receive all visiting guests with some sort of refreshment or another once they had relieved themselves of any article of clothing they wished to hand in. About 30 minutes after all the guests had arrived on board I would then, using the same team as the drinks service, start serving the hot small eats (snacks) which would be served in silver entrée dishes. The favourite snacks usually would be hot vol-au-vonts, curry balls, sausage rolls, cheese on toast, mini sausages or cocktail sausages. Once all these had been completed and the CTP was in full swing it was time to really get around fast and get everyone topped up with a refill of their glass. The best and fastest way to achieve this was to establish what was the most popular drink being drunk, normally gin and tonic or Horse's Neck (brandy and ginger ale) and get each member of staff to top water jugs up with these mixers. This not only saved time for people queuing up at the bars or waiting for their orders to be returned, but it was a very efficient way of keeping the guests happy with a constant supply of drink.

The CTP would normally start at 18:30 and close at 20:00 (one and a half hours is the accepted time) and 20:40 at the very latest depending entirely on the Captain and 1st LT to close the bars. It would be my job at 20:00hrs to approach either the CO or XO to gain permission to close bars and once authorised it would be full steam ahead to get this wrapped up, everything shut down, all bar stocks returned to the Wine Cellar, glasses returned after being cleaned by our volunteers (a few members of staff would assist at this stage) and box them up ready for the next CTP. Trestle tables had to be returned to the proper stowage positions around the ship, all gash (rubbish) ditched and finally once all guests had left a final sweep of the Flight Deck. All this would take, if organised properly, 20 to 30 minutes to have everything back to normal by 20:30hrs and all staff and volunteers having completed their jobs downing a very well deserved couple of cans of beer, either on the Flight Deck or Wine Cellar. Every ship varies but it is common practice for most ships that the crew members actually involved in these function are rewarded with a couple of beverages afterwards.

I was very fortunate with the Broadsword's ship's company as nearly every time I asked for volunteers the faithful and loyal ones always used to come forward for which the staff and I were forever grateful. If it weren't for POMA John Wicks, AB(s) Fez Parker, LREG Jan Goss, POCA Jim Goodwin, my good old mate LSA Jerry Billinger, AB(s) Steve Bullock, SA Kev Doidge, Rick Luxford, C Dave Sutton, CK Ollie Holroyd, CA Darren, POYSER Steve Wilkes and a few others which I can't remember, it would have been a very different set up to make it be as nearly as successful, if it weren't for the different departments who assisted in these functions. "Well done lads, "grogs" are on me next time we meet!"

After everything was packed away, cleaned and stowed away by 21:00 more often than not we would go to our different Messdecks, get changed into civvies (civilian clothes) and all arrange to meet on the gangway ready to "leg it" ashore and do some serious catching up at the local bars where we would find the majority of our Shipmates a bit worst for wear, understandingly as they would have been ashore probably since 16:00hrs.

HMS Endurance.

In June 1981 under Margaret Thatcher's Conservative Government it was decided under part of the defence review policy to withdraw the Survey Ship HMS Endurance from Naval Service. Six months later General Leopoldo Galtieri, in a coup took office as President of Argentina. A month later, in January 1982, the military forces started military committee meetings for a possible invasion of the South Atlantic Island under British Government Rule. Even at this stage it was still decided to withdraw HMS Endurance from Royal Naval Service and confirmed by the British Prime Minister in early February. Representatives from Argentina had meetings with the United Nations in late February and on the 1st March 1982 Argentina completely rejected all talks that were held previously in New York at the United Nations' building (seems to me trouble brewing here!)

The first day at sea, especially after such a hectic weekend in Gibraltar and the last night's binge, was undoubtedly felt by all. As we sailed passed the Gibraltar Breakwater Entrance and headed out to sea we were in company with HMS Yarmouth, captained by Commander Tony Morton, who later I had the great honour to serve on HMS Beaver as his Petty Officer Steward in 1988. He has been promoted to full Captain since the Falklands War but then was Capt "F" (Flotilla) in charge of the Squadron of Ships in the HMS Beaver group.

Before I leave the story of Gibraltar completely, a few years before when the ship I was serving on called in at Gibraltar, I took the opportunity of visiting St. Michael's Caves about a third way up on the Rock. These caves are an absolute must to go and see with the stalagmites and stalactites formed through lime deposits from the ceiling to the rock floor, but as an added bonus I was fortunate enough to be able to attend a concert actually held in the cave performed by the Royal Marine Band based in Gibraltar. Not being a concert fan myself I just couldn't believe how much of an unbelievable experience it was to hear the pronounced acoustics echoing around the caves as the band played for a two-hour evening performance. It was absolutely out of this world and has got to be a "must" if ever you're in Gibraltar and the "Royals" are playing during your trip and you're lucky enough to get a ticket.

Operation Springtrain would be one of the longest Naval Exercises to be held by Royal Naval ships, submarines, landing crafts and other supporting ships, that is RFAs (Royal Fleet Auxiliary ships), who fuelled and gave us stores during the full duration of the exercises. The Commander in Chief (C in C) who was in overall charge of this operation was Admiral Sir John Fieldhouse who would have conducted all tactical scenarios for the fleet to perform with his staff members plus senior members and staff from the Army and Royal Air Force and their staff from Northwood HQ in London. I had known Admiral Fieldhouse since 1972 when I was on HMS Aurora, a Leander Class Frigate, as a Junior Steward. A couple of months earlier I had left HMS Britannia (Her Majesty's Yacht), which was the first ever ship I joined, entirely run by the Royal Navy. In June 1971 after finishing all my basic and continuous training at HMS Ganges (1969) I went on to HMS Pembroke, the Royal Naval Supply School in Chatham, Kent in 1970 and then joined HMS Osprey in the early 1970s, before joining the Royal Yacht Britannia on the 15th June 1971.

I was to be part of Admiral Sir Fieldhouse's stewarding staff, or the proper term to use would be Retinue Staff, while he was Commodore Standing Naval Force North Atlantic (Stanaforlant). The ships of the Stanaforlant Squadron were and still are, made up out of the NATO (North Atlantic Treaty Organisation) and I believe at the time we had six other countries with their ships joining the Stanaforlant Squadron which were the Canadians, Dutch, Germans, Americans, French and Portuguese (not quite sure if the French were involved). The position of Commander of this Squadron was always held by a Naval Commodore for a period of six months for each of the countries that took part. By January 1972 it was the turn of the British Commodore to head the Stanaforlant Squadron. As HMS Aurora was now the Royal Navy's ship to represent this Squadron it would automatically become Commodore Fieldhouse's flagship for three months, as HMS Aurora would be relieved by the Guided Missile Destroyer (GMD) HMS Norfolk in April 1972.

Before joining HMS Britannia and after finishing my full Naval training I was drafted (assigned) to the Royal Naval Air Station HMS Osprey at Portland Bill in Weymouth, Dorset. I was sixteen and a half years old. At first my duties were to join the 25 to 30 other Stewards at the Wardroom in HMS Osprey which was stationed at the top of the hill (about a mile) from the Naval Dockyard. The Air Station was stationed with also the Captain's (CO's) private residence at the bottom of the hill. The Captain of the Air Station at the time was Captain Morrison who resided in what was and still is, I think, known as the Castle, with his wife and two children. After about three months I was summoned to the Chief Steward's office and asked what I felt about working at the Castle to help run the day-to-day duties in the Castle for our Commanding Officer and his family, as the previous Steward was due to join a ship and would be drafted in a couple of weeks time. At 16 years old, either way, if your Chief says I'm putting you somewhere else to work, there's no point in giving an opinion: basically "Matey, I have another job for you," would have sufficed.

Anyhow, it was agreed that I pack up my belongings and kit and make my way to the Royal Naval Regulating HQ as there was a room put aside for me in these premises close to the Castle. I have never felt so alone and miserable in my life as I moved into these Quarters. The other occupants were all Naval Regulating Staff, which really are the Police of the Royal Navy. I had a box room on my own and no mates to talk to as I had left them a mile away to take up this job. To me these people all looked like the equivalent of Arnold Schwarzenegger or Mike Tyson. Only weighing eight stone and a bit of a nervous teenager I really felt out of place and unwanted as I felt I had invaded their area and always seemed to be sneered at. It was bloody awful to start my full Naval career this way. It didn't take long for my mates to find out how I felt and we came up with a solution that two or three nights a week when all of us were off duty we would all meet up in one of the many pubs at the bottom of the hill, just outside the Dockyard for a few bevvies. That really bucked me up and it didn't take long after that to settle into my hopeless depressed state and work it into my advantage to make it more bearable whilst serving at the Castle.

At one time, after the pubs kicked us out at 23:00hrs we had managed to persuade the landlady to sell us a couple bottles of parsnip wine to take out. The one great advantage of me having my prison of a room was I was literally two minutes away from all the boozers so it was unanimously decided (foolishly) to polish these bottles off in my prison and have a bloody good laugh and a joke before they made their one mile trek to HMS Osprey. We were doomed from the moment we stepped outside the pub. Unbeknown to us at that time of night it was guaranteed a "meat wagon", being a term matelots use for the Royal Naval Police Vehicle (van), would patrol this stretch of road just waiting for the opportunity to throw you in the back for any Royal Naval Discipline Act (RNDA) you breach; whether it be for drunkenness, fighting, abusive language or whatever. We were immediately challenged and stupidly we hadn't even thought of concealing our nightcap trophies. The Naval Patrol obviously knew who I was and to my surprise just gave us all a warning and told us to ditch the two bottles in the nearest trash bin after pouring the wine in the hedge or down the drain.

Again teenagers make some stupid moves sometimes. After being warned that they would be patrolling this area again in ten to fifteen minutes and would expect that I would have gone back to my Quarters and the rest of the group to have started to make their way up the hill, after a damn good evening and definitely under the influence, this obviously seemed a very good move to get shot of this grog. So we waited for them to go and sneaked over to my box prison, with a couple of plastic cups and were just about to down the first snort when they crashed in giving us all a hell of a mouth full. You can imagine now there was no option but to put the remains down the sink watched on by all the Duty Patrolmen. I still think myself lucky to this day as we could have all been on a discipline charge, but they let the lads off with a warning and gave me another rollicking, but I can't help thinking they all knew it couldn't be much fun living virtually on my tod with people that were ready to arrest you, and me having to mix with them day after day.

After that episode things did seem to get a bit better once I really started to get settled into "doing time" in my new home. The Commanding Officer with his wife and two children (aged five and eight) had three other members of staff to run the day-to-day work of the Castle and daily chores, other than myself, and all were Leading Hands (Killocks). You had the chauffeur, who was responsible for driving the Captain anywhere around the Air Station and also for any official functions that had to be attended either at Portland or our neighbouring town at Weymouth. Also the driver's other responsibility when not needed for these duties was to attend to the garden and vegetable patch. The CO also employed a full-time Leading Cook (LCK) and a Leading Steward (LSTWD) (my immediate boss).

My duties, as the junior member of the team, were to carry out all the cleaning, washing, ironing, hovering and bed making for example. Basically all the crap jobs a sixteen year old detests doing. I remember one occasion when I was cleaning up the kiddies' room after they had gone off to school. I was dusting on top of the chest of drawers and knocked over a porcelain ornament which broke in half. I was petrified of what the Captain and his wife would say and I dared not tell my LSTD. Somehow I managed to find some glue from somewhere and stuck it together and it looked as good as new after I'd finished. I hid it behind the curtain on the window ledge to dry with the full intention of sneaking back later that day and put it in its original position. Things got a bit hectic that day and I completely forgot about it until later that evening after I'd left the Castle. Well, it was too late then, hopefully no one would notice and I'd put it back in the morning. Needless to say when I turned up for work the next day I made my first priority to head for the bedroom and return this expensive porcelain ornament. To my horror it was nowhere to be seen: not on the windowsill, not on the dresser, nowhere. Well that's it then, I thought, I've been rumbled. The next thing was to either be summoned by the Captain's wife or the LSTWD for a right dressing down. It would probably mean I'd have to pay for it and it would be taken out of my wages and with the little amount us Junior Stewards were on it'd probably take a month to pay off. To this day not a whisper, not a mention, not even a slightest indication was ever mentioned to me of the whereabouts or the accident that had occurred (I hope the kids didn't get the blame for it).

After serving at the Castle for only seven months the only other panicky experience I had was when the LSTD gave me the task of ironing the bed linen. After he had left to go to HMS Osprey I dutifully dug out the iron and ironing board from the closet. The only time I'd ever used these contraptions was in basic training and the sheets we used were all made of linen. With the ironing board set up and the iron on hot it was full steam ahead: if I'm quick I'll get this basket load of sheets cracked before he gets back. I never got as far as the first sheet as when I slapped the iron slam bang in the middle of the ironing board it wouldn't move and all I could smell was the horrible burning stench.

The bloody sheets were nylon. Who in the world would make sheets made out of nylon, I thought, and why weren't they linen like the ones I used to do and to top it all how on earth do you get this muck off the iron? Again luck must have been on my side because although I was given a right roasting from the LSTWD on his return he, as I found out later, he got the bollocking of his life for not giving me the right guidelines to carry out this task.

It is common practice in almost any job anyone takes up, especially just out of school, to have the senior members playing jokes on you or to have a bit of harmless fun. There were two occasions which I fell for lock, stock and barrel and that was when I was still in the Wardroom at HMS Osprey before being transferred to the Castle. Everytime it would be the Killocks who would try and get a laugh out of you in front of their mates and more so to the delight of the onlooking junior members who had already fallen foul of these pranks.

One such incident was when we were preparing the carving table in the Wardroom for a salad buffet and I was asked to go and see the Head Chef and ask him for a leg of liver. On another occasion we were preparing for a major Mess Dinner for about 150–200 people. For a function this size all the big mahogany tables were assembled and the legs adjusted accordingly. I was in a team of two Killocks and four Stewards all deeply engrossed in the job in hand to get all the legs of the tables on an even level. One of the Killocks suddenly announced, "Hell, this is no good. What we need here is a special tool for this job." Looking straight at me (muggins), he said, "Right, Barrie, what I want you to do is go and see the Warrant Officer Steward and ask for a long weight." Again dutifully I plodded off to see the WOSTWD and asked him for this "long weight" of which I hadn't even the slightest possible clue what it was; obviously my Leading Hand knew what he was talking about to send me to the Warrant Officer. After giving my request politely to the WO I waited and waited and waited a bit more patiently while the Senior Steward was busily writing reports and making notes. It must have been at least half an hour before I plucked up the courage to repeat my request as by now the Killock must be doing his nut wondering where the hell I must have got to. After about an hour I now must have looked quite anxious because it seemed I was getting nowhere nearer to getting this long weight thing than I was over one hour ago. After a few minutes he suddenly looked up and said, "Right you've had your long wait, now report back to the Killock and get on with your work." Which, when I did, was greeted by a bunch of laughing hyenas at my expense. What a plonker I felt then, these buggers had got me again and they were all in on it.

My orders came through to join my first Royal Naval Ship while I was at the Castle and it first came to my knowledge while we were having "stand easy" (mid-morning break) by the LCK and LSTWD who announced they had heard that orders had been received on the base for me to join Her Majesty's Royal Yacht Britannia in June 1971 (two months time). I'd already been the brunt of jokes at the Osprey Wardroom and was getting to be a bit of a veteran of how these Killocks ticked for their laughs and casually answered, "Yeah right" and left it at that and walked out of the tea rooms and got on with my duties around the house (Castle). No way was I going to be conned into thinking my first ever ship in the Royal Navy was going to be some poxy yacht with probably a couple of flimsy sails and looking something like a sailing dinghy spiniker, or fireball. Well, the jokes on the other foot now, looks like this time I'll have the last laugh with these prankster Killocks. By playing them at their own game ha! ha! – wrong! Anyhow I'd joined the Navy to go on a Warship and see the world not to be outdone by some dinghy bobbing up and down in the Solent or wherever this thing was moored.

The very next morning before the Captain left for work I was summoned to see the CO and his wife in the front lounge of the Castle and with his outstretched hand and beaming face his announcement that he had just received orders from drafty that I was to join the Royal Yacht Britannia on the fifteenth of June. You can imagine the shock I felt. What in the hell was this Royal Yacht Britannia? I almost certainly had never heard of it and never expected it to be manned by the Royal Navy – did it have guns? Was it a fighting ship and surely this can't be another wind up for me? Not coming from the CO of HMS Osprey at the Royal Naval Air Station (RNAS). Before the day was out I found out all that was to find out about this famous ship and couldn't believe I was about to start my Naval career on HMY Britannia.

HMY Britannia.

We had just heard that HMS Hermes was to act as the task force flagship and HMS Invincible had just sailed to join the main task force and were heading for the Falklands. They had sailed from Portsmouth and we had sailed from Gibraltar. Things had definitely taken a turn for the worse in the last couple of days. I think alarm bells started ringing when a party of Argentine scrap metal merchants working in the South Georgia Islands were being escorted by their military personnel, and when asked by the British Government to remove all Argentine military personnel it fell on deaf ears. This episode took place on the nineteenth of March and by the twenty-sixth of March all, if any, negotiations that had been made to resolve the build-up to any conflict had been totally rejected by the Military Junta and now had every intention whatever the outcome to invade the Falkland Islands. Dictated by General Leopoldo Galtieri, who at the time was President of Argentina, the Invasion itself was planned by the Argentine Naval Commander, Admiral Jorge Anaya, who code-named this operation "Operation Posario". The invasion originally was planned with all due sense and purpose for the 25th May 1982 as the twenty-fifth would have been Argentina's Revolution Anniversary. Another date was also considered, the 9th July, when they would have celebrated Independence Day. But because of the enormous pressure from the public sector and the enormity of Union Demonstrations, it was decided to bring the invasion date forward to April 2nd 1982. Although the British Royal Marines put up a very courageous stand at Port Stanley they were no match to the thousands of Argentinian Military Forces that had invaded with the Argentine Navy. Consequently the British Governor, Rex Hunt, reluctantly ordered the very sparse detachment of Royal Marines to lay down their weapons, where they were later transported by air and flown on to Montevideo. General Mario Menendez now took up residence in Government House. This of course made Galtieri and his Government very popular with the main majority of the public (for a short while). On the third of April the Argentinian Military Forces took control of South Georgia and the Group of Islands in the South Sandwich Area, roughly about 1,000 miles East of the Falklands.

By then at least 10,000 Argentine Military personnel had landed on the Falklands and had started to dig in; preparing dug out trenches awaiting for the inevitable retaliation from the British Forces.

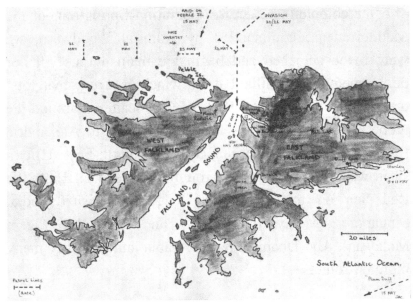

Broadsword patrol lines.

The Chief of Naval Staff, who was the British Navy's first Sea Lord Admiral, Sir Henry Leach, strongly advised the British Prime Minister, Mrs Margaret Thatcher, to deploy a large Naval Task Force to recapture the Sovereignty of the Falklands with the full backing of the United Nations, who approved Resolution 502. The task force set sail on the Monday 5th April from Portsmouth, led by HMS Hermes, the task group's flagship, who would carry the Queens second eldest son HRH Prince Andrew (Lieutenant) to take part in the duties of a helicopter pilot. During the conflict the United States' Secretary of State, General Al Haig, started peace talks and arrived in London on Thursday 8th April. Our Foreign Minister, Lord Carrington, resigned on Monday 5th April and Francis Pym was appointed Foreign Secretary on Tuesday 6th April. Things by now were really hotting up.

After completing exercise Operation Springtrain in the Mediterranean, commanded by Admiral Woodward, we were to be detached and begin the main purpose of our deployment on Armilla Patrol; which is every matelots' dream,- visiting paradise Ports of Call scattered around the globe. Starting at Naples in Italy, then on to Alexandria (North Africa – Egypt) and Djibouti (North-East Africa). Then we would have gone through the Suez Canal into the Red Sea on to the Indian Ocean and visited India, Singapore (Malaysia), Kelang and Colombo (again Malaysia), Abu Dhabi in Saudi Arabia and probably many more en-route.

On many occasions on these deployments around the many islands surrounding these countries, usually on a Sunday or weekend, we would anchor off and lower the sea boats laden with barbeque equipment: water, ice, plastic knives, forks, plates stacks of food and of course not forgetting the most important item on the agenda to be landed ashore were cases upon cases of ice-cool tinned beer. This really was going to be some deployment to be reckoned with. I remember when I was on one of those cruises years ago, before the ship's company could be safely beached a small brave party of seamen had to be landed to badger all the hundreds of venomous snakes back into the undergrowth and brush, who were out for their daily sunbathing spree – not a job for the faint-hearted: especially not my cup of tea.

It's usually common knowledge to all matelots that after scran (mealtime) at approximately 13:30 there undoubtedly would be a "hands to action stations" exercise with some sort of scenario thrown in, either a mock air attack, torpedo attack or a ship-to-ship attack against the ship. Prior to "Action Stations" being broadcasted all personnel must lash down everything around their departments and stow all loose items, either in locked cupboards or drawers. This immensely reduces the debris in the ship if damaged in a war situation by bombs, missiles, torpedoes or any other weapon the enemy wish to fire upon us. However, especially in peace time and especially just visiting a Foreign Port, it is to get the ship's company back to normality for the proper drills to be carried out and this is done at the earliest possible opportunity once the ship has left harbour.

All personnel must at this time be in proper battle dress carrying their AGR (Anti-Gas Respirators) and anti-flash (special extra gun flash clothing that is white, to cover full facial features and gloves that are long sleeved). In my case, as with all my other first aid colleagues, we would also carry a fully packed first aid canvas bag. Additionally for all crew members it is essential that everyone carries a full water bottle not only for the human consumption but it could be an absolute life saver for someone, if not yourself, with life threatening multiple burns. This drill also informs Command that everyone has reported to their posts.

Once everyone has reported their closing up to Action Station positions to HQ, and command has been informed that all ship's company is present and correct in the proper position for attack the Captain would then give the order for the ship to fall out from Action Stations and the ship then would go into normal sea routine.

Our first day at sea after leaving Gibraltar now took us to approximately 14:30hrs in the afternoon. Concern was starting to mount up as a few ships that were involved in Exercise Springtrain had been ordered to store up in Gibraltar and head for the South Atlantic. We were still heading East towards Naples and hopefully then on to the Far East. Even at this stage I'm sure at least 80 to 90 per cent of the HMS Broadsword's ship company were very confident that our deployment would not be jeopardised, and a peace solution would be very near at hand.

I almost certainly felt it would never ever get to the stage where our ships would be used for war in the South Atlantic. Anyway where in the bloody hell were these islands supposed to be in the, where did they say, ah yes, Falklands? I had to go and see a mate of mine in the Operations Room as he was bound to have a chart handy in case there was the remotest chance we were called up to join the now increasing task group of ships. After trudging along all of twenty yards from the Captain's Pantry to the Ops Room I would have met up with either one of the on-duty Petty Officer Radar, Stan Holloway(R), Ian Laurie(S), Chris Chapman(R), or Mac McMahon(R), having now had a two minute geography lesson update on what was all the fuss about regarding these islands. I returned to my normal ship's duties at 16:00hrs having made the Captain a cup of tea and placed a couple of biccies on the saucer. I again plodded on the twenty yard trek to the

Operations Room, as I'd just seen the Captain enter it a few minutes before. Almost every Captain in the Navy would have been served tea at this time by their Steward. As I approached the Captain he caught sight of me and very calmly said, "Not in the Ops Room please. PO drinks of any sort are NOT permitted. Please put the tea in my Cabin and I'll be along in a couple of minutes." That statement alone warranted respect for our Captain, as another CO could easily have bellowed, "Get that bloody drink out of here now," but always with Captain Canning, everyone was treated with great respect and the order for me to leave the Ops Room was done more in politeness than anything. Anyhow I should have known better, I had completely forgotten that hot and cold drinks were not permitted in this area, it really makes sense, why as this is literally the Main Command Post, where any war situations would have been commanded to use to combat attacks. So a moment of a little stupidity on my part turned out to be resolved in a very dignified way.

At 18:00hrs I usually asked the CO if he required a soft drink or maybe a drink from his bar then, having served his order, I'd start preparing his evening dress and make preparations for dinner which will be served at approximately 20:00hrs.

Most of the ship's company during the day would have taken the full opportunity of being at sea with the preparations for us to enter our next Port of Call (Naples). Scouse, the Wardroom POSTD, and his crew would have been busy for the main CTP once we were berthed alongside in Italy. Every Port of Call from now on would be entertained by a CTP from HMS Broadsword. You would have the Buffer, who I think was PO Dick Clayton, and his merry men preparing all the seaman ship aspects. The main task would have been to prepare the awnings on the Flight Deck. Once berthed, this is like a temporary roof made of colourful canvas, that is draped by side canvas attachments from the makeshift roof. Once finished it would look like an enclosed canvas entertainment area, something like a marquee. Then of course you would have the Waffoos (Flight Crew) preparing the Hanger and getting the Lynx Helicopter ready for the ship to be opened to visitors. This usually would take place on the second day the ship would be tied alongside. Having said that not always was this the case, it all depended on how long the ship was alongside. In some cases you could be in Port for only a couple of days and be off on the third, so it would have been impractical to hold a "ship open to visitors" day, because there just wasn't enough time. The main priority for a Naval Ship when visiting a Foreign Port was to show the British Flag and this of course was backed up by inviting all the Foreign Dignitaries to the main CTP reception on the first day of arrival. The Chefs and Caterers would be busy preparing all the delicate hors-d'oeuvres well in advance. The ME Department would be preparing the HQ Area and the cleanliness of all the Machinery Areas including all the Engine Room spaces as quite often, once alongside and after the Captain had held his private lunch or dinner party for a very, very select number of important guests, the main areas most guests wanted to visit was HQ and the Engine

Rooms. Along with this the other area that was most visited by everyone from the private functions was the Operations Room, which again would fall under the responsibility of the Seaman Department and probably the Weapons Engineering Department. Their additional responsibility, prior to getting alongside, would be to make sure both Broadsword Sea Wolf Missile Launchers were on top line for visitors' inspection.

Usually two to three days prior to a foreign visit the Scribes (Writers Department) who are responsible for the smooth accounting of the Crews' pay and financial aspects, would be in custody of thousands of pounds worth of the actual currency of the country we are about to visit; in this case the currency in Naples (Italy) was the Lire. So once lists had been submitted to the pay office of all individual Messes it would then be distributed to the person in charge of that particular Messdeck and the Captain would receive his dosh usually from his Secretary; usually a Sub Lieutenant or Lieutenant or the Senior NCO Writer.

A mammoth task for the Greenies (Electricians) would be to get ready the string upon string of coloured lights that would be assembled once the awnings on the Flight Deck had been erected by the Seaman Department. Also if the ship had to be floodlit, massive, heavy, powerful spotlights would have been positioned all around the outside of the ship from bow to stern so as to be lit up at night like a Christmas tree. The Buntings (Radio Operators) would sort out the proper flags needed while alongside and on some very important ceremonial visits would have to be ready for a major dress ship which would be hoisted from now, amidships to stern on whatever the event and this would include literally dozen and dozens of different flags that would be used. Surgeon Lieutenant Woodroof along with John Wicks the POMA (Petty Officer Medical Assistant) would make sure all the first aid facilities were checked and stocked up.

With the ship now working flat out to achieve their own department's chores to get prepared for the arrival at our first Port of Call the start of our deployment would and could never be achieved without the assistance of the Stores Department or as we call them the "Jack Dusties". Jerry with LSA John Oxley, SAs Rick Luxford, Kev Doidge, Steve Wilks and Steve Ledge would endlessly be issuing out stores equipment for every department in the ship: whether it be a rotor blade for the ship's Lynx Helicopter; engine oil for the Marine Engineering Department; all kinds of rope for the Seaman Department; glasses and crockery to the Stewarding Department; stationery for the Writers; pots, pans and utensils for the Chefs and CAs in the Galley; numerous flags for the MCO (Main Communications Office); light bulbs, wiring and lamps for the Greenies (Electrical Department). Additionally any cleaning gear to be used for the ship's husbandry, its cloths, mops or buckets, right down to a small can of Brasso which was used to clean any brass fittings around the ship, used mostly on the older class ships for the scuttles and last but not least a bottle of grog for me (only joking).

So as you can see every member of the ship's company was kept busy even if we were only sailing from port to port after completing one of the Navy's largest combined exercises in the Mediterranean.

We only had a couple of days to get our ship "Ship Shape" before we hit harbour again as we were due to arrive in Naples, if I recollect, on the morning on the eighth of April. Like everyone else on the ship and before leaving Devonport we all would have brought onboard our tropical clothing, (beach clothing, sun tan oils, sun hats) ready for this adventurous journey through the Suez Canal to the Red Sea and into the Indian Ocean.

It reminded me of when I had been on this particular patrol years before while serving on another Naval Warship and I was to be taking part in one of the oldest and greatly appreciated recreational events that very, very rarely took place on HMS ships and that was that the order "Hands to Bathe" which may be given strictly on the orders from the Captain. Usually this event would take place in or around tropical waters and what would happen is the ship would slow down to approximately one knot. A sea boat would then be launched off the ship's side by the use of the mechanical davits (crane like arms) or even a gemini board (rubber dinghy with outboard engine). A sentry would be positioned on the Bridge roof armed with either an SLR or SA80, usually it would be a Royal Marine or a member from the Seaman's Branch. This precaution was solely to ward off any sharks that might be snooping around looking for any easy freebie lunch (I think I'd be quite safe in their eyes – to them I'll probably look like a mere shrimp). A ship's roped ladder then would be attached to either the port or starboard waists (side of ship) depending on which side of the ship we could swim from, so once we'd jumped in this would be the only means to get back onboard independently, other than the sea boat which was made seaworthy only if anybody got into trouble! Yes, you've guessed it, like muggins here.

What happened was when I first ventured on this exciting exercise and being a flunky, not knowing much about the rules and regulations the Seaman Branch got up to, was that when "Hands to Bathe" was piped or broadcasted over the Tannoy System I thought the ship automatically stopped engines and would be just sitting there while we were all splashing about. I jumped off from the Flight Deck, other people were diving off from all other parts of the ship, you even had some daredevils diving from the Bridge roof and believe me that was some heck of a long dive. Anyhow there's me merrily having a whale of a time and suddenly to my horror all the swimmers started drifting away and the ship was getting further and further away. Feeling a surge of panic and not knowing what the bloody hell was going on the more effort I tried to catch up with the ship and swimmers the further I started drifting away. There was no way whatsoever I could now possibly catch up. There also must have been a slight current because within seconds the ship seemed to be steaming towards the horizon quite unaware I was now in a frantic panic (perhaps Mr Hungry shark would have to make do with shrimp for lunch after all!). To the rescue within minutes I heard this chug, chug,

chug and a voice bellowed out from the sea boat from the Leading Seaman Coxwain and said, "Hey, Barrie, what you doing mate trying to swim home or what?" They hauled me into the sea boat and after the hands to bathe had finished the sea boat was ordered back to the ship. I'd never felt so embarrassed in my life when we were hoisted inboard with the Captain, 1st LT and part of the ship's crew looking on probably thinking: the one that nearly got away. It was only later that I was put right about how you can't just stop a ship in the water without the engines running. Well that's what's life's all about, we all have to live and learn at some stage (what a plonker – that still bugs me now).

It was 20:00hrs and time to serve the Captain his dinner. The first course consisted of an iced cold caspacho soup followed by roast lamb, fresh vegetables and boiled potatoes and gravy and for savoury I served Irish bite, which is cheese on a small bit of toast and Branston Pickle and coffee to follow. The time was 20:40hrs approximately, still no news from the Signals Office in the MCO of us being ordered to join the task force, so it looked like we were home and dry. Sun-tan oil at the ready, let's look forward to the beaches and sand, tropical islands, sun, sand, sea, surf and girls. Plenty of reception parties to go to, sight-seeing trips to the local breweries, bus tours and grippo's rabbits to buy for the families at home. This is what we joined the Navy for. We'd all worked hard to get the ship ready for this deployment, now it was time to play hard. What I planned to do as soon as I'd finished serving the Captain, was to go and sort out my locker and get all the beach and swimming gear ready. Naples here we come. WRONG!

At approximately 21:00hrs, twelve hours after HMS Broadsword had sailed from Gibraltar the one and only signal that the whole ship's company hoped and dreaded would never be received finally came through. The signal flashed to Broadsword would have come from the Commander-in-Chief-Fleet (Northwold) Admiral Sir John Fieldhouse and addressed to the Commanding Officer HMS Broadsword Captain WR Canning Royal Navy. I imagine the classification would have been permitted to read such a High Priority Signal but it wouldn't take someone like Einstein to work out the nature of its contents but it would have been brief and straight to the point, probably something in the tune of: Immediately return to Gibraltar -stop- fully store ship -stop- prepare for passage to South Atlantic -stop- prepare ship for war -stop-. At 21:10hrs Captain Canning addressed the whole ship's company over the main broadcast system on the contents he had just received from London. Goodbye sunny paradise Indian Ocean. Hello stormy, cold, wet South Atlantic.

On the sixth of April, now that Lord Carrington had resigned as Foreign Secretary, Francis Pym had taken up the appointment. We had also just heard that the assault ship HMS Fearless had also sailed from Portsmouth to join the task group, probably to rendezvous at Ascension Island.

These type of ships were essential for landing amphibious landing craft and heavy vehicles; her sister ship is HMS Intrepid.

With us back in Gibraltar we followed suit of our previous colleagues who had already been ordered down South and that was to undertake the enormous task of carrying out a major, major store ship in preparation not only to expect weeks upon weeks at sea and probably months but, more to the point, prepare the ship with tons upon tons of live ammunition: ranging from exocets, Sea Wolf missiles, torpedoes shells for the bofor guns, sea skuas for the Lynx Helicopter and rounds upon rounds for the small arms used mainly by our Detachment of Royal Marines and the ship's crew landing party if there were ever a need to land the ship's landing teams. This gruelling ordeal was going to take us to the eighth of April when we would yet again sail from Gibraltar laden right up to the Gunnels with every possible imaginable item one could carry on these ships and with every possible nook and cranny being utilised for storage space. So from our one million pound each missile to our two pence potato, we slip and proceeded out of Gibraltar in company with HMS Yarmouth who have had their fair share of hard graft and like us have also done a mammoth store ship. Actually, now thinking about it, most of the live ammunition would have been done while we were anchored off at the Ascension Island where the missiles would have been transported to the ship by helicopter (Navy language "vertrepped") for safety reasons. I don't think Her Majesty would have been amused if the Navy was to be blamed for re-naming the

"Rock" of Gibraltar the "Rocks" of Gibraltar because our missiles went off while anchored alongside in Gibraltar. After leaving Gibraltar at 16:30 we now had a seven to eight day passage to the Ascension Island, accepting that our would have been cruise had definitely gone to the dogs for sure, so now's the time to make the best out of a bad situation.

After leaving Devonport as "white as a sheep" (appropriate phase to use for the unexpected fate of our future destination), and catching up on a bit of bronzy bronzy on our passage to Gibraltar, I decided to do the same now on our passage to the Ascension Island, and get a bit more of a tan. We all tried to grab half to three-quarters of an hour on the Upper Deck tanning ourselves, usually during the hour and a quarter lunch break There was usually a mad rush at midday to get to the front of the scran queue, have our nosebag, then make our way to our individual Messdecks or cabins, get changed into beach gear, grab a towel, sun-tan oil and take a large towel or wicker mat to lie on as the midday sun had made it impossible to lie on the steel metal deck without sufficient coverage. You'd be surprised where people dig out their deck chairs, camp beds, rubber matting and lilos – in all sorts of hideaway places around the ship for this ritual time of day relaxation. People will go to all sorts of lengths to find just a tiny, tiny space to stow their gear for sunbathing.

Of course this didn't exclude the Captain wanting to get his two pennies' worth of the sunrays in at lunchtime. He'd have a quick lunch around noon and then be off with sun hat, towel, sun cream, foldaway chair all in tow, making his way to the Bridge roof for his bit of bronzy bronzy and be back down to change at around 13:05, before the whole ship got back to the afternoon chores when "Out Pipes" was broadcast and "Hands carry on with your work" at 13:15hrs.

Everyone was designated a certain area on the Upper Deck, the lads would use the foc'sle and Flight Deck (if the ship was not at flying stations). Petty Officers, Chief Petty Officers and Warrant Officers would share both Sea Wolf Deck Areas and the Officers would use the Bridge Wings and Bridge roof. Never could understand why we just couldn't all mumbo-jumbo wherever but so I'm told it's a "matter of principle" – lads one area, NCOs another area and Officers in their area. Anyway everyone used to manage to find a spot somewhere to squat down, and at 16:00hrs when secure was piped and you weren't required on watch or duty this again would be an ideal time to venture outside for an hour or two before the sun went down.

The ship tuned into the World Service News and like every other Naval vessel and supporting ship involved in the build up of the task force we were eager to hear how the negotiations were progressing or so it seemed more and more the other way – not progressing. Mr Al Haig had arrived in London on the eighth of April for talks with the newly appointed Foreign Secretary and also the Prime Minister, Mrs Margaret Thatcher. Surely this could be resolved. HMS Broadsword's morale was always quite high although we'd missed out on our original deployment. We all expected any day to receive some sort of signal to stand down or continue on your visit to Naples as peace talks had been established but alas we were still steaming South to the Ascension Island. Two days later on the tenth we learned Al Haig was in Buenos Aires in Argentina and was doing his bit again. He's like a yo-yo on a piece of string and would be back in London on the twelfth of April. As the British Government declared an Exclusion Zone to protect the sovereignty of any country legally by UN Law against hostile invasion then things must be getting very serious.

On the twelfth of April 1982, this order was precisely given as announced in Parliament: a 200-mile exclusion zone was now in force around all the Falkland Islands. It was at this time that some sort of reality of feeling around the ship started to set in. Training was intensified throughout the ship and very noticeably by our Royal Marine Commandos led by Mean Machines Sergeant Bill Leslie, Corporal A Wimpenny, Marine C Lima, MNE PK Wilson, MNE K Sadler, MNE DC Whitehouse, MNE AM Goulder, MNE GW Morris, MNE D Pearce and MNE MA Elston and you couldn't ask for better a Commando Team than this bunch. Bill and I often used to have a good yarn in the Petty Officers' Mess Bar over a jar or two. Even if it was just talking shop it made a pleasant change to have a natter other than normal ship's routine. Although the compliment of the ship's company onboard was about 256, when the Royal's embarked in Devonport for our now non-existent deployment it was not only a question of finding these lads a bunk but a Messdeck to put them in. So from day one the Marines were accommodated in different sleeping quarters around the ship. Typical RMs' determination: it didn't take long to overcome this minor obstacle. How on earth they managed to pull this off it beats me. Somehow, somewhere by talking to someone they managed to find a compartment, turn it into living quarters and move in. Bloody good for them; I'd hate to know how many people they might have upset for that manoeuvre. Anyhow the main thing was the majority of their unit were now in a much more commanding situation for essential tactical discussions and future debates on the endless training programmes, which, if called upon for real, they could respond efficiently because communications between the team would have been essential.

I had the great privilege, once they had settled into their new homes, of being invited one evening for a couple of tinnies, tell a few jokes and have a good laugh. It may only be a small gesture to some but I felt quite honoured.

In 1954 I was fostered out to an absolutely loving family with three other children, one boy and two girls: Tim Jackson, Trudy Richards and Anne Nagle. Tim and I were born in the same year and Trudy and Ann were two and three years older. Our foster parents were Winnie and John Vestey. Winnie was a full-time nurse and John a Fleet Street editor for The Times. Right up to the day they passed away we all called them Auntie and Uncle and loved them dearly. They in turn had three children Micky (who started his career as a Sub Lieutenant), Jo and Pippa. It was Pippa who took over responsibility for Tim and me as foster parents with her husband Ray. We were about eight and had moved to a village called Dunkeswell not far from Honiton in Devon. How in the world they managed to bring up four children of their own, Debbie (eldest), Caroline, Simon and Michael, as well as us two is quite an achievement in its own and again we thank them and love em to bits. It wasn't until later that I found Simon had joined the Royal Marines and unbeknown to us at this time we would both be preparing ourselves Land and Sea for the possibilities to fight if and when our country was ordered for war! It's quite understandable that I should think of Debbie, Caroline, Simon and Michael as younger brothers and sisters, which to me they are, and I'd known them all since birth and we all grew up together happily. I was to hear more about Simon's plight on the Falklands later during the conflict. I thought it would be quite respectful to mention that Devonport being a Naval Port with Plymouth its city, that Aunt Winnie's sister Aunt Pidge (maiden name Piegeon) actually took office as the Lord Mayoress of Plymouth in the late 1960s (1966–1967), and it was at one of the receptions held in the Town Hall that the conversation got around to the Navy as I was only just thirteen. Well it looks as if it paid off, because two and a half years later I signed the dreaded dotted line as we used to call it then.

"You're committed mate!"

"I'm in."

Listening constantly to the World News we found out that since the eighth of April Canberra had been commissioned (commandeered) by the Government to enable Royal Marine Detachments 40 and 42 Commandos also 2 Para

Regiment to board. She sailed from Southampton to join the now ever growing task force. We were due to arrive at Ascension in two days on the sixteenth. By now the MCO had received hundreds of signals. One of which I learnt was that the Brilliant Group commanded by Captain John Coward, Royal Navy, onboard HMS Brilliant (Type 22 Frigate) had left the Ascension Island with ships HMS Glasgow (Type 42 Destroyer), HMS Sheffield (Type 42 Destroyer), HMS Coventry (Type 42 Destroyer) and HMS Arrow (Type 21 Frigate).

It was on the last departure from Gibraltar that I just started jotting down notes on scrap bits of paper of events, thinking this will all be over shortly once we call their bluff: again "WRONG". As things progressed so did my heap upon heap of bits of paper until I think one of the lads in the MCO mentioned, "Why don't you start a diary or something? If we can help, we can pass on any info that might be useful." Well, as it turns out the Captain's Pantry was literally right opposite the Main Communications Office (MCO), where all the signals were coming in by the bucket full, so what the hell, why not start a diary if these lads (LRO Heighton (Hedge), LRO Weir, RO Morton, RO Beasley, RO Tainton, RO Porter, RO Halliwell, RO Yeo, RO Cheney, RO Marsay, Ro Harrow, Ro Green, RO Foster and RO Allen) were willing to keep me updated with signals (which they all did constantly) I might as well go ahead and put pen and signals to paper. These people were a god-send for the diary. If one watch were to change over duties the other watch would then resume the endless traffic of incoming signals. I would guarantee to get at least half a dozen signals pushed under the Pantry door to the relevance of what was going on around us in the fleet. Many a time I would unlock the Captain's Pantry door at 06:30 to prepare and to get the Captain's morning cuppa for 07:00hrs and prepare breakfast and literally find the deck covered with information on what was going on; not only signals but snippets from probably days old newspapers from other members of the ship's crew. It soon got around that the Captain's PO Steward was starting up a diary and when you think about it I probably was the ideal person to do so as most of my time was spent up and around the Captain's Quarters for any requirements that might be needed or even, at short notice, from other Senior Naval Officers who might need to visit Broadsword; Admiral Woodward being a high possibility. If the SCO (Ship's Communication Officer) were to find out his lads were shoving signals through my Pantry door he'd probably have had a fit but like all the Officers onboard Broadsword they were of a good sort. I can proudly say Broadsword was a happy ship's crew and always would be regardless. Like all the other ships, the amount of pressure Commanding Officers and Crew were about to undertake in the next couple of months would be tested to the maximum. For the last few weeks on Exercise Springtrain mock exercises were put into force for exactly this kind of attack on the fleet but then it was more like games: this however might be for real. We also had information that at least 7,000 troops of the Argentinian Military Personnel were on the Falklands.

It now seemed war was imminent and it was therefore decided to commandeer the P+O Liner Uganda to act as a

Hospital Ship. The ship at the time was actually on a cruise in the Mediterranean. So I imagine her passengers weren't happy when they were bundled ashore in Naples so the ship could then sail off to Gibraltar to get kitted up with all the high-tech medical supplies and equipment and then bring onboard all the doctors and nurses needed to man the floating hospital. I'm sure the MOD would have compensated in full the passengers at a later date for their paid tickets and the inconvenience caused to them. The same day Brilliant Group left the Ascension. Admiral Woodward also departed from Ascension to fly his flag in HMS Glamorgan (Type 42 Destroyer) to meet up the next day, April fifteenth, with the Carrier Group led by the Aircraft Carrier HMS Hermes, commanded by Captain Middleton, Royal Navy. Hermes would be the flag ship throughout the rest of the campaign. At this time this is where HMS Alacrity, HMS Yarmouth and HMS Broadsword would also meet up with the Aircraft Carrier and our first and foremost role from then was to act as Goalkeeper, which basically means to say we flank the Carrier to defend her from any incoming attacks from either quarters: in a nut shell we get zapped first.

The Antrim Group were also at the Ascension. They had been there since the tenth of April led by HMS Antrim (Guided Missile Destroyer) in company with HMS Plymouth (Leander Class Frigate) and RFA Tidespring. RFA Fort Austin was responsible for replenishing HMS Endurance (Ice Patrol Survey Vessel). Endurance was the first Royal Naval Vessel on the scene at South Georgia when all this flared up, to disembark the scrap metal

HMS Glamorgan at Ascension Island.

workers from the Island. Once fully fuelled up and stores received onboard the Antrim Group with Endurance they would now sail for South Georgia with RFA Tidespring and RFA Fort Austin would head North to rendezvous with the Brilliant Group. RFA Appleleaf would also follow the Brilliant Group. The Royal Fleet Auxiliary Ships (RFA's) are literally the bloodline for the Royal Navy for supplying fuel and essential store to the ships and with so little armament to protect them I salute the Fleet Auxiliary Crews not only in a time of war but also during the peace times. Officially now on the fifteenth of April Admiral Woodard now flies his flag on HMS Hermes and on the sixteenth we all arrived at the Ascension for the continuous work of storing ship. At anchor the scene was absolutely overwhelming, with ships dotted all around us in all shapes and sizes and looking into the air, well, if you imagine you have just disturbed a wasps' nest and you are surrounded by dozens and dozens of angry workers, this scene would fit the bill almost exactly, with the amount of helicopters airborne all doing their bit to get every ship stored up as soon as possible before we commenced our journey down South for battle.

* * *

It was mid-afternoon and the ship was at anchor. The weather scorching hot with hardly a breeze of air around; thank god for the ship's air cooling system, inside the ship it would be literally unbearable without it.

"Please don't let the air conditioning throw a bloody wobbler now."

As things had started to quieten down I heard a few of the lads had dug out their fishing rods which have been secretly hidden in various nooks and crannies around the ship. So with a couple of hours to spare on my hands I decided to pop down to my cabin and get changed out of my tropical white shorts, socks, white shoes and tropical shirt to something more practical such as my tropical blue shorts and shirt and don a pair of sandals. I then decided to make my way to the Quarterdeck where most of the fishing enthusiasts would have got set up. Just walking down the main drag en-route to the Quarterdeck it was such a sense of excitement to witness crew members popping out of doors and hatches and coming up ladders from various Messdecks laden with tackle, rods, hooks and flies in boxes, making their way to the Main Galley at first to scrounge from the Duty Leading Chefs and Duty Chefs whatever they could to use for bait. Moments like these you absolutely treasure; who would ever think we were on the verge of war? The atmosphere around the ship certainly didn't warrant this whatsoever.

"Hey, Taffy." I bellowed as I saw him emerge up the ladder from three para Messdeck proudly boasting a sun and fishing titfer and all the other essentials needed. "How's it going, mate?"

"Hi, Baz. OK, mate. Well, I've got my bait sorted out half hour ago before these other buggers twigged on, so hopefully at least I might manage to get a decent spot on the Quarterdeck before it gets overcrowded."

We walked down to the Quarterdeck together and talked about our families back home. He had all the update letters from his girlfriend back home and like myself had taken the opportunity to phone loved ones, families and friends before we departed and sailed out of Gibraltar. We both came to the same assumption even now that give it a couple of days: "You'll see" and the whole affair will be sorted. It was only a matter of time before the Argies backed down. They're just testing to see just how far they can go with the Brits.

Anyhow having convinced our families of just how we felt it must have been some sort of relief to them and to reassure them if "we" weren't worried then damn well they shouldn't be, and if they could have seen a video of what the ship's crew were doing now it would definitely have convinced them likewise. Taff was a Leading Seamen

Missileman and spent most of his time when on duty in the Operations Rooms and if not there he either was sorting out Seamanship stuff or involved in the manning of our sea boats. One of his duties could easily have involved being the Coxwain of one of the sea boats, to the aftermath debris of a depth charge firing and that was to retrieve not only what was left but to also to the whole ship's delight, pick up all the dead edible fish – mostly snapper – that would fall victim to the ship's Gunnery Exercise. This of course took all the fun and enjoyment out of fishing and was a cheat way of getting a cheap lunch (of course your Admiralty Lordships wouldn't see it that way, costing goodness knows how many thousands of pounds for each firing!).

It goes without saying that day was going to be an adventurous day where ever you managed to find a spot to throw your line over the side. I just wish at times like this I had remembered to bring along the little rod I had at home, it didn't really occur to me until now. I stayed with Taff for about half an hour, once he'd got himself settled in a reasonable spot with other crew members on the Quarterdeck who, as I wandered around were using lines from large and small rods and a couple had resourcefully taken the initiative to just tie a length of nylon to a block of wood, attach a hook, apply whatever bait they had, sling it over the side and hope for the best. Believe it or not nine times out of ten they hauled in some unfortunate sea critter lurking in the depths.

"Well, I'm off back into the ship, it's getting too bloody hot out here for me and as for the activity going on all around us with ships of all shapes and sizes still being stored up by the endless number of helicopters still buzzing around like locusts in the afternoon sun. Time for me to pop back inside to cool off for a while."

No sooner had I closed the inside watertight door and made my way back passed the Laundry who should be coming out of the Sick Bay just along from the Laundry but me ole buddy Petty Officer Medical Assistant (POMA) John Wicks. He also now had his chores around the Sick Bay complete and was going to take a wonder around the Upperdeck on the lively activity that was going on. I explained that Taff and probably seven other people were fishing aft but no luck on any catches yet. Apart from my main duties of Stewarding, my main role at Action Stations was to be in charge of the after First Aid Crew, with Scouse Bradburn taking charge of his team at the Forward First Aid Post. John would then oversee both his Crews with Surgeon Lieutenant Woodroof and advise, teach and demonstrate all there was to know about all and everything on the medical side as First Aiders. John and I would quite often meet up in the POs' Bar at 21:00hrs and catch up on all the gossip around the ship and discuss any points. Reference first aid matters basically, talk shop for a couple of hours, but always done with sincerity and many a time the points brought up would be beneficial to both of us professionally.

"Barrie mate, while I think of it I've just written a memo to the Jimmy, reference to placing a message on tomorrow's Daily Orders that during the dogs (16:00 to 20:00 I think or is it 16:00 to 18:00? Anyhow 16:00 onwards) that any First Aiders that can be spared from their duties are to muster in the Sick Bay for training."

Now what are we training for this time was my response. Surely we've learnt everything there is to know and we've all been through these scenario exercises literally dozens of dozens of times – what now?

"Ah yes, Baz, I know. But not everyone, if any of the First Aid Teams has been trained up to administer an intravenous (I.V.) drip, which requires the insertion of a sterile needle into the vain and blood stream to supply the red blood cells with protein from the liquid in the drip to the body. This of course would be administered to anyone injured who has lost a considerable amount of blood and would be of a life or death situation to any First Aider. The latter should never arise if the teams have been properly trained and briefed."

"OK John, I'll make sure I'm available for tomorrow's session and I'll try and inform as many of the teams as possible between now and then."

A few minutes later the "Doc" and I went our own separate ways around the ship.

I suppose it must have been just after I'd served the Captain his afternoon cuppa that a commotion at the other end of the ship erupted. So not being nosy (I lie), I made my way down the ladder to two Deck and challenged the first crew member I saw and asked him what the hell was all the fuss about. AFT "Taff" is fighting like mad to land a shark was the reply as he also was racing down to the Quarterdeck with me close on his heels. What's he trying to haul in I thought "a Great White" or whatever the species of sharks were here in the Atlantic. Needless to say when we arrived the Quarterdeck was swarming with crew members. Let's face it this was the highlight of the day so far and it goes without saying that anyone who thought they had found a quiet peaceful spot for fishing, I'm afraid their hopes were completely dashed now, and would be for the rest of the afternoon. I don't know how long Taff and the fish had been at battle with each other but guessed for at least a good half to three-quarters of an hour. Anyhow he had successfully managed to reel it inboard to the delight of the ship's company and to this day I still didn't find out what sort of shark it was, but it can't have been any bigger than two to three and a half feet long. I would imagine probably a Sand Shark, which would be quite unaware that on this fateful day it would be for the Broadsword Galley Pot and made into shark fin soup, which we would have a taste later that evening.

Progressing now into the evening and chatting to Captain Canning about the fishing event, after serving him his 18:00hrs cocktail (orange, ice and water), we were both looking forward to an evening's entertainment of Horse Racing held on the Flight Deck which would be organised and run by the ship's Chief Petty Officers (well done to the Chiefs). To break up the monotony of the last few days the Chiefs, with the approval of the Captain, had decided to start and prepare for this event a few days earlier. The event which was due to start at 20:00 would consist of a race track simulation laid out on the Flight Deck and up to six horses made of hardboard from our Chippy's Shop, individually coloured for example in red, blue, white, green and be ready lined up at the starter's post. Punters then would have the opportunity of placing bets at the allocated deck positions, then, starting from track one to six a massive dice would be thrown from a plastic bucket for each horse in turn. Around the course and more or less on the principles of snakes and ladders there would be set backs or advance bonuses from start to finish, for example back two paces, miss a throw, take another throw, forward four paces and of course the worst of the lot if you were in the lead and nearly at the finishing line and had the misfortune in landing on the square, yes, you've guessed it "Back to Start". You would have very, very little chance of getting back to the leading front runners. Mind you it has been done before on a couple of occasions I've known. Well, with the barbeque food set up by the Catering Department and cases upon cases supplied by NAAFI Manager, Kevin O'Kane, and the NAAFI Assistant, Steve Edwards, it turned out to be a very enjoyable and relaxing night. It also gave us a chance to let off steam, get out of uniform in exchange for any outrageous outfit. On this occasion most of the crew were sporting jockey get-ups: caps, riding sticks etc.

I really must commend the Chiefs, they always know how to organise a bloody good night. I remembered about an hour before all this was about to start meeting CPO Skilleter or as most of us were to know him as "Billy Whizz" along the passageways between Decks all dressed up for the fun night. I think his role was either to be a commentator or dice thrower. Billy was an absolute natural when it came to entertaining and was forever having a good laugh and a joke with the Troops whatever rank or rate.

"Barrie, don't forget to remind the "old man" to bring stacks of cash with him tonight for a flutter on the gee-gees. All profits made go to the ship's charity."

"Don't worry, Billy mate." I replied. "Captain already knows and is eagerly waiting to place bets before the first race starts."

Gambling in the Royal Navy is illegal. The only exception to the rule when it is 1) Authorised by the CO 2) Profits must go to a proper registered charity 3) Monies paid in and out for whatever the entertaining function should be happening, must be run properly by an NCO or Officer; in this case Chief's Mess Members.

It must have been about midnight before the last of the stragglers finally departed from the Flight Deck and like always before the end there was a mad rush to the beer dump to see who can buy the last few cans from the NAAFI Staff, before it dries up. It was evenings like that when I'm glad I wasn't the duty Petty Officer at sea working alongside the MAAs and just because the Flight Deck had been cleared you could bet your bottom dollar the partying didn't cease. Here it takes ages to get the Crew Members to quieten down. You can guarantee a few of the Messdecks, including my own, would have taken their high spirits below Decks but usually everyone had exhausted the use of their vocal cords by a damn good sing-song. The ship was thankfully at peace around midnight to 01:00hrs and everyone was tucked up in bed-e-byes snoring their heads off. Luckily for me I never managed to get clobbered for the DPO Sea Roster; I only get stung once the ship gets alongside in port anywhere around the globe.

Dutifully at 16:00hrs the following day with anxious mixed feelings about the sticking in needle and vein thing I made my way towards the ship's Sick Bay, situated aft on Two Deck. The Sick Bay door was open and most of the two First Aid Teams had already arrived and were in deep conversation with both John and our Surg/LT. A few minutes later the remaining team turned up with the exception of the Wardroom Duty Steward who had to be in attendance to serve tea to the ship's Officers, and would be trained separately at a later time during the day. After a brief introduction of why a silicone drip was needed in emergency cases we then had to know how to administer the fluid into the bloodstream. If you get a bit squeamish about a normal common injection or jab you want to try sticking a needle into someone and if that's not bad enough you have to find a suitable vein for the liquid to flow into the bloodstream. I can tell you now it's hit or miss as our lot found out as we were prompted by our Doc to perform the grotesque exercise on each other. I can tell you now it took some of us a few attempts to get it right and we weren't allowed to leave the Sick Bay until we did. Once this mission was accomplished by all, bruised and leaking like sieves we sombrely went back to our duties or whatever we were doing before we were summoned to, in my eyes, the worst practical first aid training I'd ever come across. I suppose it's the reality at the end of the day, we could be in a position to actually have to do this and possibilities were getting more and more highly likely as the war got closer and closer to our doorstep, or should I say hatchstep. This uncomfortable hour of training was going to be invaluable to some of our First Aid Teams within the next month and a half. As we all staggered out of the Sick Bay I made my way to my Cabin to lie down for an hour. Halfway down the main drag I met up with Jerry.

"Bloody hell, Baz, you look awful. Sure you don't want to visit the Sick Bay?" "Bugger the Sick Bay," was my answer. "I've seen enough of that area for one day thank you very much." That left him wondering what the hell I was on about but I explained to him later over a couple of bevvies in the Mess.

I also bumped into Billy Whizz and told him what a good night his Mess had organised at the horse racing. Billy was the Senior Rate in charge of the Sea Wolf Missiles with Bob McGregor and the job for the Sea Wolf Missile Teams was to get the missiles up from the Magazines about four Decks below from the Ammunition Compartments and by using the hoist up to Two Deck disperse evenly the missiles to the Firing Launch Areas, so as to be ready for firing from the OPs Room position by command.

It was actually Billy who took a great amount of interest in my diary and gave me a lot of encouragement to see it through to the end. Well, Billy mate, here it is twenty-five years later, but as the saying goes: better late than never.

The day before we sailed from Ascension on the seventeenth the Commander in Chief and Major General Moore flew from London to meet up and brief Admiral Woodward and Commodore Clapp (in charge of the Amphibious Ships) with Brigadier Thompson. He then apparently flew back to Britain that same day so it looked like we had had a visit to Ascension Island by the Big Wigs or in Military terms "Top Brass", from London. What now? No doubt we would find out all in good time.

Now with the full Carrier Group stored up completely on the eighteenth and led by the Flagship Hermes, Broadsword, Glamorgan, Yarmouth, Alacrity and our supply ships RFA Olmeda and Resource, we were ready to sail from Ascension Island. Unfortunately HMS Invincible (Carrier) hadn't yet completed stores but was later to sail that same afternoon and caught up with us soon afterwards.

Reality now started to take a grip as all ships in the Carrier Group were ordered into defence watches, which means to say every crew member, whatever branch or rate, would be required to report to their allocated position around the ship for an eight-hour shift in order to be in a state of readiness for an incoming attack by hostile forces. In other words we were one step away from action stations and when that happens try and imagine yourself at a football match and for argument's sake some incident occurs in your stand that sends everyone running, ducking and diving in all directions to reach whatever destination they think would be safe for them. This is the best way I would describe it, but bearing in mind, although it is a panic situation because everyone knows the ship is now under possible attack, with everyone running up and down ladders, dashing in both directions along passageways, diving through different compartments and slamming shut watertight doors behind them, as they have reached their now different allocation for this highest state of readiness for an imminent attack on the ship, it is absolute bedlam. The difference here from an incident on a football ground terrace and a British Warship is the football supporters are absolutely blind to the sudden horror they have now been forced into and will instinctively try for any means of escape out of the chaos that surrounds them in the sudden danger that faces them, their families and friends. In a Warship, however the adrenalin is, like the football supporters, racing through our veins, but we have the advantage of knowing, unlike our supporter football friends, of exactly where and the direction where we have to get to in order to defend our ship before danger strikes from any weaponry used by the enemy. At the time the order is given to go to defence watches every crew member from the Captain to the most Junior Member of the crew has to carry their own battle bag, wherever they go around the ship, on or off watch and even to the loo. The battle bag consisted of anti-flash hood and gloves, life jacket, action overalls (or coveralls; whatever you like to call them), water bottle with a special drinking tube (purpose is for expected gas attack and respirators are ordered to be put on), gas respirator, plastic drinking mug, ear defenders (used mainly for the Gun Crews and Flight Team) and surcoat for whatever you represent; in my case and the First Aid Team, white surcoat displaying the Red Cross sign. In addition for the First Aid Teams, if this isn't enough to lug around, a canvas first aid bag fully topped up with various types of bandages, plasters, eye solution, morphine, note book and writing implement, marker pen, syringe needles for silicone drips and the bottle and an extra water bottle. Bloody hell, it's enough to haul your own battle bag around the ship hour after hour but to carry this extra additional stuff, it's "fucking knackering". But if it's going to save lives at the end of the day, so be it – a water bottle on its own after a few hours seems like you're carrying a lead weight, and with all the other gear you look like a stuffed waddling duck bobbing around the ship. If you had wings there'd be no hope in hell you'd ever get off the ground.

My role as the Captain's Petty Officer Steward ceased as soon as defence watches were ordered. I assumed a completely different area of responsibility at another post which was to man the switchboard situated on Two Deck at the other end of the ship in HQ1, right next to the Marine Engineering lads in the Main Engineering Control Room. This place is something else if you were to see the system used to monitor all the four mega-powerful engines. If all the warning lights were, for example, to light up you'd think you were on Kirk's space ship Enterprise (hardly unlikely they would). I used to take great delight every time when on watch to witness them going through their safety checks and see all the lines of panels light up with the numerous different coloured lights, for whatever purpose. Although I thoroughly respected our Captain it was a great opportunity for me to get away from the everyday monotonous routine in the Captain's and Wardroom Areas and meet up and work alongside crew members who were a completely different Branch (trade). It was inevitable that I would, at some stage, be on watch with my other fellow Petty Officers in the ME Department who were Mick Brennan, Dave Pickup, Dave Ogden, Kim Robinson, Bob Butler, Pete Heron, George Bowham, Andy Jenkins, Peter Tabenor and Simon Giles. Every one of these Petty Officers was always ready to assist me in my new role in HQs, whenever they were on watch with me, although I had nothing to do with their department. It just goes to show there is a lot to be said, wherever you hear it, that we all work as "a team". It doesn't happen very often on our more modern day Warships, but on the older types it was more or less a tradition for the ME Department to scrounge some grub from the Main Galley during the day if you knew you were on the night/morning shift and take it down to the Boiler Room to heat up and have a good old nosh up at two or three in the morning.

We were in our fourth day of defence watch routine and the date was the twenty-second of April, a Thursday. HMS Brilliant had been ordered to detach from Brilliant Group to join and assist the Antrim Group. HMS Sheffield, commanded by Captain Salt, now took temporary command of the Brilliant Group. Between leaving the Ascension Island and now we had believed to have made one enemy submarine contact. We were in company with ships HMS Coventry (Destroyer), HMS Sheffield (Destroyer), HMS Alacrity (Frigate) and our faithful old friend the Blue Rover, our Royal Fleet Auxiliary Ship, to replenish us all with fuel and stores. The twenty-seventh of April was to be a very sad day for everyone in the Task Group. Although a landing was made by two helicopters on the twenty-second the mission was aborted due to the crash of two Wessex helicopters on South Georgia Glacier. But all teams were safely rescued by HMS Antrim's own helicopter (thankfully no life was lost on this occasion). But again while on a sortie HMS Hermes' own Sea King helicopter sustained engine failure and was forced to ditch. Although all the crew members, apart from one, managed to escape we lost our first casualty at sea, a Petty Officer Air Crewman by the name of POAEM KS Casey. This undoubtedly was a very sad loss for Hermes, but also for the rest of the fleet. Our hearts went out to the man's family and loved ones.

I'd often pop up to the Captain's Quarters between defence watches just to see if the CO was OK, although now it wasn't my place to do so while in the defence watch routine. On my first visit I couldn't believe the transformation in the Captain's Day Cabin. Everything had been moved around in order to make it into a "War Room" Area; there were charts, maps, easels, notices and diagrams of ships' positions plastered all around the Area. Well, if it's got "this far" perhaps there isn't a hope in hell of turning back now, were my immediate thoughts when I saw the layout in his Quarters.

On the twenty-fifth of April we learned at 09:00 that HMS Antrim, with HMS Plymouth (Frigate) had been constantly bombing bombardment shells on the Georgian Islands and they were soon recaptured by our SBS (Special

Boat Service) Teams (who are equivalent to the Group Force SAS) and the Royal Marines. Also the old, I mean, old submarine, "Sante Fe" was disabled by HMS Plymouth's Lynx Helicopter firing one of her Sea Skuas. HMS Plymouth and Antrim both witnessed surrender documents from Captain Largos who at the time was the Commander of the Argentine Forces on the Georgia Island (signed on HMS Antrim) and Lieutenant Alfredo Astiz who signed his surrender document on HMS Plymouth. The whole of the Santa Fe's submarine crew were captured and held as prisoners on the Naval Warships Plymouth and Antrim. We received a signal that evening addressed to all Commanding Officers and Crew Members which was requested by the Senior Military Argentinian Officer (Captain of the sub): "Being well looked after by the British Royal Navy."

HMS Plymouth.

There were reports that the Argentines' 707 spy plane was trying to penetrate the Task Group so HMS Hermes launched two Sea Harriers to intercept and destroy it if it got too close. With all this going on and with the surrender and recapture surely all this must now start to wrap up and come to a close so we can all get on with our business and perhaps we might even rejoin our original deployment jolly. I mean it had only been a few weeks when we were involved and the shit hit the fan.

"Come on, someone make a decision."

NO SUCH LUCK.

On the twenty-eighth of April the British Government ordered the 200-mile exclusion zone surrounding the Falkland Islands. It goes without saying the whole ship's company by now was ear-glued twenty-four hours a day to the events in London by means of World News on the ship's radio. There was absolutely no room for any other crap to listen to on any other channel or station. Two days later on the thirtieth of April the Main Task Force of the British Royal Navy arrived in the Exclusion Zone. America by now had given their support for Britain.

"War Now Awaits".

I honestly could see some kind of retaliation, from either the Argentinian Naval Forces for capturing one of their subs and taking all the crew members prisoners or again by the Argies' Ground Forces now we had now taken back South Georgia. It looked like at any time: "The Fight Is On"

The US Secretary of State had completely exhausted all his peace options to both countries and had to stand down or back off and watch from a distance to see which "Best Man Wins". I must admire Alexander Haig though for all his efforts. I don't think anyone could have been more of a go-between in President Reagan's Administration for peace than him. Nevertheless war was imminent.

We were all aware that the Argentine Navy had left port and were out there somewhere with the Frigates, Destroyers, Cruisers and Subs. It only needed a matter of time to find out exactly where.

"HANDS TO ACTION STATIONS, "HANDS TO ACTION STATIONS" sounded at 11:40hrs throughout the ship on the first of May 1982. Two aircraft contacts had been detected on Broadsword's radar screen in the Operations Room.

"Fuck it's started for us already."

There was a great urgency throughout the ship to reach our place of duty at Action Stations and report it to Command once we were all at our posts. It was now my job to check that all my First Aid Team were closed up in the After First Aid Area in One Mike flat. That was situated just forward of the Sea Wolf Loading Area, Hanger and Flight Deck. Once I had made my report that the After First Aid Post were closed up I then briefed my team and paired them off ready for any attack that would be expected from enemy aircraft and to deal with any casualties inflicted by any number of injuries expected either by fire, shrapnel, loss of limb, head injuries and all kinds of unexpected events that could possibly take place in the next half an hour. The adrenalin was at its highest point and all of us were very tense waiting, just waiting for the announcement, "Incoming Aircraft" or "Incoming Missiles".

"This is for real."

We could have very well become a target in the next few minutes and I could sense the slight fear in my team and detect it slightly in their eyes as they undoubtedly could in mine. The two aircraft when first reported were believed to be 150 miles away and heading in our direction. That was five minutes before, "AIR RAID WARNING RED" "AIR RAID WARNING RED" bellowed on the main ship's tannoy system. This is the highest state of readiness for an immediate threat by enemy aircraft. We could be attacked at any moment.

"Please god, get our Sea Wolf or Exocet Missiles locked on to these aircrafts and zap the shit out of them."

11:45am enemy aircraft identified as two Mirages who had fired missiles 50 miles out. This was believed to have been done as they couldn't risk coming any closer due to the fact they were running out of fuel and were unable to find their own re-fuelling tanker. Two Harriers were scrambled from HMS Hermes to intercept and the Argentinian missiles launched made no impact or damage to any of the Task Group.

"Hands to Action Messing" was piped at 12:00hrs (lunch), which is a speed feed while still closed up at Action

Stations. Believe it or not, but the Chefs and Catering Department did the whole ship proud by providing a very nourishing and filling "Pot Mess", which was basically a hot stew. I have never heard of anyone complaining about this veg, meat and potato stew. If anything some of the lads would have loved to have it on the regular menu once in a while. The term "Speed Feed" means exactly that: you have minutes to get to the Galley, scoff down your grub, wash it down with a cuppa or mug of water and get back to your Action Stations to allow the next Team Members to feed. Usually I would send my Team two at a time allowing my Team Leader to go in the first or second pair so as to allow myself to proceed for a nosh up once he returned. Once all personnel had been fed and watered in my section I would then make the appropriate report to HQ that all the First Aid After Crew have wined and dined and are all back on Station. Ironically my reports went directly to the section where I was closed up at defence watches, in exactly the same position as when my role in the ship changed yet again, once Action Stations had been ordered. Mind you HQ was now the prime command area for all reports to be monitored throughout the whole ship. All, I mean all, sections and compartments had to report in that personnel were at their proper Action Station Post by their Section Leaders, in my case it would be me for our First Aid Teams. The other major role for HQs, who in turn report to the ship's command, that is the Captain, would be to monitor all fire, floods or damage caused by an attack. This would be done on a massive damage control board with the whole of the ship's layout from the funnel to the bilges and would be marked accordingly where the damage occurred by using different coloured stencil pens shaded in diagonally, for example, fire indicating colour red, flood would be blue and electrical damage green.

Before we even went to Defence Stations, let alone Action Stations, I vividly remember one glorious evening after having supper, going on the Upper Deck and leaning over the guard-rail armed with a brew in a plastic mug and thinking to myself, on a very rare occasion you were left alone with your own thoughts and were extremely lucky if you managed to do so, if the main threat to this ship was to come about the biggest threat of all must surely come from aircraft. Are we prepared for that I thought? All the Gun Crews have exhaustedly been practising continuously. The Sea Wolf Teams also have had many good firing runs as had the Exocet Crews and Torpedo Teams for subs, but yes, aircraft were definitely going to be the punch to us by the Argentine Airforce. How true this assumption was going to be. As time went on all the Gun Crews were geared up so it was wait and see. Like all matelots on ships it's only natural to think you are part of a team that is the best in the fleet and understandably everyone's opposites on other ships are always trying to outdo their counterparts in one way or another. And why not? It's all done with great professionalism and respect with a bit of skylarking, jokes and fun thrown in just for good measure.

Most of our Royal Marines would have joined up with our Gun Crews at this stage, but obviously they could be called upon at a minute's notice to stand down and be prepared to make an assault shore side once given the appropriate information and green light. If any ship's Gun Crews be it small arms (Bofors), Sea Wolf, Exocet or whatever, were going to give the Argies a bloody nose it would be the Broadsword lads. So with this thought I drained the last dregs of my now cold tea and feeling a lot happier with myself I went back inside the ship.

At 12:00hrs we got reports through to the MCO that nine Sea Harriers had just returned from a sortie, after an apparently very successful bombardment on Port Stanley Airstrip. We were still closed up at Action Stations and at 12:56 "Air Raid Warning Red" was piped again over the Broadcast System. By 13:00 three Mirage aircraft were identified on radar. These aircraft are supersonic fighters and would be lethal to our ships if engaged, but for some reason or another they altered course 110 miles away and the ship went to stage "Air Raid Warning Yellow" which is one drop down from red. I wondered where are they pissing off to now to cause havoc. With no threat in our vicinity the ship relaxed from Action Stations at 13:30hrs and we reverted to our normal Defence Watch routine but it was still my official shift on watch so I plodded off to finish my watch at HQ.

We were to go back to Action Stations again on the first of May at 19:25 and HMS Hermes sent CAP (Cover Aircraft Protection) to intercept Mirage aircraft. It was reported later that one of the aircraft was shot down and the other Argentine Mirage returned to its base. Also a raid was taking place to the West and six Harriers were scrambled to assist. Our first Action Stations on the first of May was at 10:00 and HMS Brilliant was sent by Admiral Woodward to investigate the radar contact which this time came from underwater. It is believed that Brilliant had fired two of her torpedoes at the contact but later it was decided the contacts may have been whales. She (Brilliant) returned to the Task Group at 10:15. At 10:30 we were approximately 180 miles off Port Stanley and the flagship had eighteen miles to sail before she could send her Sea Harriers for a bombardment at the Port Stanley Airstrip. At 10:50 another nine Sea Harriers were sent to continue the bombardment. We fell out of Action Stations at 11:10. The first day alone we had been to Action Stations three times and this was just the beginning. We have had our first taste of war inside the Exclusion Zone and by now we had all realised there was no turning back. This was for real: it all depended on who was going to win.

Whilst closed up at the 19:25 Action Stations it was reported twelve Mirage aircraft were attacking the Task Force in all directions. HMS Glamorgan, Alacrity and Arrow seemed to be the main targets and Alacrity seemed to have had one casualty. At 21:00hrs after we had fallen out of Action Stations and everything had quietened down our Captain addressed the whole ship's company over the main broadcast system. The Task Force had two Mirage Aircraft brought down by Sea Wolf Missiles and also one Canberra aircraft (which was given to Argentina by the Brazilians). The British Fleet had encountered no loss of aircraft in this wave of attack. The atmosphere in the ship was not one of jubilation although we were pleased with the results but there seemed to be an uncanny silence throughout as if everyone was in a world of their own. Although we were still in Defence Watches conversations when off watch were very short which could be expected because once you were off watch you had eight hours to sort your own life out; that is write home, eat, sleep etc and it didn't take long before you were back on watch again for another eight hour shift. It was like a zombie routine and takes time to get used to. No more attacks on the first of May.

Although I'd been closed up at Actions Stations since 08:00hrs I had a feeling it wouldn't be long during the forenoon before the ship was flung again in complete disarray by the Argentines' Air Force. Sure enough at 10:00 the company was ordered to Action Stations. You can't help feeling sorry for the blokes you had just relieved two hours earlier, who by now should be well into their noddy-land sleep. Fortunately we were stood down at 11:00, one hour later, and reverted to our normal defence watches. At 12:00 a Mirage aircraft was spotted on the radar screen but was no immediate threat as it was reported to be heading away from the ship. It seemed to be going back to its Airforce Main Base.

Although it may seem to have been a very high tension routine which involved both closing up for Defence Watches, with Action Stations thrown in now and again for good measure, believe it or not we did have a very rare opportunity to relax with our Messmates and Sunday 2nd May was no exception. Like most Messdecks around the ship, including the Wardroom and the Captain's, morale needed to remain at its highest possible level at all times. One thing to combat this, although it might not seem too much of a issue to many people in civilian life, was to hold a film show once a week in our Messdecks. Myself being a Petty Officer would hold it in our Recreation Mess. The lads would rig up a film show in the Main Dining Hall Area, the Chiefs in the Chiefs' Mess and the Officers, where the Captain would be invited, would arrange a show in the Wardroom. When I say film shows I mean the proper McCoy of reel to reel movies, using the proper projector equipment and a proper foldaway full-length movie screen. It's quite amazing but every ship I have served on you would always find at least two or three trained projectionists on the ship to operate the equipment for the crews. If, say, the POs hadn't got a trained man to operate the system (heaven forbid for a Senior Rates' Mess), we would ask one of the Operators to show the film, who in turn would be rewarded either by our cash float or, more times than many, would be quite content with a few jars of beer during the movie. It is the Captain of every ship who decides if and when he wants the Messdecks and Wardroom Bars locked, with the distribution of alcohol to be issued either during peacetime or war situations; the Captain's word is final. Fortunately we were never given the order to lock our bars so that Sunday evening at 20:45 it really was a blessing to sit in our own environments with a pint and just – just for a short while – relax and be subconsciously oblivious to the goings on around us. The movie we chose to see that night was "Wild Geese" with Richard Burton and Richard Harris.

At quarter two eleven reports were flashed around the Task Group that the Nuclear Powered Submarine HMS Conqueror had fired two torpedoes at the Argentines' Cruise Ship, General Belgrano, which had consequently sunk with the loss of over 400 sailors. The Cruiser was apparently outside the Exclusion Zone but it was still decided by Admiral Woodward, the British Task Group Commander, to warrant a threat to our Naval Ships.

I can only speak for myself but I can imagine, from one sailor to another, that there would not have been a lot of jumping for joy. The fact was that they had just sent 400, although enemy, fellow sailors to their deaths, mostly teenage boy sailors. As we were all aware the Argentine Navy recruited so many of these young lads with hardly any experience in their job, let alone to be faced with war, and yes, it brings up the well-known saying "War is a nasty business", whatever side you are on. But you still can't help thinking a spark of anger towards the two Foreign Secretaries representing Britain and Argentina, with the support of both Governments, not being able to come to a peaceful solution before lives were lost. Anyhow who am I to say? I'm just a mere steward!

At 23:59 London confirmed the sinking of the Argentine Cruiser, General Belgrano, by announcing on the World News Main Radio Station.

From an eight Defence Watch Routine we were now settled in a six-hour watch system with me being part of the Starboard Watch and reporting to my place of duty at 02:00hrs to relieve the Port Watch HQ personnel. During the evening two enemy tugs were under fire. They inflicted very little known damage until later we were to find out that these tugs had opened fire on a Sea King helicopter. Two Lynx Helicopters were scrambled to these tugs which had apparently been converted to "Gun Ships" and during the Lynx attack one "Gun Ship" was completely destroyed with no survivors and the other damaged considerably.

Action Stations were ordered at 10:00 on the third of May (why was it at this hour again?). At 10:15 it was reported that the Argies' Aircraft Carrier had been plotted 200 miles West of the Main Task Group (I didn't know they had one!). At 10:16 a contact was picked up on radar four miles to the East of the Main Task Group; we were heading South. A Sea King and Lynx were sent out to intercept the contact. HMS Glamorgan (Destroyer) made a signal to ships that she had just sailed passed two life rafts and reported no survivors. It is presumed that these must have come from the tug boat (converted to a Gun Ship) that was sunk during the night. At 10:45 Royal Marines landed on the Falklands to act as Scouts and were dropped off by Sea King helicopters from HMS Hermes.

I could not help thinking while I was on the passage down from Ascension Island about what the people were thinking of all this at home. It must have been bad enough just to read a national newspaper headlines plastered over the main front page "Britain at War". As for us all involved in the Task Group we got a tremendous boost to hear that back home not only were a very high percentage of the British public behind us, but not all of this tremendous Task

Group could have been put into action and made possible without the dedication, loyalty and bloody hard work (literally twenty-four hours a day) of our Naval Dockyard Personnel in Devonport (DML) and Portsmouth's Dockyard Workers whatever trade or task they were professionally tasked to do. A great admiration was felt by all of us for the impossible to be achieved. My hat definitely goes up to all the Dockies for the role they played in this 1982 conflict.

As I've probably mentioned before nothing seemed to matter now about the lost cruise we were supposed to have undertaken. This was literally being in the front line to defend our rights for British Rule on Territory and I was feeling twenty feet tall to be part of it for our Country and would have absolutely hated it if I had been grounded at some shore established running a Wardroom Mess and being unable to have the privilege of serving in one of the Warships. Let's face it, I'd served sixteen years already, all of peacetime and would have felt as sick as a dog if I had not been where I was then. This doesn't mean I'm a warmonger by any means, but I wouldn't have missed this opportunity for the world to serve my Queen and Country: "NEVER". It was, we all felt, an absolute honour to do so even if we were shit-scared of the consequences or the outcome.

The rest of Monday 3rd May passed reasonably peacefully and our Captain addressed the ship's crew for the second time at 19:45, to inform us that a second wave of Royal Marines had been airlifted to the Falkland Islands, again during the early hours of the morning. I wondered if

Simon (Neill) was amongst the Royals in this detachment. As I mentioned before, Simon is the younger son of the foster parents who brought me up as a child. The Captain also mentioned that there would be a possible attack by Vulcan aircraft on the Port Stanley Airstrip, but this would undoubtedly depend on the weather conditions for it to execute this operation. The Captain signed off.

Raids were carried out during the night and again at 06:30 to bombard Port Stanley Airstrip by the Vulcan aircraft. In the meantime we were ordered back to Action Stations at 09:30 on the Tuesday May fourth, for the sixth time since the first one at 10:00 on the first May. The threat was, as you might have guessed, "Air Raid Warning RED", surface warning YELLOW (no immediate threat to enemy surface ships) and sub surface warning RED. Now this meant not only was there an immediate threat by air but we obviously had an immediate threat to this ship by Submarine torpedoes. Reports were being made to us by Intelligence that a large air raid was forming up; this was probably due to the attack on the airfield by our Vulcan Bombers. Reports were coming through that during the Vulcans' raid a Harrier Jump Jet shot down an enemy aircraft while acting as protection cover for the Vulcans and it was also reported that 120 survivors from the Belgrano had been saved. By 11:00hrs all states of readiness were reduced down to State "YELLOW". We could fall out of Action Stations and go back to the six-hour Defence Watches.

The fourth of May proved one of the most devastating days the Royal Navy had witnessed for many years and was a day of reality for me and the fleet that it had finally really sunk home with no question of a doubt that Great Britain was "AT WAR". Until that day arrived I still had thoughts that it would all be over within a few days although incidents had occurred beforehand with the Santa-Fe (Submarine) and the Belgrano. Also the taking of South Georgia and in a short space of time being yet again liberated by the British Forces; surely this would soon be over.

Everything changed at approximately 14:20hrs when we were ordered to Action Stations for the seventh time. What we were about to learn was absolutely incomprehensible. One of our most modern and sophisticated Destroyers had received a direct hit from one of the deadliest missiles a Warship could encounter: an Exocet Missile. It was fired by an Argentinian Super Etendard Aircraft at HMS Sheffield, amidships Starboard side, and ended up through into the Mains Operations Control Room which couldn't have been a worse area for a missile to hit, apart from the Ammunition Compartments. The Exocet that destroyed Sheffield was a surface to surface/air to surface missile and as mentioned was fired by the Fighter Bomber aircraft the Super Etendard. More or less on the moment the Exocet locked in with it deadly cargo the Sheffield was doomed. The impact immediately caused disastrous results to the crew on HMS Sheffield with twenty ship's company being killed and dozens of fires igniting throughout the midship section. Any Maritime Seaman will always tell you the thing to fear at sea is fire, and the extent of damage it causes and still is to this day. The most powerful missile to use against Warships is the Exocet, which is 4.7 metres long and has a wing span of 1.1 metres, weighs approximately 670 kilogrammes and has a deadly warhead of 165 kilogrammes and its range can reach up to 65 kilometres. Although Broadsword was only twenty nautical miles from HMS Sheffield we were not ordered to break away from our role as goalkeeper to the Aircraft Carrier. Instead Admiral Woodward sent in two other Frigates, a "type 21", HMS Arrow, and a Leander Class Frigate, HMS Yarmouth, who at that time was being commanded by Commander Tony Morton who consequently became my last Full Four Ringed Captain to serve under on HMS Beaver in the early 1990s, before I left the Royal Nay in 1994. These two Frigates were immediately sent in to assist Sheffield in any way and the reports that were feeding back to the Task Group was that she was encountering many, many fires onboard and that there were many crew members dead and injured, with the Captain possibly being amongst the dead (but not confirmed at the time). Later we were to find out that their Commnding Officer, Captain Salt, had indeed survived the blast, which crippled his ship, which later sank.

We meanwhile at 14:30 (ten minutes after hearing the fate of Sheffield) had taken the precaution of firing "chaff" in the air. This is ammunition fired above and around our ship which releases metal deflections to confuse any incoming missiles as it would lock on to these metal filings before they would strike the ship. Apparently this has saved many a ship in the past. While still closed up at "Action

Station" at 15:00hrs we had another threat on radar and a periscope had been spotted 30 miles to the South. At 15:30 HMS Glasgow (Destroyer) and 24 miles to the South of HMS Broadsword, had a sonar contact and was in pursuit to investigate.

16:06 and four torpedoes had been fired on HMS Arrow who was assisting the rescue of HMS Sheffield Crew Members. Either the enemy hadn't a clue how to online or properly set torpedoes or it was a chance to fire and run at will I don't know because all four torpedoes missed and the submarine legged it.

16:10 and no further contacts so the ship was ordered to fall out of Action Stations. Before everyone properly closes up to Defence Watches it's not hard to imagine why every possible urinal unit and toilet traps were being engaged in use. Before getting back on watch a wise matelot will make full use of the bog while he possibly can. No one can possibly know when you will have time to go for a piss or shit. Once closed up at Action Stations and fully booted and spurred with all your clobber on, it was virtually impossible to use such luxuries as these. Anyhow if any Section Leader, such as me, was to be approached at Action Stations and someone wingeing for the heads the only possible reply would literally be, "No, tough shit". Which I'm afraid they would have to go through the embarrassment and discomfort of doing just that.

The whole ship was absolutely stunned by the news of HMS Sheffield and had fallen into a sombre mood, mostly in respect for our fellow Shipmates but, more to the point, from the disbelief I saw in a lot of our own crews' faces (me included).

"How, HOW could this be happening? This can't be for real."

I think as the day moved on the more we really started to get to grips with the absolute danger, reality and above all the essential purpose of what exactly our individual responsibilities were. For at "WAR", fighting a war, in the South Atlantic what we were fighting for really became second priority. Number one as we all felt, and I mean number one, from the Captain to last crew member was that at all costs and to the bitter end "SAVE AND DEFEND THIS SHIP". I guarantee the Falklands now came secondary. This ship had been home to many crew members for some two to three years and was now home to members who joined before leaving. Guzz and be buggered if we were going to be blown out of the ogin (water) without a fucking good scrap.

The more the day wore on you could feel the tensions arising in the ship's company and by evening you knew you just knew that **"HMS BROADSWORD WAS NOW READY FOR WAR"**. Don't get me wrong, we definitely were before but this definite change of mood in the ship's company was like the trance spell had been removed and you knew the time for every ounce of professionalism and skill was to be made with the one goal in mind and that was to win at whatever costs. But again I must emphasis priority number one:

"DEFEND AND SAVE THIS SHIP"

Everyone was anxious to hear more news of how HMS Sheffield was coping with her dreadful blow and we were all rooting that if anything could done to save the ship and keep her afloat their ship's company would viciously fight to achieve this, but alas this was to prove an impossible task.

At 18:00hrs Captain Salt (Royal Navy) of HMS Sheffield gave the order to abandon ship (an order no Captain of any seagoing vessel ever wants to give). The crew members now had no choice but to do exactly that, and that means getting off by whatever means, as soon as you can. HMS Arrow and HMS Yarmouth were both at hand to pick up all Sheffield's crew members who had jumped from any position they were in and falling with their bright orange survival suits and life jackets into the icy and bitterly cold South Atlantic water. Apparently while all this was going on Yarmouth was fired upon by Torpedo Tubes but it was reported that all had missed as the ones that were fired on to the Arrow (I can't really say if these sub sightings reported were accurate but they are definitely logged in my diary on this day).

Here we go again. Action Stations were piped at 18:45 "Air Raid Warning RED". The ship must have closed up in record time with reports to HQ that all crew were in their action positions and ready. Two aircraft had been picked up by radar and were heading straight for the Task Force. It was later confirmed that one of the aircraft was one of our Hercules, heavens knows what happened to the other one!

The Captain announced to us the abandoning of HMS Sheffield and we could possibly be expected to take aboard surviving crew members. At 19:16 we reverted to normal defence watches with no immediate threat by enemy to the Task Group.

Every Captain will whenever possible take on fuel and at 21:50 we did exactly that and topped up all our fuel tanks, finishing at approximately 23:15. The night went through fairly peacefully with me being on my Starboard Defence Station in HQ at 02:00hrs. We also learned that it was decided to take the survivors of HMS Sheffield on to two RFAs (Royal Fleet Auxiliaries) who were then flown back to the United Kingdom once the Tankers had reached Ascension Island. Unfortunately it looked like the war was over for these lads.

I was relieved at 08:00 by my Port watcher counterpart and headed straight to the breakfast queue at the Dining Hall. Then it was a quick shit, shave, shampoo and I was off to my rack to get my head down, ready to relieve my mate at HQ in six hours time (please god no Action Stations – we're all knackered). Bloody great, I managed to get a few undisturbed hours kip.

To bring the morale up for us all and raise our high spirits even further, there was nothing more welcome than the mail, which was so gratefully received from Fort Austin and which we eagerly brought on board. Needless to say there weren't short supplies of volunteers for that task. We were also to learn that the RFA Blue Rover had sacks full of mail for Broadsword, so as you can imagine this gave a tremendous boost to every crew member on board. The RFAs are like our fairy godmothers and more so at times like that.

"Hats off to the RFAs and Crews. Cheers Mateys!"

I went back on watch at 12:00 (midday). At 19:55 the Captain addressed the ship's company with news that although HMS Sheffield was still on fire she was still afloat. The fire had spread throughout the entire ship and now there were two options for the Royal Navy: Option No.1 – Sink her now with our own ships or: Option No.2 – Leave her for bait with the intention that the enemy would take so we could zap them if they came within range. The Captain finished his broadcast to us stating the decision was now for the Admiral to take.

I was back on Starboard defence watch at 20:00hrs and was relieved at 02:00hrs. I heard that while off watch we had two surface contacts 80 miles to the South. Apparently, this was to be confirmed as two rocks sticking out of the sea! While returning to Defence Stations at 08:00 we heard on the Main World News that there was a possibility that the Argentine Government was hoping to have talks for a cease-fire (watch this space). Two contacts were picked up from our Aircraft Carrier, HMS Hermes, and Sea Harrier Jets were scrambled to intercept at 11:50hrs on the sixth of May (Thursday). The OOW made an announcement that there could be a possibility that we might be able to send off all our own mail in the next couple of days, transferring over to a ship heading for the UK. So obviously this gave us the incentive to whenever we could get pen to paper so as not to miss the opportunity of landing/transferring our personnel letters to a ship bound for England. By the time I went off duty at 12:00 there was still no news with regards to the two Sea Harriers that were scrambled from Hermes an hour before. We were all eager now to get to the Dining Hall for the midday nosh up as fast as possible so as to get to our own private rest place to start writing home to our families; hopefully they were fully updated by our Government, exactly what's going on out here, but letters to each other are never a substitute as to how each of us all feel. A letter is so much more understood personally by everyone; be it mum, dad, girlfriend, wife, brothers, sisters or cousins. We all knew they were thinking of us as we them. The bond of love seems to intensify tremendously whenever a person is facing danger but the love on both respects will always be strong (if this makes any sense!).

"Bloody hell, not again. Are these people ever going to give up?" The ship yet again was ordered to "Action Stations" at 18:00hrs (this made it nine times in less than a week) "Air Raid Warning RED". HMS Invincible the second Aircraft Carrier supporting the Task Force, has reported to the fleet that five aircraft had been detected on radar. Also the Destroyer HMS Glamorgan had another two aircraft on radar at the same time. Intelligence had informed the Task Force that a very large number of aircraft had left Rio Grande Airstrip which was to the South of us and were heading our way. One could not help thinking this is going to be one hell of an air to sea battle any moment now. Four minutes later the Captain ordered "Chaff" to be fired into the air above and around the ship to confuse the enemy of our exact location, and to decoy any missiles away from Broadsword. Another broadcast was made, this time from our Principle Warfare Officer aircraft (PWO "A"), who announced that although there were no radar contacts on our screens for at least sixty miles caution must be maintained on the possibility that the enemy aircraft could be flying at a very low altitude to avoid being detected by our radar. At 18:20 Glamorgan said an error may have been made on their original contact. Well, better be safe than sorry is all I can say.

What we all heard on the London Main News dashed all hopes of this conflict being resolved. Apparently Argentina had refused all proposals by Mr Haig over a cease-fire. Mr Haig was expected to be in London on Friday 7th May at approximately 17:00 local time for talks with Mrs Thatcher.

By 18:35 we had come down to "Air Raid Warning YELLOW" and had been given the command to relax our anti-flash protection clothing and ten minutes later we went back to Defence Watches.

At quarter to eight that evening the Captain addressed the ship's crew. Firstly, sadly to announce that two Harrier Jets, sent out at 11:00 that morning from HMS Hermes, unfortunately it was believed, that they had collided in mid-air due to poor visibility and very bad weather conditions. It made me think it's bad enough we lose our Fighter Pilot Officers in combat but to lose two brave officers due to weather conditions makes it more unjust. We all felt a sad loss for those brave pilots in the Fleet Air Arm.

My grandfather, Frederick Fieldgate, after serving in the Second World War chose a career in the Fleet Air Arm and like me started his boy training at HMS Ganges. But grandfather, being more ambitious than me and determined to climb the ladder managed to get a commission after serving many years as a Wireless Operator and ended his career in the Fleet Air Arm as a Lieutenant Commander. Ironically my youngest cousin Mark Fane also decided to join the Fleet Air Arm about two years after the Falklands War. I think with Mark it was probably a difficult decision to make after leaving school, to join either the Royal Navy or the Royal Air Force, with whom my uncle, his father, had served his full "twenty-two years" and retired as a Senior NCO (Non Commissioned Officer). Robert Fane, my uncle, had many stories to tell regarding the Air Force, as did grandfather regarding the Navy, so what better way to start in life and get the best of both worlds and then to join up with the Naval Fleet's Aircraft. So even before this war and after, my admiration for the Officers and Crew in our Fleet's Aviation had made me more aware of what their job was, as our family has always been associated with this particular lifestyle and as for Mark I know he thoroughly enjoys and enjoyed working with aircraft. Although only serving for five years in the Navy he had no trouble in securing an Aviation position at Stansted Airport and is still there to this day.

The Captain ended his speech on the note that HMS Sheffield was still afloat and raging fires were still burning. After they did finally manage to burn themselves out it now looked like a detachment of Royal Marines would be sent in to probably set charges in order to sink her. We are yet called to Action Stations at 22:58. Yes, what else could it be but "Air Raid Warning RED"?

We took on fuel again at 00:50 on the seventh of May and then went about our normal Defence Watch changes. Nothing of importance happened during the night and it was not until 11:45 that we got some idea of the situation for the future when the Captain addressed the ship's company over the main broadcast. He announced that London should be expected to order a full scale landing on the Falkland Islands in approximately ten days time or even sooner. Therefore there were one or more options for us as the Task Group to try and minimise the odds and that was take out the air threat so as to minimise the harassment to our forces from the enemy. The Captain had said he put a plan to the Admiral which in turn would have to be approved by Whitehall (more bloody red tape) and that was to send ourselves in charge of a small force of Naval Ships consisting of another Type 22 Frigate (like ourselves) which would be HMS Brilliant and two Type 42 Destroyers which would be HMS Coventry and HMS Glasgow. The idea would be that we all sail at high speed West and North West, but remain within the fleet. The idea was to see how they would react before the main landings took place but more to the point to draw them away from the Mainland (watch this space). Before the Captain signed off he assured us all the political solution was far from solved. We closed up for our eleventh Action Stations at 18:10 with the familiar announcement of "Air Raid Warning RED". What the ship's company were now starting to wonder was the only threat we seem to be getting was by air. Where in the hell were their Ships, Cruisers, Carriers and other vessels. Although the Belgrano had been lost surely they must be building up a Naval force somewhere. I couldn't help thinking that suddenly we were going to get the full force of their Naval fleet in the very near future and if that did happen it would almost certainly be joined by a massive air strike in combination. But the question we were all asking: where in the bloody hell are they?

The Operations report at 18:15 was that a radar tracker had been detected flying around the Task Group and Invincible reported fast moving aircraft were heading towards them at 18:25. The Captain ordered "Chaff" to be fired and it seemed the aircraft were coming from the West. We had yet to pick them up on our radar screens in the Ops Room. At 18:30hrs HMS Invincible launched two Sea Harriers. She also got airborne two of her Sea King Helicopters to detect any possible activity of Submarines in the area. Broadsword took station to act the role we were originally supposed to do and that was goalkeeping on the Task Group Flagship HMS Hermes and by now we were heading South. Coventry reported aircraft fifty miles to the West. Although there seemed to be a lot of aircraft miles away from us it looked like they didn't seem an immediate threat (YET!). We therefore stood down from Action Stations and reverted to "Air Warning YELLOW". It was now quite clear Britain and Argentina were at war, therefore the 200-mile Exclusion Zone enforced on the 28th of April had been changed dramatically to a twelve-mile Exclusion Zone around Argentina.

WHAT? "Surface Warning RED" (being a threat from sea) was made on our twelfth time to be ordered to Action Stations. Was this when we were going to see something of the enemy Naval Force? The time was late morning on the eighth of May. At 11:04 two unidentified contacts on the surface had passed HMS Glasgow at a very high speed. All ships had them on radar but were doubtful exactly what they were. Two helos were sent out to investigate. This may be hard to believe but it is now thought that the two bogus contacts could well have been the remains of a recent "Chaff" firing which had come zooming down and along the surface. (Work that one out!)

The enemy tracker aircraft was back again and reported to be 150 miles to the West. We had already closed up to Action at 15:35 for the thirteenth time. It seems the tracker was flying a figure eight flying tactic, which is a pattern used for other aircrafts to follow. There were two Harriers airborne 100 miles to the West and Hermes had launched another to intercept. By 16:00 the enemy aircraft were reported to be now 200 miles away so we stood down from Action.

When a ship has to re-fuel at sea or take on vital stores (eg mail!) everyone immediately involved in this evolution is fully trained to deal with, if the situation arises, emergency breakaway. This is practised time and time again on exercises by scenarios on mock exercises, which would mean if under attack from air, sea or underwater we could immediately deal with the threat as routinely as tying your shoe laces. So it was absolutely essential this may have to be enforced as war had been declared. Our fourteenth call to Action Stations proved we had to do exactly that at 18:58 in the evening of the eighth of May. We were about three-quarters of the way through re-fuelling and taking on stores when the "Emergency Breakaway. Emergency Breakaway" was sounded. The threat could come from anywhere but of course as expected it was aircraft. The two Captains on both vessels that literally were attached to each other had to make immediate and decisive decisions. There is absolutely no room for error. If this means axing all the pipe lines and cables attached then so be it. The threat came from this blasted Tracker again, but the real danger was to be two Mirage Jet Fighters picked up SW of the Task Force. Again CAP was used (Cover Aircraft Protection) to intercept these and the enemy aircraft returned to the Mainland.

It is believed that one of their Hercules Aircraft had made a drop to the Argentine Troops on the Falkland Islands and the two Mirage Fighters were there to escort her in once the coast was clear. We reverted to Defence Stations. It was getting quite a regular thing with our Captain. He was on the broadcast again at 19:45. Well, thankfully at least we were all being well informed by our Captain on the daily events so it was all ears and let's see what he has to say. (I hope someone was bringing him a cuppa now and then). After going through the events of the day, don't forget we were still, believe it or not, on the eighth, the Captain went on to inform us that HMS Brilliant would be detached from the Task Force sometime that night in order to attack and destroy one of their Merchant Vessels anchored off the Falkland Islands. Also there would be a raid by the SAS (Special Air Service) again that night. This all was to start to get things hotted up a bit. The Captain finished by saying that although we had to do an Emergency Breakaway not so long ago during the RAS, we would be glad to hear not only was it executed very successfully but we managed to get 95 per cent of our fuel tanks topped up and I'm sure to everyone's delight we also managed to receive many sacks full of mail from the RFA. Overall quite a good result under the circumstances. The Captain signed off and no sooner had he than there was a pipe made throughout the ship which was heaven to hear, which was mail was ready for collection from the Regulating Office. Once again morale was boosted up to an all-time high. Bloody hell, it made you think at times like that, it's good to be fighting for real for our Country because you seem to get tons of letters. I received letters from people I'd never even heard of before. But they were apparently part of the family or friends of the family. Times like those really bring a nation together and the feeling in your hearts for your folks at home is stronger than ever, which I know is mutual.

HMS Alacrity, the Type 21 Frigate in our Group, had been detached, her orders were to carry out a Naval Gunfire Support (NGS) on the Falklands and the Leander Class Frigate, HMS Yarmouth, had been given the daunting task of linking up to the Destroyer HMS Sheffield in order for her to tow the Destroyer away from the area. The Admiral has decided not to send in the Royal Marines to set explosive charges. At 01:50 then minutes before I started my 02:00 Starboard Defence Watch a pipe was made by the OOW that Broadsword would be detaching from the Main Task Force at 03:00 with the Destroyer HMS Coventry. We were to also carry out an NGS off the Falkland Islands. Additionally we were ordered to try and target the area where the Support Hercules Aircraft were and bombard accordingly. Our role now had somewhat changed from goalkeeping for Hermes, but we were now goalkeeping for Coventry.

As the Admiral decided to have Sheffield in tow by Yarmouth it was not quite clear why he wanted to keep her afloat but as mentioned before this could be a tactical move to take advantage of our doomed Destroyer and use her as bait. I can remember the majority of us all thinking because of the horrific amount of damage the ship must have now surely endured, she must be very close to either capsizing or even just sinking, surely she can't stay afloat all that long. Anyhow the grand old lady still had life in her and was obviously not going to go quietly. The rest of the night went without a hitch and I think our NGS firings went OK.

We were back to Action Stations again at 08:30 but were soon reverted to our Defence Watches. Just as bloody well this was now my time off. The Brilliant and Alacrity had rejoined us after their continuous bombardment zapping on the Island. We were all eight miles off the Falklands. Sorry, we still were at bloody Action Stations and we are about to do another NGS with Coventry at 09:15 and were now four and a half miles off the Falklands. HMS Coventry locked on to two enemy aircraft picked up by their radar 24 miles away and locked on with her Sea Dart Missiles. Because of the very poor visibility it seemed the two enemy aircraft decided not to do an approach attack and changed course and were heading back to their base. As no other threats were imminent we stood down from Action Stations. It was time for me to grab a quick nosh and a couple of hours kip while the going was good before yet again I'd be required on watch at 14:00hrs. Two Harrier Jets were scrambled at 11:40 to investigate (wait for it) yes, another rare thing to report a "Surface Contact" (basically a ship) and what they confirmed to be was the Argentines' Spy Trawler, the Narwal. This was the ninth of May and orders for the Harriers were quite specific and that was to sink it. After a few shots were fired on the Trawler the crew members surrendered. Well let's face it, they didn't stand a chance anyway.

The Lynx Helicopter from HMS Coventry was airborne at 13:00 to do a recci on the Falklands before we did our NGS firings. Once complete Coventry opened fire and dispersed eight shells. Unfortunately she endured problems on the guns so it was decided for us to withdraw on the firings in the area for the time being until it was rectified.

Two hostile aircraft were now heading towards us from the West, possibly they could be their Hercules Support Craft at 130 miles, but two fighters were also detected at 110 miles. This was recorded at 14:05 and 14:10. The two fighter aircraft were 70 miles and the Hercules at 110. It was left up to HMS Coventry to open fire at 48 miles. The two fighters orbited the Hercules. At 14:18 Coventry fired two Sea Dart Missiles at targets and a third one minute later. Somehow the Super Etendard Fighters managed to avoid all three missiles. Must have been their lucky day. They were joined by another two fighters (could this be it for us!?). Were we about to get zapped? The time was 14:19, but to everyone's surprise between 14:30 and 14:50 it was definitely confirmed that four Mirage aircrafts were on course for an attack. But wait a minute, what the hell was going on? One minute they were 48 miles away and closing, now there were reports that they were 100 miles away. Surely these pilots weren't blindfolded. Well that's how it was. Before you knew it, all aircraft were flying away from us and it wasn't long before we lost contact completely with the fighters and also the Hercules aircraft. The only explanation I can think is they had strict orders only to protect the Hercules.

It was still Sunday 9th May and at 16:30 we got reports that the Argentine Government had officially confirmed that they had surrendered the Trawler Narwal to our Forces. Between now and 18:00 we got several contacts with aircraft and were continuously changing our state of alert from Air Raid Warning RED only to revert to the lesser state of YELLOW a few minutes later. However at 18:00 a Pucara enemy aircraft was picked up on radar. HMS Coventry again engaged Sea Dart and this time the Sea Dart found its target and the Pucara was destroyed. At 19:05 things quietened down during the early evening and the ship fell out of Actions Stations at 19:30. We were still on station to carry out NGS firings during the night and were relieved by the warships HMS Brilliant and HMS Glasgow. HMS Coventry and ourselves then sailed to return to the Main Task Force. We re-fuelled our ship at 08:00.

At midday on Monday the tenth of May the ship's company got an update of things to expect or not to expect from our CO over the main broadcast. Basically no one was quite sure what the programme was. He explained we were still awaiting orders from the Admiral but hopefully the ship would know a bit more by the evening. It was later that we all found out the not so unexpected: that at 07:20 that morning, while under tow from HMS Yarmouth, in very rough weather conditions HMS Sheffield listed over heavily to Starboard and slowly sank. I can imagine the shock or panic of the Yarmouth crew in desperation to cut, chop, hack away the tow rope so as not to take her under as well while Sheffield gracefully went to her resting grave. What a great loss to the Royal Navy and of course her crew; a sad day for her Commanding Officer and Shipmates.

Finally at 19:45 we were informed that orders had come in for Broadsword and Coventry to detach from the Main Task Force, by the way, Coventry had now solved her problems in the Gunnery Section, and to proceed to the Falklands and relieve HMS Brilliant and HMS Glasgow and to continue the NGS firings. At approximately 04:00hrs the damage made by our Sea Harriers to the Spy Vessel Trawler Narwal must have been more serious than we all thought because at 20:15 she sank while being commandeered by the Royal Navy. Fortunately all our lads managed to get off safely. Anyhow, knowing the Navy they had without a doubt got all the enemy secret equipment off, with any documentation, before she finally went down.

The whole of the ship's company by now had completely settled down and accepted that the day-to-day events during war now came to us routinely and to always expect the unexpected. Broadsword I'm sure, like all the other Naval ships around us, could not have been more ready or alert for any situation than we are then. It's pointless at this stage to say what the conversations were except the talk around the ship would basically be about the events of the day, be it during the day or indeed during the night. But I can tell you now for sure every one of us every minute was thinking about our families at home and hoping that someone in the UK was there to comfort them. In a way they also were going through a war of their own. It was very comforting to hear that a special Naval team had been set up for all families to attend to give them comfort, hope, love, support and above all reassurance, and to prepare them for our return once peace had been established.

It was also reported that at 02:00 HMS Alacrity challenged one of their Tankers believed to be carrying fuel and ammunition for the Argentine Forces on the Island and after giving the Tanker plenty of warnings to no avail, Alacrity opened fire and sank it.

Tuesday 11th May brought Broadsword and Coventry uncertain confidence as both Frigate and Destroyer each had weaponry problems. During the night and morning watch our orders were changed and we had to get back to the NGS firing position where we were the day before with HMS Coventry. While returning to our original position we hit very rough seas. Being in the South Atlantic is not like being in some millpond. On the contrary the weather out there can get quite nasty and the previous night was no exception. Unfortunately although our Sea Wolf Missile Systems were quite high up on the superstructure the seawater managed to penetrate the Sea Wolf Tracking System causing it to be flooded out. Consequently it made the whole system useless at that time for any firings forward of the Bridge. Even at midday the wind was howling, the seas were heavy and rough and visibility was virtually nil due to rain and fog. Coventry still had the same re-occurrence problem with her Main Guns and to cap it all there was a very strong Submarine threat at hand.

"Shit! We really could be sitting ducks now."

Both ships, after reporting the defects and problems to the Task Force Commander, were ordered back to re-join the Task Group if we couldn't get these problems sorted out as soon as possible. I think we did manage to resolve the problems and stayed out on Station. The rest of the day passed peacefully which takes us through to 16:00hrs on Wednesday 12th May.

As usual both Defence Watches Port and Starboard did their change over and guess what? Lucky for me – it was my turn to be on watch – Starboard watch. I was on duty three quarters of a hour when at 16:45 came our first major report of an attack. The two Naval Warships under attack were the Type 22 Frigate, HMS Brilliant and the Type 42 Destroyer, HMS Glasgow. The threat came not only from one aircraft but four Skyhawk Fighters all of which are carrying deadly bombs. They had been picked up on radar coming in from the North. Brilliant opened fire immediately using her Guided Missile Sea Wolf System and triumphantly scored two direct hits, splashing two Skyhawks. The third was lucky and escaped the onslaught and flew away to the West. At this stage neither ship sustained any damage then, twenty-five minutes later, another wave of four. This time the Skyhawk Fighters attacked the same two ships and 40/60GPMGs were used for this attack and Glasgow was hit by one of the aircraft bombs which unexploded entered through the Port side of the ship carried on through the Engine Room space (all above the waterline apparently), exited below the waterline then passed through the Starboard side, miraculously causing no casualties. The prize was for us another two Skyhawks shot down and two sent with their tails between their legs.

"Bravo Brilliant and Glasgow."

HMS Glasgow was ordered back to the protection of the Task Group and at 20:00hrs we were ordered in to take up her position.

It had now been confirmed that the supply ship that HMS Alacrity sank yesterday was the Argentine Supply Ship "Isla de Los Estados". 20:00hrs brought us to our normal update of events from our Captain who stated both countries were continuing with their attacks; the ship would be expected to re-fuel sometime and on completion we would then take up HMS Glasgow's original position; also somewhere in the Task Force (it was just trying to pinpoint where) there were sackfuls of mail for HMS Broadsword. Actually it was not until 10:30 the following day, Thursday thirteenth that we did actually manage to re-fuel, closing up special sea duty men at this time and the pumping of fuel got under way at 11:40. There was an attempt to bring mail onboard at 16:10 but weather conditions were too foggy to make an attempt so it was decided to leave this until the weather improved. After we changed watches at 20:00hrs Starboard watch being the oncoming watch the Jimmy (1st Lieutenant) made an announcement over the main broadcast to inform us that at approximately 01:00 the next morning ourselves and the Flag Ship Carrier HMS Hermes would detach from the Main Task Group and sail to the North side of the Falklands to enable the landing of several parties of the Royal Marine detachments and SBS (Special Boat Service) by helicopters. He also informed us that the Captain had received a letter from the Captain of HMS Sheffield who stated that what probably saved a lot of his crews' lives was the mere fact the order was given throughout the ship to put on anti-gas-respirators (AGRS) when the missile struck the ship and also to put on anti-flash hoods as the majority of burns came from around the neck and the AGRs combated a lot of the smoke filled areas.

At 23:00 orders were changed and we were to remain with the Main Force and not proceed with the landings. To everyone's delight mail was received onboard by helo via our Supply Ship, RFA Regent, and at 14:55 the ship did a major store ship. When this happens it literally involves every member of the ship's company whatever rank or rate. Once we are alongside our Tanker and lines from ship to ship have been secured the "Clear Lower Deck" pipe is made and it's all hands in from Officer to Sailor. The sooner all of us can get these stores inboard the sooner we can detach from our Tanker as both vessels on this evolution are dangerously vulnerable to attacks from all quarters and to do an Emergency Breakaway at this time could have some catastrophic consequences. Luckily all went very well as mentioned by the Captain on his 20:00 update speech and all in all we managed to get all stores and fuel onboard in a couple of hours. As he put it: A good, quick, slick RAS stores this afternoon. Well done to the whole of the ship's company. "The mission," he added, "That we were supposed to carry out yesterday and was postponed, will now be carried out tonight in company with Hermes and now also the Destroyer HMS Glamorgan and the ships will then re-join the Task Group at approximately 11:00hrs Saturday 15th May."

Additionally on Sunday afternoon we again were to be detached from the Main Task Group, this time in company with Coventry and Brilliant and to sail this time to the West side of the Falklands to knock out, zap, splatter, sink, destroy or blow up any air, sea, or surface enemy forces that were around. We were expected to do this continuously for at least three days, taking us up to Wednesday the nineteenth of May. This obviously meant that the Main British Invasion was very close at hand. During our last stores RAS we managed to get onboard another sixteen Sea Wolf Missiles which brought our total Sea Wolf arsenal to seventy missiles.

"Hell, we can do some damage to their aircraft with this lot."

Saturday the fifteenth brought good news from our Sea Harrier on HMS Hermes. Apparently during the night wave after wave of these aircrafts were sent in to bombard Port Stanley Airstrip which resulted in the destruction in no less than eleven of their aircraft, which were stationary on the airstrip. They consisted of six Pucara, one Skyvan and four 734s. By the way, these were knocked out by the Ground Force SAS, not the Harriers; the Harriers were responsible for causing huge damage to the Airstrip. It was also reported the SAS managed also to destroy an ammunition dump and radio shack.

"Heck these lads must have been busy during the night. Good show."

The more grief we could give their aircraft taking off the better chance we could get our lads landed for the time the Main Invasion would take place. Again another change to our orders for Sunday: we were now to remain with the Task Group and await further orders. So on Sunday we took advantage to get our weapon system up to scratch because we had had problems with the forward Sea Wolf Tracking System. We rendezvoused with the Frigate HMS Yarmouth to carry out Sea Wolf test firings using her gunfire from their 4.5 guns as targets. This eventually started at 12:30

and all Gunners Teams were ordered to close up to their positions. I'm not quite sure how all this works, but at a guess I suppose Yarmouth fired shells (4.5) in the air then Sea Wolf tried to knock em out. Anyhow at 13:20 the first Sea Wolf was launched on Yarmouth's 4.5 shells and forty minutes later a second was fired; both were successful hits. We were now back on top, with our weaponry systems onboard 100 per cent ready and now awaiting for the main landing for the Invasion, which was rumoured, should be that week sometime.

The Captain gave his long speech yet again at 19:45 Sunday evening as follows: "We were going to detach from the Main Task Force this evening in company with HMS Hermes but have just this minute received another signal to postpone the order to detach. Presumably we were going to, as originally planned, land the SBS and the Royal Marines Teams by helo. HMS Brilliant sailed to the West of the Falklands early this morning to identify two shipping vessels alongside Port Stanley. If she however is unable to identify one of the ships NOT being their Hospital Ship she has strict orders to destroy it. Unfortunately Brilliant was unable to identify which was their Hospital Ship so withdrew from the area under carpet darkness. So Harriers were sent in from Hermes who were able to identify both vessels, none of which turned out to be their Hospital Ship and immediately opened fire. After the attack the report came back that one of the ships was sinking and the other one was on fire and they will probably fly in tonight to polish them both off if still afloat." The Captain also warned us that it was the Argentines' Navy Day the next day

(Monday 17th May) and this could spark off a major attack on the Task Force. So as we hadn't been at Action Stations for some days now we must be fully alert for tomorrow so as to not be "caught napping". Finally the Captain finished by adding there is yet more mail for Broadsword on our main Assault Ship HMS Fearless, but unfortunately the very earliest for us to retrieve it would be on Wednesday 19th May, or possibly later but there would be absolutely no chance before. The Captain then signed off.

The last time the ship was at Action Stations was at 08:30 on the ninth of May at 11:15. On Monday 17th May it was our sixteenth time called up for Action Stations and this was only for half an hour as an aircraft was getting too close for comfort. Fortunately an hour before we had managed to re-fuel and take on 200 tons worth. Another ship had now appeared in the Task Group or should I say was now immediately involved and that was our second Aircraft Carrier, HMS Invincible. We detached with Invincible at 18:30 on the Monday evening leaving HMS Brilliant to take over our role as goalkeeper to HMS Hermes. Radio silence was ordered at 19:00hrs to both Warships and all communications had to be done by light. Our Lynx helicopter was on alert fifteen in preparation for a surface search and was armed with two Sea Skuas as the Captain pointed out on his evening broadcast our mission was to sail in company with Invincible, head West off the Falklands, land a helicopter of troops from Invincible then both ships were to sail straight back to the Task Force. Our speed would be no less that 27 knots; anyone will tell you that is quite some speed in nautical terms. Once returned to the

Main Task Force we were ordered (situation permitting) to re-fuel immediately. Normal Defence Watches changed over at 20:00hrs Starboard (me) on Port stand down.

Although we were well into the war we heard that a peace proposal was presented by the United Nations' Secretary General Peres de Cuellar but was immediately rejected by Britain. It made me think, if we have got this far in the conflict with the loss of life on both sides, why in the hell should either side give in now. It was much too late for negotiations for peace talks now at this stage. No, this was a case of WIN or LOSE, so be it. This proposal was put forward and rejected on Tuesday 18th May. The rest of the day passed with no incidents to Broadsword and we re-fuelled our ship with the supply ship RFA Olmeda and managed earlier than thought to receive our much awaited mail from HMS Fearless, which was flown in by helo. We were told there would be a possibility that our own letters could be transferred the next day, so you can imagine a lot of scribbling was going to take place whether on watch or off watch. As promised mail was closed at 18:30 on Wednesday nineteenth and transferred over to RFA Regent who was due to sail to the UK. At 18:45 there was a Squadron Battle Group Meeting in the Captain's Cabin which our own Mess President attended, POEL (Petty Officer Electrical) Dave Phelps. Wednesday evening brought the familiar voice of our Captain throughout the ship and it was to no one's surprise for us to learn that no diplomatic solution had been achieved to end this crisis (oh really!). HMS Hermes and Invincible, our two Aircraft Carriers, had been working flat out transferring twenty Sea

Harrier jets from the Container Vessel the Atlantic Conveyor. It's astonishing the amount of tonnage these vessels can carry; the Harriers were just a fraction of her cargo. Deep inside her cargo bays there could be anything from Jeeps, Landrovers, helicopters to millions upon millions of ammunition shells for the Heavy Armoured Tanks. It would be a bitter blow to the British Forces if this ship was to go down before landing her precious cargo. As the Captain continued his brief he informed us that at midnight tonight we were expected to join up with the Amphibious Battle Group led by HMS Fearless with all her other landing craft ships around her: Sir Galahad and Sir Tristram to name just two. Also carrying thousands of Marines was the Cruise Liner Canberra which the British Government commandeered when war broke out. Surely we had to be getting bloody close for a full scale landing now. As the Captain explained our primary role was to protect the Amphibious Landing Ships. There were rumours the invasion would take place the next night under complete darkness but as everything was highly top secret we could only guess, but our job at hand right then was to protect these ships and all our troops onboard.

At 03:00hrs on Thursday 20th May the Task Group (ourselves included) met up with the Amphibious Group. I counted that there were twenty-one ships in this part of the force alone. At ten minutes past eight our Captain was flown over to HMS Fearless by Lynx Helicopter for top secret briefings regarding the Main Invasion and returned to HMS Broadsword at ten minutes past twelve. It was needed to take advice from the Commanding Officer of HMS

HMS Fearless.

Sheffield and although we were still in Defence Watches it wasn't as yet necessary to carry our respirators and anti-flash hoods and gloves until now. The whole ship's company had been ordered to do so now in preparation for the Main Invasion. That was the first time for a long time I could literally feel the immense tension in the ship's company. We were completely psyched up for a full scale air to ship battle at sea and believe you me there were a lot of worried faces on ship and we all knew more than ever that a possible attack was imminent now from any quarter. It wouldn't take long for the enemy to work out, if they hadn't already done so, that the gathering of this force together must mean one thing and one thing alone: INVASION.

When I came off watch at 12:00 (midday) I went to the Dining Hall and grabbed a spot of lunch, consisting of a couple of pork chops, peas, boiled potatoes and gravy. I've never been a great fan of puddings so skipped that course. In desperate need to get a bit of fresh air after being cooped up in HQ1, I went to my Cabin and collected my instamatic Kodak camera. I knew there was a hell of a lot of activity top side and as things were reasonably quiet decided to take a few snapshots of this Historic Naval occasion. Let's hope I live long enough to get them developed and not have the misfortune of being sunk, I knew the weather was quite foul outside by taking a quick tour of the Bridge and looking out of their many windows. So after donning a couple of navy jumpers and a waterproof foul weather jacket I took myself to the Upper Deck via O1 Deck Door, the same area the Captain's Cabin is situated. It took quite an effort to get the screen door open as it really was blowing a bastard; I would say at least a force eight gale was in progress. It was drizzling with rain and misty, but I was so grateful to get the fresh air into my lungs I actually enjoyed the wind and rain in my face. In a way it was heaven after being so long cooped up below decks, days on end. Although the weather was misty the evidence of all the activity around us was clear to see. I could see HMS Antrim forward of the line of ships who seemed to be the leader of the formation. Astern of her was HMS Ardent, then HMS Plymouth followed by HMS Yarmouth, then HMS Brilliant and it was so good to see the first ever ship I served on in 1970, the Leander Class Frigate F56 HMS Argonaut. I'll never forget the many happy times the lads and I had on Argonaut when I was a mere sixteen year old. They say the first ship you have is usually the happiest time in your career. It really brought back memories those so many years ago and even to this day once you have a happy crew it always remains so throughout the lifespan of Naval Service.

HMS Argonaut.

All these ships were on our Starboard beam. On the Port side we had the sister ship to HMS Fearless our assault ship which was the other assault ship HMS Intrepid then there was the Ferry Norland and the Norsen Ferry. Obviously these were carrying troops and equipment. Looking out at the Norsen Ferry it was quite alarming to see it pitching and rolling in the rough seas so much, right in the middle of all the ships. It was quite distinctive to see the brilliant white liner Canberra carrying a vast amount of our Royal Marines personnel. I now know that Simon Neill, with whom I had the privilege of being raised in his family, was now actually onboard the Canberra, after just completing a gruelling exercise in Norway in company with HMS Fearless. I couldn't help thinking at least we were giving him a lot of protection with all the Naval Ships surrounding the Canberra.

"The more fire power the better that's what I say, Si. GOOD LUCK MATE!"

Then we had the Sir Percival who was the Leader of the Landing Craft Vessels consisting of Sir Geraint, Sir Tristram and Sir Galahad and on their Starboard quarter were the Auxiliary Store Ships RFA Stromness, RFA Fort Austin and RFA Tidepool. The whole scene from the Upper Deck on Broadsword was immensely impressive. I have never seen such a large gathering of Naval Vessels since we had the Silver Jubilee in 1977 for our Queen when she reviewed the Naval Fleet off Portsmouth. I then was serving on the Guided Missile Destroyer (GMD) DLG HMS Fife and then, after the review as was customarily done she ordered "Splice the Mainbrace," which means every serving naval personnel is issued the tot of rum ration "Free". Only the serving monarch can issue this order throughout the whole fleet.

After about three quarters of an hour and slowly freezing my butt off and taking numerous snapshots I headed back inside the ship for a nice hot cuppa. It doesn't take long on any ship for word to spread for whatever reason. No sooner was I inboard the ship and securing the upper deck screen door through which I went out and walking down the main passageway on one deck than the news soon reached me from the matelots along the passageway that our task as of now was to lead and protect the landing crafts in this Group with Sir Percival and the rest of the "Sir" crafts and to prepare ourselves for the Main Invasion which would now, so I heard, take place tomorrow. But having said that rumours soon get around a ship and you cannot guarantee they are absolutely correct unless you officially hear it over the main broadcast system from the old man. So in the meantime I just watched this space; no doubt there would be an announcement from the Captain all in good time to confirm these rumours or chatter that was going around.

15:05 "here we go again". Action Stations sounded for our seventeenth time since the first of May. Apparently intelligence had signalled to the whole Task Force that aircraft had taken off from Argentina and were heading for the Task Group. HMS Brilliant and us took up positions on the flanks of the ships we were protecting with the Assault Ships Fearless and Intrepid astern and Antrim's Group forward leading all the Main Group in the sector. Our Flagship Hermes had launched Harriers for cover air protection (CAP) to intercept the incoming aircraft and at 15:20 had sent a further two jets to the West. Fortunately no ships were threatened on this raid and we fell out and went back to our normal defence watch system at 16:05. Almost immediately the Captain was on the blower again obviously now fully aware that the buzz had got around the ship that an Invasion could be the next day by the British Forces so had decided to bring the normal 20:00 brief forward to this time to keep us updated for the events to come. The Captain started by making it quite clear that the Main Invasion would take place tomorrow morning with the first landings being done by the two main Assault Ships HMS Fearless and HMS Intrepid.

What we were are about to do in Naval terms was an Amphibious landing which would take place near Port San Carlos on the Northern Coast of East Falklands. The first wave was to commence by Fearless and Intrepid at 06:30hrs on Friday 21st May. The second wave was to follow approximately one hour later at 07:30 to 08:00hrs and this would be achieved by the Canberra Group of ships and at approximately 09:00 the Broadsword Group (our group) was to bring in the final wave of the Landing Crafts in the Sir Percival Group. We would then patrol these waters and await the inevitable air attack, which would undoubtedly come. But when? It was anyone's guess. HMS Hermes and HMS Invincible our two Aircraft Carriers were to be stationed approximately 50 miles to the West of the Falklands ready to intercept any hostile aircraft by using the Harriers who would add more to the protection of the Landing Forces in this Sector.

Although I was still at Defence Watches I did manage to call in on the Captain now and then and as the attacks hadn't yet been all that many I could more or less carry on my normal Captain's duties. The Captain retired at approximately 22:20, I remember saying to myself I hope he manages to get a reasonably good night's kip. I had a feeling, as I'm sure everyone else did that the next few days were going to be hell. Five minutes later, once I'd squared off the Pantry and stowed everything away in the cupboards and, with my own key, I locked up and made my way towards the Petty Officers' Mess for a pint with John Wicks, the POMA (Petty Officer Medical Assistant) who I knew was waiting for me as we had arranged to have a game of

HMS Invincible leaves Portsmouth Harbour for the Falklands.

Uckers (similar to Ludo). The bar closed at 23:00 but we managed to scrounge a couple to the side before the pumps were finally closed and padlocks were secured. I finally got my head down around 00:15 to 00:30 feeling very relaxed after a couple of bevvies and a chat with our other fellow Mess Members. During the night Naval ships Glamorgan, Antrim and Ardent had been nominated to continue the NGS firings on Fox Bay with the assistance of Harriers from our Flagship. We found out later they had managed to zap their ammunition dumps. One thing I do remember before I finally went into noddy land and closed my eyes was thinking that this is going to be the day, May twenty-first, when bloody hell is going to let loose, once the

Argies find out we have started the assault to take back the Falklands. I imagine they'll chuck everything they've got at us. Oh well, let's see.

A signal had been passed on to the whole of the Task Group to all ships which read: from CTG (Commander Task Group) Rear Admiral Woodward, "The eyes and ears of the World are upon us. Be steady in rescue, strong in battle and merciful in victory". More or less to the minute, as previously planned, HMS Fearless and HMS Intrepid moved into the Falkland Sound. At 06:00 **"THE INVASION HAS STARTED"** and at 06:30 our Troops were on the beaches and at precisely 07:00 Canberra moved in to land her load of Troops and equipment. Helicopters were also used to assist Canberra as well are the Landing Crafts. We started our approach at 08:45 and were just outside the Sound with Sir Percival and their Group. They moved in at 09:00 according to plan. By now the Invasion to recapture the Islands was well and truly underway. The Landing Craft went in and started to unload all the Artillery Guns and at 10:20 Broadsword was at "Action Stations". At 10:22 we sailed through the Inlet East and West of the Falklands. Two Sea King Helicopters were airborne for the detection of any enemy submarines patrolling this area. It had been reported that there were two but believed one has returned to base with engine or electrical faults. By 10:25 we had now taken up a new position patrolling this time North to South and were ready for any forthcoming attacks from all quarters due to the commencement of the Invasion. It was decided to relax anti-flash hoods and gloves at 10:25 and by 10:45 we were well in the Sound. HMS Invincible and Hermes with CTG still onboard were well out to the North and South of the Islands at approximately 130 miles and had already launched a good number of their Harriers ready to destroy any incoming enemy aircraft. If however any did manage to break through the cordon then it would be up to us and HMS Brilliant to wipe them out. When we finally reached the centre of the sound at 11:20 HMS Brilliant started a shore bombardment eight miles away from us to the South. Two enemy Dipper Helicopters had been picked up in the vicinity and were trying to contact their Submarine or Submarines. In the meantime our own Lynx Helicopter was scouting the area for any surface ships that might be hiding in any of the inlets or coves.

Before things started hotting up our Sea Wolf Crews carried out Sea Wolf Missile transfer to the forward and after tracking systems. These have to be brought up from four decks below and placed on a hoist (lift). They are then put on specially adapted transferring trolleys and moved to the AFT/FWD sections accordingly, which requires four to five members of their team for each missile moved. Not surprisingly as they are twice my size in height although I'm only five feet five inches tall. You couldn't help noticing the strong smell of oil and grease as these missiles were wheeled passed us in the after section First Aid Post in One Mike flat which is just forward of the Hanger which carried our Lynx helicopter. Once the missiles passed our Action Station position they were then transferred through two watertight screen doors and eventually hoisted up to the Main Tracking and Firing Point. The whole process really takes some effort and time, hence why there are always ready reserves at hand on all Action Stations with a full back-up team to supply more if needed from the main magazines forward – phew! It made me knackered just watching them. Don't forget they've also got a ton of kit on like the rest of us, no wonder why First Aid Teams carry one extra bottle of water, not only for burns but obviously for dehydration.

I think it goes without saying that it would be quite clear that our First Aid Teams could expect casualties in the next few days of battle so the Surgeon Lieutenant and John (POMA) had decided to have an additional First Aid position other than the one forward in the Wardroom and AFT where my team and I were located in One Mike flat. It had been decided to call and use this first aid post as the "Emergency Operating Theatre" and it would be located and manned in the centre of the ship's Decks, midship as close as possible, which will be the Petty Officers' Mess situated on Two Deck.

My duties now changed at Action Stations and Jono the AFT Section Leading Hand now took over and was in charge of this team while I took over the EOT with the assistance of Caterer Darren Poyzer. Darren's role usually was with the FWD First Aid Team and was also required to assist when Action Messing was piped which basically meant help feed the ship's company from the Dining Hall once Command had ordered to do so. Darren also was my assistant in an emergency as well as the SURG LT and POMA as this area now became an Operating Theatre with the proper operating table transferred from the Sick Bay (based AFT) and with the full sterile hot equipment system and all the surgical instruments at hand in a proper plastic roll up sheet with individual pockets to hold the various tools for the job. Also along with the bottles and bottles of fluid needed for major blood transfusions if required. Once settled in the PO's Mess I couldn't help but chuckle to myself and thinking if a bomb hits now and I get zapped at least I got clobbered in my own "Fucking Messdeck".

While things were still reasonably quiet at 11:25 I took the opportunity to get my blank bits of paper I'd got in some of my pockets and wrote a few notes for my diary which I had done since we started going to Action Stations from the first of May. While now closed up at my new Action Station Post I could distinctly hear gunfire which apparently was the Destroyer Antrim carrying out Naval Gunfire (NGS) on the shoreside battery positions on our Starboard side.

HMS Intrepid had now up anchored and was on the move after successfully unloading her cargo of equipment and disembarking the troops. She was sailing to do her secondary landing on another point around the Island for her second assault. In the meantime Hermes and Invincible were still keeping their positions out at sea 130 miles away and continuously supplying the essential air cover for the Invasion. Surprisingly no aircraft had been spotted yet! And it was 11:25 in the morning of May 21st!

We fell into a routine for war on the feeding of the ship's company and this was done by Order of Command by the Captain. Only if the ship was reasonably safe would the

Supply Officer, with the Senior Caterer, inform Command that the Chefs were ready to accept the ship's company in stages at the Main Canteen and Galley Areas, for what we call "Speed Feed". This means exactly that, there is absolutely no time for idle chat with your oppo – you get down to the Galley, down your nosh, have a quick drink then piss off back to your post. This is done once Command has given the green light by means of every Officer or NCO in charge of their particular sections who will send away twenty-five per cent of their teams to the Canteen. All teams and the whole ship's company must be fed in thirty minutes maximum which, give credit where it is due the Chefs and Caterers did an absolutely fantastic job every time we had to "Speed Feed". The means on this occasion was steak and kidney small round puddings (matelots nickname this dish Baby's Head for some reason or another. I suppose the round puddings remind them of a baby's head! Who knows?), followed by fresh fruit, oranges, apples or banana. Drink was a plastic cup of orange, tea or just plain water, with a crusty slice of bread. The main dish was served with various veggies and potatoes (mashed I think). This had to be consumed in minutes, as I mentioned, to allow the other Messmates to get to the Galley within the thirty minutes for their grub.

The Galley was situated on Two Deck more forward than AFT and just below the Wardroom Deck, so if your post was right down AFT, for example the Flight Deck Crew, to speed feed was an arduous task in itself. To reach one end of the ship to the other there were several doors and hatches to go through. Don't forget the whole ship was closed down for war, so all watertight hatches and doors were shut, clipped and locked down and this had to be done on the way to the Speed Feed Area and then back again. Every door or hatch opened had to be closed after you immediately and with all your clobber on believe you me it's a mission and a half to grab a spot of nosebag (grub).

Right in the middle of Speed Feed (sods' law) we got an air contact and were ordered to fully put on our anti-flash hoods which were hanging around our necks. Thankfully we found out by confirmation it was one of ours anyway and then were told to relax anti-flash. Our Lynx helicopter returned onboard at 12:10 after being sent out in search of enemy surface ships and the Speed Feed finally finished at 12:15 (fifteen minutes over: not bad though).

At 12:31 three waves of our aircraft flew over us and were heading to attack the bombardment sections shoreside. Ardent's Lynx helicopter picked up on radar two enemy A4 Bombers and went to try and intercept. The time was 12:55 and at 13:15 the order "On anti-flash" was piped again with the warning "Air Raid Warning RED". Somehow I got the feeling that this time it must be for real. My feelings and predictions were soon confirmed, because at 13:29 we were under attack by six A4 Bombers. We immediately fired our Sea Wolf missiles at the targets and scored a hit which means to say we splashed (destroyed) one. We also opened fire with our Bofors which are the anti-aircraft guns positioned AFT of the Bridge Section.

"Shit, all hell's let loose topside".

I was sure lunch "Speed Feed" would surface any minute now, I felt as sick as a dog; nerves obviously. The most nerve racking thing when you are closed in a ship is that you can hear all the commotion going on but can't see a damn thing. It didn't take a genius to work out that the Argentines now had realised that they had been caught napping to allow the Invasion Force to have began since the early hours of the morning and by the looks of it they were coming out in force. The report by Ardent's Lynx helo earlier on was a sure indication of the presence of the two A4 Bombers that we had been rumbled. It was just a matter of time what and who was going to be hit or destroyed and by whom.

Six minutes later at 13:35 my question was answered: HMS Antrim had been seriously hit AFT by this wave of Dagger aircraft which I believed to be of FAA GRUPO 6. Unbelievably the bomb which entered her had not exploded.

"Bloody hell if a bomb can do this amount of damage unexploded, what the fuck is the damage going to be when these UXBs do explode on impact?"

In my new Command Post at the EOT I could hear a lot of gunfire and plainly heard the WHOOSH as one of our Sea Wolf missiles was launched. I was waiting in anticipation as I was certain assistance from the First Aid Teams was bound to be called for. No way with all the fire power going on topside could we possibly have got away without someone sustaining some sort of injury.

"Bloody good luck to us mind you if we have this."

This was short lived as at 13:41 the dreaded pipe was made which is for the after First Aid party to muster in the Tiller Flat (secondary position for steering the ship). We had been hit by gunfire and had casualties mainly from our Flight Deck Crew and also the Chinese Laundry Man had apparently been injured during this attack as his laundry was close to the Tiller Flat. That was where our casualty was and it would be Johno and his team who assisted all personnel in the After Area. Three injuries were sustained in the Flight Crew, all from shrapnel.

Our Lynx helicopter was out on our Flight Deck and also had been damaged by gunfire. There were also reports that we had a fuel spillage on the Flight Deck. The last thing we needed now was a major fire AFT but the Flight Crew soon had this threat of fire under control.

I was pacing up and down the PO's Mess with a thousand and one things going through my mind about what horrendous injuries we might expect to come. Can we cope? Do we have the right equipment? Will the Surg Lt and POMA be here if surgery is needed? If this place catches fire where were those escape routes again? Although I'd been all through this dozens and dozens of times I had to keep reassuring myself to keep calm and of course expect the unexpected.

"Fuck this is it".

We had well and truly got right in the middle of their retaliation on the Invasion Assault. At 14:00hrs after being treated and patched up by Johno's First Aid Team, four casualties were brought to me in the PO's Mess. As mentioned one of which was the Chinese Laundry Man and three were the Flight Deck Crew Members, all having sustained shrapnel wounds. In a way I couldn't help thinking I was glad for their company as Darren had been sent back to the Forward First Aid Team in the Wardroom to bring them up to full support and I was definitely feeling a bit jittery there on my tod.

It was announced over the main broadcast system at 14:50 to expect another air attack by another four A4 Bombers carrying 1,000 pound bombs. These A4 Bombers are better known to us as Skyhawks, which are very fast and deadly. Ardent picked up two aircraft contacts to the West (ten miles) and Sea Harriers had intercepted Pucara aircrafts and successfully managed to splash one of them (shot down). HMS Antrim was completely unable to fire any of her guns as the Gunnery System had been wiped out and at 15:30 I received my fifth casualty, again from the Flight Crew, with shrapnel injuries. Also HQ1 informed the ship's company that all damage to the After Section of the ship had all been temporarily repaired and Broadsword was still fully operational.

We were next confronted by the Skyhawk A4 Bombers at 16:05. The ship was ready for the attack as was HMS Antrim. They were five miles away, but wait a minute, Dog Fights were in progress.

"Yahoo!"

Two of HMS Hermes' Harriers zapped and splashed them both in a matter of seconds and were back to join their ship only to be relieved by two more.

"Cheers! Waffos" (Fleet Air Arm)

The Catering Department while all this was going on had organised urns of tea to be strategically set around the ship and we all in turn got to these points for a very welcome brew. Jim (POCA) and his team sure knew when to refresh the lads although it may only be a cuppa.

"Thanks, Caterers. Much appreciated."

John the POMA made a visit to my First Aid Post in the Petty Officers' Mess and after having a chat with me during which I gave him a full update of my patients he injected penicillin into a couple of the crew who were in real agony. I was also told by John that another four casualties were in the Wardroom of our Forward First Aid Post on One Deck and all had been treated accordingly. Again all had the same symptoms, mainly of shock and shrapnel wounds, so all in all on that wave of attack alone we had received nine casualties. It's a miracle that the injuries were not more serious.

Action Snacks were announced to report to the Galley or Canteen which consisted of a slice of Bakewell Tart and again as for Speed Feed all had to be done very quickly with, on this occasion, only one Team Member of the Section sent to the Canteen to collect all the Team's Action Snacks and bring them back to their individual Team Members.

We learned at 16:45 that so far six enemy aircraft had been splashed, but at this stage it was still not sure whom the credit should go to. HMS Brilliant had two helicopters dipping for Submarines and at 17:20 the "Air Raid Warning Red" again sounded. At 17:30 two Sea Wolf Missiles were launched (whoosh – whoosh!) and Leading Seaman Ball on the FWD Tracking System managed to shoot one of the Mirages (different aircraft now) down.

"Good shooting, Alan mate!"

We had now been hit yet again and a party of damage control people did what we call a blanket search. This meant the patrol went around every Department, Store Room, cubby hole, Passageway, Cabin and Messdeck and completely blanket searched the area, hence Blanket Search.

Before any of us could do anything the order "BRACE – BRACE – BRACE" was repeated because of an expected hit either by missile or bomb. This basically means every member of the ship's company has to grab hold of a secure fixture such as a metal rod, bar, pipe or even just something solid to hold onto ready for the bomb or missile to strike so as not to be thrown into the air on impact. This would obviously result in more injury to yourself that the actual weapon used against us. This pipe or announcement was made every time an attack weapon came in and the word "BRACE" was repeated three times.

Our tenth casualty was again from the Flight Deck. By fuck these lads were getting a right pasting down there. This time it was no less than our own Flight Commander, Lieutenant Commander Jones, who had sustained facial injuries caused by shrapnel.

"Blimey, it must be hell down there on the Flight Deck. There can't be many more of the Flight Crew left for the Argies to zap."

Again Sea Wolf Missiles were fired and the bofor guns opened fire under the TV Control System in the OPs Room. We could see that No.4 Barrel Missile had chased two Mirages heading for HMS Brilliant, which was also tracked by Leading Seamen Evans (Taff). The missiles missed but did cause the Mirages to drop their bombs, which missed anyway.

We were still under attack half an hour later and the time was 18:35 and still the day was far from over. Very bad reports were now coming into the ship that HMS Ardent, the Type 21 Frigate, had been seriously hit and was leaning over to her Port side. This now seemed much, much more serious than first thought. Ardent came under heavy attack by Daggers and the A4 Skyhawks. She had been hit by at least five bombs while patrolling in the Grantham Sound and it looked as if the Skyhawks finally made their mark as the order by their Commanding Officer was given to abandon ship. Again HMS Yarmouth was close at hand to pick up survivors from the ship and also from the freezing icy-cold Atlantic waters. We joined the rescue operation and were heading for her and it wasn't long before we sent in two of our Diver Swimmers to rescue two of the Ardent's crew who were on our Port side. The information we learned later was that Ardent still had an unexploded bomb lodged in her belly somewhere and it could go off any second. The order to abandon ship on HMS Ardent must have been around 18:35. At 19:00 I headed towards the Flight Deck and could see clearly the Ardent on fire with smoke bellowing from her Stern. It would take a hell of a time to get near enough to put that out and with an unexploded bomb lodged in her the risk to other fire fighting crews was far too high. Unbeknown to me then, but two years later I was going to join one of these Type 21 Frigates, HMS Avenger. It is with great sadness whatever ship you're on to see any ship in difficulty, on fire, and worst of all sinking. Anyhow, Ardent was still afloat and I just wondered if there was any hope at all to salvage and save her for her crew.

At 19:20 we were all ordered to put on full anti-flash. HMS Yarmouth was now steaming towards the inlet and heading towards Canberra to transfer all the remaining crew from HMS Ardent and we had taken up our normal sea station in the Sound and were carrying out patrols North to South. We picked up aircraft on our radar at 19:40 and believed them to be 120 miles and heading in our direction. By 20:00 this gap had closed to 80 miles and there seemed to be four enemy aircraft but at the last minute all contacts veered off or returned to their airbase. It was now getting quite dark and clear to see the Ardent well on fire and as night drew near we were quite confident by 21:00 that all attacks by aircraft had now ceased for the day and so we fell out of Action Stations. This was our first full day over since the Invasion began and phew, what a day!

We got an address from the Captain the next day, Saturday 22nd May at 08:00 who announced that he was very pleased with yesterday's performance, especially to the Lookouts on the Bridge Wings and the Gunnery Teams on the bofor Guns. Also our team in the First Aid Crews got a chuck up as we did receive a few minor casualties. He went on to say as far as the war went we were extremely lucky to suffer only minor injuries in the Sound and after receiving all the reports it was confirmed that we had shot down, between all of us, at least seventeen aircraft consisting of a combination of Mirages, Pucara and Skyhawks, but unfortunately we lost one of our Harriers. All of us knew that HMS Ardent sustained serious damage and was still on fire. It was also reported that HMS Brilliant received a shell that went straight through her Operations Room, fortunately causing no casualties. HMS Argonaut also suffered damage on her bows and we ourselves were slightly damaged Astern and shell holes were struck for'd just after of the Bridge Section Starboard side. The Captain continued by adding that the Argentine Airforce could not afford to lose seventeen of their aircraft a day. He added it would be unwise for us to stay in the same position today as yesterday and also we could not use our full capability of the Sea Wolf range with the mountain range in between, therefore we and the Type 42 Destroyer HMS Coventry had been despatched from the Sound with Broadsword's role to act as goalkeeper to Coventry. Our new position therefore was to patrol North West of the Islands and to knock out the enemy aircraft before they reached the Islands. This is where we were at a great advantage, he continued, to use the Sea Wolf missiles at their greatest potential. However HMS Brilliant had been ordered to stay in the Sound and use the rocks either side as cover and protection from enemy aircraft, but again Brilliant also had Sea Wolf missiles and we were the only two Naval Ships in the entire Battle Group to carry the them. The Captain then signed off by saying, "That's all."

We were back to Action Stations for the nineteenth time at 11:00hrs and the ship's company went through the Dining Hall for "Speed Feed" which was all done in forty minutes and the whole crew was fed by 13:15. Action Snacks were issued at 15:45 and consisted of a slice of Bakewell tart (yuk!). Beggars can't be choosers as the saying goes and fifteen minutes later Action Stations were relaxed and we reverted to our defence watches at 16:00. Two hours and fifteen minutes later "Bloody Hell" we were back to Action Stations "Air Raid Warning RED". Suspected five Mirage aircraft coming towards us, range 60 miles but minutes later they changed course. Another hostile aircraft was detected at 230° range, 51 miles. At this point the ship started a zig-zag course and increased speed. Within the next hour it was confirmed that the six Mirage Fighters suspected were for one purpose only and that was to act as protection for either one if not two of their Hercules aircraft delivering Cargo, Stores and Troops to the Islands. Our recent contact at 51 miles seemed to have veered away from our direction so this was no threat to us. It was confirmed that the Hercules had landed and the Mirage aircraft returned to the Mainland. We had two of our own Sea Harriers in the area but they were in desperate need of re-fuelling and could do so on the West side of the Islands as they would never have reached HMS Hermes on the fuel they had and would have had no other option but to ditch.

At approximately 223° at a range of 60 miles were two of the contacts but apparently there seemed to be too much of a crossfire position, whatever that means. Again it was the Argentine's Hercules and it looked like they were going to escape being splashed. With no other threat we fell out of Action Stations at 19:30.

Sad news reached us all at 20:00 and as we learned that HMS Ardent, the Type 21 Frigate, had finally lost her will to stay afloat and had sunk. Very sad news for her Commanding Officer, Officers and crew. She actually sank just off the Falklands Islands. It was also reported that our landing crafts Sir Galahad and Sir Tristram had successfully managed to beach, but on a sadder note HMS Argonaut F56 (my ship in the 1970s and one of the happiest ships I have ever had the privilege to serve on; always, always a happy crew) had sustained massive damage and was literally a sitting duck in the water. Being unable to move the main damage was to the Bow section and would have to be towed out of the danger zone area sometime.

The rest of the day and the early morning of Sunday 23rd May went unhindered and it seemed now like clockwork. Yes, you've guessed, it we were back to Action Stations at 11:00hrs but this time we'd taken the initiative for the inevitable attack by the Skyhawk dawn raid patrols. Again the ship's company speed fed at 11:35.

"If we keep this up the "Doc" won't be dealing with cuts and bruises but bloody ulcers."

While this was going on we had the Harriers carrying our CAP Patrols (Cover Air Protection) over the Task Force. Speed Feed finished at 12:25 and we were all back at our posts around the ship.

Every time the ship was closed up at Action Stations the electrical lighting was reduced considerably and you felt you were in a ghost ship environment. What was distinctly noticeable were the green and yellow exit and arrows pointing in the direction for your escape route in an emergency, as they were very strongly illuminated, glowing like glow-worms. Of course if the whole ship was to loose 100 per cent lighting these life saving direction signs would save many of the ship's crew and lead them to safety out of the ship to the Upper Deck. When you're closed up hours on end the conversation with each other is very limited and it was best to leave everyone to their own thoughts whether it be fear, thoughts of home or simply how will I react if this happens or if that happens. I'm damn sure I did.

Some of us, although this was not permitted, managed to get hold of a novel or book from somewhere and others dozed awaiting for the next situation to take shape. When the ship was fully dressed for action and full anti-flash had been ordered your hoods up over your face, it got very hot and not surprisingly and naturally if you're not occupied with something to do apart from wait, you will find yourself nodding off. So it was essential that the Team Leader (i.e. me) kept an eye on this and to now and then bark, "You wake up. Stop nodding off."

Reports came through at 13:20 that an Argentine Tanker, which had been spotted to the South, had been attacked by our forces was now on fire. HMS Yarmouth's Wasp (helicopter) was scrambled and ordered to fly out and finish it off. We also learned that Sea King Helicopters had been dipping their sonar equipment and had had one supposed submarine contact. Depth charges had been fired but no results had been released to us. Harriers on the other hand had three helicopter contacts of two Pumas and one Chinook. One Puma was destroyed and the Chinook was damaged, but landed safely. Unfortunately the Harriers couldn't persue the attack as fuel was getting critically low for them, but their reliefs were ordered in to finish them off.

Still staying with Sunday afternoon at 14:45 more reports were flooding into the ship that the Harriers had destroyed all three helicopters mentioned earlier. The update on the tanker was that it had sustained two large holes, which I imagine must have been inflected by Yarmouth's Wasp and was listing to Port very badly and it was still on fire. Our own Lynx helo was launched earlier and the pilot and crew reported back to Broadsword a "racket" which, so I'm told, means a contact to the West. We opened fire with our Bofors at 16:40 and a minute later Sea Wolf missiles were launched. It was confirmed later that the Fwd No.1

misfired, but No. 2 barrel (under tv surveillance control) possibly splashed a Skyhawk; the aimer being Leading Seamen Lynch.

"BRACE – BRACE – BRACE." We were now under attack. The whole crew was in a position holding on to anything they could that was a permanent fixture, in readiness for whatever we are going to be hit by. We were under attack by four A4 Bomber aircraft. This was literally happening while we were all reading our letters from home from the last mail drop and had been delivered to us only minutes before. We had been strafed by gunfire on the first wave of attack and were now carrying a full blanket search of the ship to check for any damage inside. It looked like we'd only got superficial damage and the First Aid Teams were in full readiness and awaiting the information of where, if any, we had casualties. As soon as HQ1 received the information we in turn would respond or another way we knew will be over the main broadcast either from the Officer on the watch who would make the necessary pipe or again from the Main Head Quarters.

"Fucking shit, things are now getting quite bloody hairy."

I ordered all my First Aid Team to check every Compartment around our immediate area for damage. Those areas consisted of Senior Rates' Cabins, Stowage Areas for the Weapons Department and other Storage Areas. All my team reported back to me that there was no damage in our area. I expected to see the Damage Control Party very shortly so as to report to them. This team usually consisted of four to five personnel and their job immediately after an attack was to sweep through the ship and gather reports from each section reporting damages to pass on to HQ1 and in turn then to Command. I also reported to HQ1 no damage as soon as the First Aid Team reported their findings to me and to keep the Officer in charge up to date on our situation. I was also in communication with the Surgeon Lieutenant (Surg Lt Woodroof) and John our Petty Officer Medical Assistant. It was vital we all communicated as often as possible and keep updated on every situation. My communications to HQ1 were done by using the ship's pick-up phone situated in 1 Mike Flat where our After First Aid Team were situated and I used the Storing Phones to contact the medical team or I phoned the Wardroom where the head of the medical team would be or the Sick Bay by using one of the ship's ordinary phones. So I had got plenty of means of contacting the appropriate personnel if one should fail or get wiped or knocked out.

HMS Antelope's mast had been damaged by a passing bomb which crashed into the sea just in front of us. As I found out later it missed us by five feet above the Bridge, but the explosion we all heard was the bomb that exploded 25 yards on our Port side. Our boys on the Sea Wolf missiles managed to zap two of the Skyhawk A4 Bomber aircraft. We just hoped the Sea Wolf System didn't jam if we got another incoming raid which no doubt there would be. Although a lethal weapon they do tend to jam at the wrong times when needed. The actual full name of the aircraft attacking our group of ships who were responsible for the extensive damage were the A-4B Skyhawks of GRUPO5.

The Captain received HMS Antelope's Lynx onboard after the raid carrying Antelope's Captain to discuss the damage occurred on this Group of Ships. We relaxed once we lost contact with the aircraft raid. They had obviously done as much damage as they possibly could for the day and probably gone home for tea! Wrong again! 18:00hrs brought us back to full alert, this time by a report from HMS Invincible, our second Carrier, who reported she had three Mirage Etendard aircraft approaching our direction at approximately 120 miles.

"Looks like these bastards aren't going to leave us alone after all."

One group came in to zap us while another group waited in the wings to take over the zapping duties once those buggers had dropped their load. The three Mirages were coming in from the West "FAST" and were doing a low run into the Falklands Sound. Luckily we had CAP in the air and one of our Harriers shot one down while good old HMS Yarmouth zapped and splashed another. An Argentine pilot from one of the aircraft was seen to have jettisoned into the sea and no doubt was picked up by one of our nearby vessels. It was reported we had no less that six CAP Harrier jets protecting this part of the Task Group. It was also now reported that HMS Antelope was sailing amongst the protection of the larger ships at a safe distance as during the last full air raid attack she received a 1,000 pound bomb which had lodged itself in one of her Engine Room spaces unexploded.

It was nearly dark by 20:30 and we were warned to expect more attacks but doubtful: in any account be prepared. At this time Broadsword had sailed out of the Sound towards the RFAs to give them some protection and also to make full use while on this patrol of re-fuelling and it had been decided that we would carry out an RAS (refuel at sea) sometime later that evening.

The assessment of damages of this one day on both accounts was as follows:-

Argentine Losses: 10 Aircraft:

2 Mirage Fighters

2 A4 Skyhawk Bombers

2 Puma Helicopters

1 BelleGusta (whatever that is?)

1 Chinook Helicopter

2 Others? (Not sure which)

Royal Naval Damage

Although HMS Antelope had mast damage she was quite OK but much more serious was that she was carrying a

1,000 pound bomb in her Engine Room which needed to be defused by experts as quickly as possible.

At 20:40 Broadsword had its evening meal. So far all was quiet and by fuck had the ship's crew got a lot to talk about on this one day of events alone. The atmosphere was somewhat semi-jubilant but serious. I really got the feeling, because I certainly felt it myself, of relief that really we had had our first real, real challenge combat to combat and survived. This had released a lot of tension amongst ourselves, individually of any uncertainties we were harbouring beforehand now that we had literally come face-to-face with the enemy and were still afloat and had also managed to strike back with the weapons and destroy enemy threats; the ship's confidence and morale had boosted up to an all high.

"But not too much to go and shout and scream about. This is NOT, NOT the time to get the Grog out!"

If the events of the day hadn't been enough what we were about to witness was going to devastate all of us. While having our evening meal it got around the ship like wild fire that HMS Antelope had exploded. We all knew she carried a deadly bomb onboard which hadn't exploded and we also knew that the ship's crew were all safely off the ship while the Special Bomb Defusing Team were trying to make it safe before the crew returned. There were four men of the Bomb Disposal Unit who boarded HMS Antelope (two being Antelope's engineers) once all the ship's crew were off and all were wearing special blast protection gear and carried sensitive listening devices to check the mechanism of the bombs. Antelope had two unexploded bombs onboard and it was then the first bomb exploded and killed one of the four Bomb Team instantly. Although the night sky was pitch black the explosion of Antelope lit up the whole of the Falklands Sound. As I watched Antelope burning and dying I knew it wouldn't be long before another of our ships would be sent to the bottom and Antelope finally gave in and sank in the early hours of Monday morning, the twenty-fourth of May. I believe the remaining three heroes of the Bomb Team managed to get off safely before she finally went to her resting-place. An eerie silence seemed to come over the Falklands waters in the Sound once Antelope vanished beneath the waves.

We carried on with our defence watch routine as normal at 02:00hrs on the Monday, twenty-fourth, and were due to re-fuel Broadsword at 03:00hrs and were anxiously waiting our turn in line, as there are two other ships ahead of us also ready to refuel, before we could make our approach alongside the Royal Fleet Auxiliary ship. Unfortunately by 06:30 we were still unable to get alongside and we were showing less than 50 per cent of fuel in our tanks. As the Captain had virtually been up all night he decided to get his head down for maybe only a few minutes. I shook the Captain with a cup of tea one hour and fifteen minutes later, at 07:45, on his request and he managed to grab a quick breakfast before addressing the ship's crew over the main broadcast where he started off by saying, or should I say, giving everyone a good chuck up for yesterday's performance. We had managed between all of us to knock out at least 25 per cent of the Argentine Airforce so far and they could not possibly at this rate keep the attacks up for long. Our mission that day, in company with the Destroyer HMS Coventry, was to sail out of the Sound and to lure in their aircraft for the Harriers to attack. We will have full manoeuvrability of our Sea Wolf Systems both forward and aft as they make them more freely to use to splash the targets. The Captain signed off.

HMS Invincible lookouts spotted something but nothing seemed to be showing up on radar. Also our shore intelligence hadn't reported any take-offs as of yet but rather to be safe than sorry we closed up for Action Stations at 10:45 for the twenty-second time. Someone actually suggested that what the lookouts may have possibly seen, believe it or not, could have been an albatross as these birds are huge once they have made full flight and they definitely nest around these Islands. The visibility was very poor, so it could have easily been mistaken for just that, but at 12:50 we got definite confirmation from shoreside intelligence that aircraft had taken to the air so all there was for us to do was to see if they were heading in our direction. By 14:15 three Mirages or Daggers Fighters were definitely heading in our direction. This was confirmed by our Operations Team and CAP was already on their way ready to confront in a dogfight. It didn't take long for the reports to come in that the Harriers had successfully shot down all three Mirages or Daggers who were heading towards us. Another wave had gone from our Amphibious Group and this time the enemy aircraft consisted of Mirages and A4 Bombers. Again CAP reinforcements by our Harriers were at hand

and in this air battle they destroyed yet another five Mirages; in all making a total of eight enemy Mirages or Daggers shot down.

"Hell, these Pilots are the best".

The Amphibious Group was very vulnerable as they were just laying off in the Sound and still transporting Troops and stores ashore along with artillery and ammunition. We heard that the Batteries shoreside also zapped a Mirage or Dagger, now making the total nine. At this rate the Argentine Airforce wouldn't have any more aircraft to fly, let alone the pilots to fly them.

Sir Galahad had been hit and had a 1,000 pound bomb lodged in her which was unexploded. There had to be something drastically wrong with the timing firing mechanism on these bombs as we should have lost many of our ships if these bombs had gone off and they could definitely have had the upperhand in this war. The other two Landing Crafts to receive damage on this wave of attacks were the Sir Lancelot, again damaged by an unexploded bomb and also the Sir Gerraint for the same reasons. Imagine the loss of life if all these bombs had gone off. Since the first May there were reports from all our forces, RAF, Army, Navy, Royal Marines, Paras, Merchant Seamen that our loses so far were 73 dead and 86 injured. I'm not sure if this was accurate up to the fouteenth of May but I'm sure it couldn't be far off. I'd got a gut feeling without a shadow of a doubt this war was far from over, with probably worse to come. These are the Royal Naval damages from the first to the twenty-fourth of May.

Saturday 1st May

HMS Alacrity – Type 21 Frigate Slightly damaged by bombs with near misses.

HMS Arrow – Type 21 Frigate. Same as Alacrity – slightly damaged by cannon fire.

HMS Glamorgan – Guided Missile Destroyer (GMD) Slightly damaged by bomb with near misses (all off Stanley) by Daggers of FAA GRUPO 6.

Tuesday 4th May

HMS Sheffield – Type 42 Destroyer. Mortally damaged on the South of the Falkland Islands by an Exocet missile fired by a Super Etendard Fighter aircraft. Once the Sheffield completely burnt out HMS Yarmouth took her under tow but in rough weather she finally sank on Monday 10th May.

Wednesday 12th May

HMS Glasgow – Type 42 Destroyer. Moderately damaged off Port Stanley by an unexploded bomb dropped by an A4B Skyhawk of FAA GRUPO 5. The bomb actually passed through the hull and the damage took some days to repair and shortly afterwards she returned to the UK.

"Her war is over".

Friday 21ˢᵗ May

HMS Antrim – Guided Missile Destroyer (GMD). Seriously damaged in the Falklands Sound outside San Carlos waters by an unexploded bomb which was dropped by Daggers of the FAA GRUPO 6. The UXB (bomb) was finally removed but the damage took some days to repair.

HMS Broadsword – Type 22 Frigate (our ship). Slightly damaged outside San Carlos waters by cannon fire from Dagger of GRUPO 6.

HMS Argonaut – Leander Class Frigate (my old ship). Slightly damaged outside San Carlos waters by rockets and cannon fire from Aermacchi aircraft MB 339A of CANA 1, and then seriously damaged by two unexploded bombs dropped by A4B Skyhawks of FAA GRUPO 6. Removing the UXB and carrying out repairs took a number of days and although declared operational she soon sailed back to the U.K. "Another ship out of the war".

HMS Brilliant – Type 22 Frigate. Slightly damaged outside San Carlos water by cannon fire from Daggers and GRUPO 6 (but different attack from our ship on Broadsword).

HMS Ardent – Type 21 Frigate. Badly damaged in Grantham Sound by bombs. Hits UXBs (more than five) and near misses dropped by Daggers of GRUPO 6, then mortally damaged by bombs from A-40 Skyhawks of CANA 3 ESC off North West Island. Ardent sank the following evening.

Sunday 23rd May

HMS Antelope – Type 21 Frigate. Damaged in San Carlos water by two unexploded bombs dropped by A-4B Skyhawks of GRUPO 5. One of the bombs exploded that evening while being defused and she caught fire, exploded and sank in the very early hours of Monday morning.

Monday 24th May

RFA Sir Galahad (Landing Craft). Damaged by unexploded bomb and out of action for some days.

RFA Sir Lancelot (Landing Craft). Damaged by unexploded bomb and not fully operational for almost three weeks.

RFA Sir Bedivere (Landing Craft). Slightly damaged by glancing bomb all in San Carlos waters probably by A-4C Skyhawks of FAA GRUPO 4.

Imagine if all of the nine unexploded bombs did actually go off. What situation would the Task Group have been in? I dread to think of it. As it so happens out of the nine only one exploded while the team of the Bomb Disposal Unit were trying to make it safe on HMS Antelope. This war wasn't over yet by a long shot.

I sent a member of my First Aid Team to collect the Action Snacks, which had been announced over the main broadcast. They were ready for collection from the Main Galley; this was piped at 16:55. We were still getting reports in and the most satisfying was to hear that the aircraft attacking our RFAs (Landing Craft) in the Sound were really getting a hammering and had been well and truly shot to pieces in one way or another. A good bit of news we heard at five to eight was that a number of ships were to join the Hermes Group and the first ships despatched back to the UK would take our mail for us. So it was pen to paper right then as mail was due to close onboard at 21:15 and as it was all quiet we fell out of Action Stations at 20:30hrs.

We were all aware that it was Argentina's Forces or Independence Day the next day, so one or two things could happen: either they back off to enjoy their celebrations for the day or they come out in full force and throw at us everything they've got. God only knows what would happen. I honestly imagined they would give it a rest for the day but as I've said before: always expect the unexpected. You never know, would we actually see anything of their Naval Fleet?

I do my normal 02:00 shift on Tuesday 25th May and was due to be relieved at 08:00. In between those times the ship managed to refuel at 06:30 and topping us up with fuel. There is one thing I failed to mention: when I was to take up my new role at Action Stations in the Emergency Operating Theatre, our Petty Officer Writer Geoff Wright (Shiner) took over my role in the After First Aid Post with of course I believe the assistance of Johno. So this position was fully manned at all times by a professional team (Sorry mate, I forgot to mention it!). The Leading Hand in charge of the

Aft First Aid Party could have been Dave Sutton or Johno, I'm not quite sure but what I am sure about is the First Aid Teams really had done a fantastic job in both sections, forward and aft. The twenty-first of May undoubtedly proved that.

A few days previously we had met up with the Atlantic Surveyor which is a massive Container Ship. We knew it was very important to protect this ship, like all the others, as she was carrying very important cargo to be landed on the Falklands for the Ground Force Personnel. Some of her cargo consisted of no less than three Chinook helicopters and eight Wessex helicopters, not to mention thousands upon thousands of rounds of ammunition. In addition I imagine were tons of food stores. So I can see why the Troops ashore were anxious to get this ship in to unload her of her cargo.

From the first to the twenty-fourth of May our ships had been under constant attacks and this book reflects exactly as I saw as I have written as per my diary log whilst in the Falklands War.

I would now like to include other members of the ship's company who have added their versions again starting from the first of May until the twenty-fourth. This now is their account from Spider Webster's website on HMS Broadsword during the Falklands War '82 and he has given me kind permission to use the following information supplied by the crew members.

At 0600 on 1st May a lone Vulcan bomber attacked the airfield at Port Stanley having been re-fueled in flight by Victor tankers from its base in Ascension – the round trip covering 6000 miles. One bomb hit the runway putting a large crater across it. At 1000 the ship went to Action Stations as HERMES launched 11 Harriers on bombing runs on Port Stanley and the airs trip at Goose Green. This strike produced three more small craters on the runway at Port Stanley as well as damaging many of the surrounding airfield buildings.

Throughout the day there were several calls to Action Stations for air raids but no enemy aircraft came near the main force except for two Canberra bombers looking for the carriers. However GLAMORGAN, ARROW and ALACRITY were bombed and strafed as they were bombing Port Stanley from close in shore.

These ships suffered minor damage but thankfully nobody was killed. The Harriers intercepted some of the attacking aircraft shooting down two Mirages, two Canberras and chasing many more back to Argentina. One of these fleeing aircraft was shot down by its own Argentine troops on the Falklands. The bombardment continued overnight and then the group in shore returned to the main force at the completion of a very successful day.

Initially Sunday 2nd May was very quiet but it livened up in the evening with the news that HMS CONQUEROR had torpedoed the Argentine cruiser, GENERAL BELGRANO. The action took place 35 miles outside the TEZ, which caused a few ruffles around the world, but the action was explained when MOD stated that the cruiser had been sunk because its six inch guns posed a threat to the Task Force. Waves of euphoria, tinged with sadness for the men now fighting for their survival in the icy seas, swept through the ship. Surely the actions of the past two days would bring the Argentine Junta to its senses and show them that we meant business?

The Argentine cruiser General Belgrano.

Monday 3 May again saw a first for the Task Force. A Sea King on a surface search mission was fired on from two small surface vessels to the north east of Port Stanley. HMS Coventry's and HMS Glasgow's Lynx aircraft attacked the vessels with the newly acquired, but as yet unproven, Sea Skua air to surface missiles. One patrol boat sank and the other was severely damaged.

During all the action BROADSWORD had been performing her customary role as goalkeeper for HERMES. This involved the ship maneuvering upthreat, very close to the carrier to enable Sea Wolf to protect both ships from attack by missiles or aircraft. Our part in the conflict seemed to be along way from the action but the happenings of Tuesday 4 May brought the horrors of war that little bit closer. We had secured from our regular, dawn action stations and eaten lunch when suddenly we were called to action stations. There seemed to be a lot of confusion. At first it was announced that SHEFFIELD had suffered an internal explosion; it was then thought that she has been torpedoed; but it finally became clear that she had been struck by an Exocet missile fired from a Super Etendard fighter/bomber. It was unbelievable. "How could the aircraft have got close enough to deliver the missile". "Had any more Exocets been fired?" The answers are now history and weren't then of any concern. What did matter was whether we could save the crew and the ship.

The missile had ripped a hole in the ship's side and had started numerous fires. Her main problem was in containing the fires and when it was discovered that her fire main had been breached and all power lost, all the ships sent over portable fire pumps. It was to no avail – the flames got worse and after a four hour battle the ship was abandoned. HMS ARROW took off most of the survivors and the injured were rushed to HERMES for treatment. A sobering day for all. Argentina was beginning to even the score. To hammer the point home a Harrier was shot down over Goose Green and the pilot was killed.

During the following day the weather clamped and the ships remained in the eastern corner of the TEZ to think through the previous day's attack. Slowly the initiative was being lost but morale still remained high and people felt happier in the evening when it was announced that the SAS would be using their High Altitude/Low Opening technique to drop in over the Islands. Very little happened in the fog of the next few days except that unfortunately two Harriers collided in mid-air and both pilots were lost.

Fuelled by this success (excuse the pun) BRILLIANT and GLASGOW attempted the air blockade of Port Stanley on the 12th. Again nothing happened until late in the afternoon when both ships were attacked by Skyhawks. Four aircraft attacked from low overland and GLASGOW's Sea Dart was unable to engage them. However BRILLIANT attacked with Sea Wolf in the TV mode. The first two aircraft were hit by the missiles and the third in his efforts to maneuver clear of the other aircraft flew into the sea. Loud cheers echoed around BROADSWORD when news of the success was received. Sea Wolf had done exactly what the makers had specified. When would be our chance to have a go? The euphoria didn't last long for further news quickly followed and this time it wasn't good news. A further wave of Skyhawks had attacked the ships and at the critical moment BRILLIANT's system reset and was unable to fire. Both ships were bombed and strafed, one bomb leapt through GLASGOW's engine room and out the other side fortunately without exploding. GLASGOW limped for home BRILLIANT as escort and I suppose you could say that honours were even that day. There were no casualties in GLASGOW but her time in the TEZ was to be short lived and after a patch up by the Fleet Maintenance Team in STENA SEASPREAD she returned to the UK on 26th May.

Fog again struck over the next few days and there was little action. Unfortunately a Sea King ditched killing 21 members of the SAS – some of them heroes at the retaking of South Georgia. Their loss stunned the Task Force. When the fog lifted the Harriers resumed the bombing of Port Stanley airfield and on 15 May HERMES, BROADSWORD and GLAMORGAN detached to do something special. What happened is now a piece of military history. The "Raid on Pebble Island". Men of the SAS bouncing back from the shock of losing their friends and colleagues in the

Sea King attacked Pebble Island, under the supporting fire of **HMS GLAMORGAN**, destroying 11 aircraft. It was a brave feat which they carried out without loss of life on their part and early the following morning they returned to HERMES, and the three ships slipped away east.

After the trouble with water ingress in the forward Sea Wolf tracker it was decided to carry out test firings against 4.5" shells. This was carried on the 16th and we shot down 2 shells which were fired from YARMOUTH. On the same day. Sea Harriers strafed two Argentine supply ships in a bay in West Falkland so things began to go our way. However again we suffered a setback. A Sea King got into difficulty a long way from the ships and managed to make it to the Chilean coast but unfortunately crash-landed. The crew managed to survive and were eventually found by the Chileans much to our embarrassment. However the Chileans recognised that the aircraft was in distress and after a brief stay in Chile the crew were returned safely to Britain. Thinking that no more Sea Kings could fall in the sea proved to be an error when a fifth speared in, this time the crew were rescued.

At about this time everyone began to wonder when the landing would be - if indeed there was to be a landing. Talks were still going on at the UN and there was always a glimmer of hope. the 19th saw

Canberra.

the arrival of the assault ships, FEARLESS and INTREPID, the LSLs, CANBERRA and all the other troop and equipment carriers of the Merchant Navy. GLAMORGAN continued to bombard the islands and the Harriers bombed two Sisters mount.

Invasion – 21st May

The following day saw the talks finally breakdown and we were told that the invasion was to go ahead and that the landing would be on the 21st at San Carlos water off Falkland Sound on the west side of East Falkland. The ships formed up and split into two groups. The carrier group remained to the east and the troop carriers and assault ships guarded by ANTRIM, BROADSWORD, BRILLIANT, ARDENT, YARMOUTH, PLYMOUTH and ARGONAUT headed for the beach-head with 4000 troops and all their vital supplies. This was the day that would win or lose the battle. We had to get all the troops ashore.

Sir Tristram, Sir Galahad and Canberra (the great white whale).

One hit on the CANBERRA and all would be lost. Surely this was the moment for which the Argentines had been saving their remaining air launched Exocet? The weather was on our side – misty with lots of low cloud to hide our position. As we set off from the carrier group on the evening of the 20th May we waited and waited for the inevitable air attacks, but non came. Maybe we could do it after all! We pressed on towards our goal. During the night creeping ever closer to the landing area, GLAMORGAN and the Harriers were carrying out diversionary bombardments of other possible landing sites and when at last as we in the Sound were putting men ashore, the SAS and SBS attacked strategic positions to add to the Argentines' confusion. As dawn broke on the 21st we had achieved the beginning of the end for the enemy occupation of the Falklands. Every single soldier of the original 4000 was put ashore safely and after few skirmishes with some Argentineans a beach-head was established.

HMS Intrepid.

The first aim had been completed, men ashore with sufficient supplies to hold their ground. However it now had to be defended and this task fell to the escorting frigates and destroyers. What happened over the next five days proved to be the highlight of the war from a naval point of view. They were days of sadness, horror, jubilation, thankfulness, pain and joy.

Bomb Alley – Day One

During the latter part of the assault, BROADSWORD's job had been to escort the

LSLs, SIR TRISTRAM etc and protect them from the two S209 submarines of the Argentine navy. Once the landing ships had entered San Carlos Water, BROADSWORD returned to Falkland Sound to sweep the area just in case the submarines were lurking there ready to attack the landing ships at anchor. We found nothing, so as dawn was breaking BROADSWORD took up her air defence station in the South with BRIILIANT, PLYMOUTH, YARMOUTH, ARGONAUT, ARDENT, ANTRIM and the undefended FORT AUSTIN. At 1020 the ship went ot Action Stations and the Lynx was launched to carry out a surface search of nearby coves to establish whether there were any lurking patrol craft which might attempt an attack. The crew found nothing and returned safely after one hours flying. Sea Harriers were more lucky and two of them found some Argentine helicopters towards the southern end of the Sound. They attacked with cannon and shot down one Chinook and one Puma. Back on BROADSWORD everyone was looking at the sky awaiting the inevitable air raid. The day was crystal clear with bright sunshine – a total contrast to the previous day. The weather had certainly favoured us on the 20th but it changed sides and favoured the Argentines on the 21st. Initially it was peaceful not unlike summer holidays in the Western Isles. The only thing that told you otherwise was the sound of Antrim's guns as she pounded the shore. Suddenly this was all to change. A lone Aeromacchi appeared and attacked FORT AUSTIN, dropping bombs but fortunately not with any degree of accuracy. Still it acted as a warning and sensibly FORT AUSTIN moved into the more secure anchorage alongside the assault ships, then all hell let loose. The air was filled with attacking aircraft, mainly Mirage and Skyhawk, and the battle raged for over six hours. Every ship in the sound came under attack that day.

ANTRIM battling bravely fired her Sea Slug at some attacking aircraft but the odds were too great and she was hit by bombs and rockets around the flight deck. Fortunately the bombs did not explode which was just as well because one passed through the Sea Slug magazine. However the damage was sufficient to put her Sea Slug and Sea Cat systems out of action so all she could do was to sit out the rest of the day. BRILLIANT's turn came next. She was hit by cannon fire and one shell passed clean through the Operations Room damaging important cabling which severly affected her Sea Wolf system. Sea Harriers were fighting the bravest air battle since The Battle of Britain. A handful of airplanes were having to fly repeatedly from their carriers 150 miles east, yet were taking on and beating the faster Mirage and Skyhawk. One flew over the top of the ship and fired a Sidewinder at a departing Mirage which dipped and crashed into the hillside when hit. BROADSWORD was

striving to get Sea Wolf away but the close
proximity of the land was preventing the system
from operating correctly and the opportunities to
launch the missiles were scarce. However when it
did strike it was a spectacular success. Unseen by
most, a group of four aircraft attacked from low
over the hills. Fortunately Leading Seaman Ball,
the missile aimer on the forward system, saw the
incoming aircraft on his screen and fired a missile
in the TV Mode. It was a tremendous
achievement, steering the missile towards nothing
more than a black dot on the screen. Many people
on the flight deck, who were looking in that
direction, didn't see anything until the missile
exploded under the aircraft's port wing. It was a
good ob that the flight deck team saw this for it
alerted them to the attack and enabled some of
them to engage the other incoming aircraft with
gunfire while others took cover in the hangar. Two
delta shaped silver Mirages winged over, flew
round the stern and attacked the port side with
30mm cannon, strafing the hangar and the flight
deck. Shrapnel bounced around the hangar
injuring several of the flight but mercifully no one
was killed. This action brought it home that we
were at war. A second attack on the
BROADSWORD was met with withering fire
from the starboard battery. Cannon shells burst
into the ship's side, one narrowly missing Sergeant
Leslie as he slipped trying to direct fire at the

escaping aircraft, and a piece of shrapnel ripped through the windproof jacket of Seaman "Oscar" Whild. Several other members of the battery who were armed with SLRs were also hit by shrapnel. The battle went on. ARGONAUT received two direct hits from bombs and again they failed to explode. One landed in her main magazine leaning on live Sea Cats and other ammunition! Crippled, but not dead, she limped into San Carlos Water to better shelter.

Still the attacks went on with no sign of them dying away. The Harriers were managing to knock some out of the sky but because they were heavily outnumbered inevitably others got through. Although the escorts were suffering badly they were achieving their aim of protecting the beach-head and equipment was still being landed and the positions ashore were being consolidated. The last attack of the day proved to be the saddest of all when a combination of Skyhawks, Mirages and Aeromacchi's attacked HMS ARDENT. They bombed her hangar and flight deck killing most of the Flight and causing her to list to starboard. Her weapons were crippled and she was heading out of control for the shore so she dropped her anchor.

The aircraft attacked again splattering the flight deck where the doctor was attending a dying man. The doctor was blown overboard but remained conscious and was picked up by BROADSWORD where he recovered after being treated for exposure.

HMS YARMOUTH came alongside the stricken ARDENT and took off the survivors to end a sad but successful day. 17 aircraft had been destroyed by Harriers and the escorts while a Lynx had quietly disposed off an oiler hiding in a cove. Darkness came and with it safety-at least for the next few hours. Tomorrow would be different because we all hoped the Rapier Batteries would be established to give the ships and the beach-head added protection.

Bomb Alley – Second Day

It was decided that to remain in the Sound would be suicidal so the remaining ships moved into San Carlos Water on the 22 May after carrying out submarine sweeps overnight. Here they would be assisted by the Rapiers. BROADSWORD was detached with COVENTRY to attempt a missile trap further west and intercept any aircraft which were heading for San Carlos. We waited and waited for the attacks or news from San Carlos but nothing happened except for one speculative strike by a Pucara in San Carlos. Perhaps the Argentines were resting or watching the UK Wembley Cup

Final on TV. One Harrier was a little more successful sniffing out and destroying a fast patrol boat.

Bomb Alley – Third Day

May 23 dawned bright and clear. BRILLIANT was in need of repairs and COVENTRY was detached to the carrier group so we took brilliant's place in San Carlos Water. Here we were supposed to have a better chance because we were protected by high ground and the long awaited Rapier, and it was thought that the only way that the Argentines could attack was through the narrow gap at the head of the water. How wrong we were. The aircraft came in low and fast, swooping down valleys on either side. Earlier in the day we had seen success when ANTELOPE's Lynx had fired a Sea Skua into a freighter and the Harriers had shot down two Pumas and Bell helicopter, but now the boot was on the other foot. There were several attacks during the day, some more memorable than others. All were frightening but some seemed comical in retrospect. Sea Cat chased Mirages and just when they seemed to be gaining they ran out of steam and fell in the water like something from a Tom and Jerry cartoon. Other missiles and 40/60 fire hit the hillside in pursuit of one jet, scattering a herd of cows who left a trail of dust that even the Roadrunner would have been proud of. After the comedy came the tragedy. ANTELOPE who a replaced the unfortunate ARDENT was the subject of a particularly ferocious attack in which received an unexploded bomb. She defended herself valiantly shooting down one aircraft and destroying another which hit her mast and cartwheeled into the water just yards ahead of our bridge. We ourselves then became the subject of a determined attack, Sea Wolf took one and 40/60 another, but somehow one aircraft launched two bombs which looked as if they were going to end Broadsword's war. The approach of the bombs, fitted with air brakes was very slow and everyone on the upper deck froze as they watched them draw nearer. Again God was kind and the first one fell short and the second passed over the bridge and exploded in the water 30 yards away. Meanwhile ANTELOPE had limped up the harbour to shelter amongst the assault ships. Yarmouth's sea Cat shot down another aircraft and dusk approached, signaling the end of the day's battle. There was a lot of joy around because many aircraft had been shot down and we had suffered only light casualties. The Navy had also not lost a ship. However this was all about to change. Shortly after dark ANTELOPE exploded as a bomb disposal expert attempted to defuse the unexploded bomb in the engine room. The explosion broke the ship's back and she quickly caught fire. This marred an otherwise successful day and set many minds wondering just how long we could hold out in Bomb Alley, by common consent we had decided San Carlos Water should be named. Early the next day ANTELOPE finally sank.

Although my heart goes out to the families and friends of those they lost in the conflict so far, I especially would like to send my condolences to the family of Mark Stevens, serving onboard the Type 21 Frigate HMS Antelope which received severe damage on the twenty-third of May, when Mark died. Like me, Mark was a fellow Steward and doing exactly the same duty as myself as part of the First Aid Team and also as I was he had been closed up in the Petty Officers' Mess awaiting to attend to casualties that occurred during battle. Mark died when a bomb entered the ship and careered through the Petty Officers' Mess killing him instantly. As any Commanding Officer would be, Captain Tobin of HMS Antelope would have felt a great loss to lose one of his crew as would all of Mark's fellow Shipmates.

May peace be with you and your family, Mark.

Tuesday 25th May was Argentina's Independence Day and we were all more than aware that their full force of attacks whether by land, sea or air would almost definitely happen and hit us with all they have. For the Naval Task Force it would undoubtedly come from the air as we knew that their Naval Force had remained in harbour since the sinking of their Cruiser, the Belgrano.

02:00hrs brought me once again to Defence Stations closing up at HQ1 and at 06:30 we were taking on more fuel with one of the Royal Fleet Auxiliary Ships and at 08:00 I was relieved of watch and went off to grab a spot of breakfast. The Task Force Commander Admiral Woodward called today the Argentines' Forces Day (not Independence Day) and sent signals to all Commanding Officers to expect more attacks on our ships with the very high risk of incoming Exocet missiles (as the one which sunk HMS Sheffield). But he also added as its foggy it may not be likely! HMS Broadsword took up position as the day before but a little farther up from her original station.

"Air Raid Warning RED" blasted over the main tannoy system at 12:45. Two Recce aircraft had been detected on the radar screen. We hear one had been shot down by a Sea Dart, but the other managed to escape into the hillside. Five minutes later we reverted to state one condition yankee and at 13:00 the ship went back to normal defence watches. Two A4 Bombers were picked up at 15:25 and by now we were again at full Action Stations. HMS Coventry splashed one (shot down) and it seemed the other had been destroyed in the Falklands Sound. These Bombers were first detected by our Rothesay Type Frigate, HMS Yarmouth. Today was normally a big celebration for the Argies of their successful bid for Independence from Spain in 1810, so although by late afternoon at approximately 15:45 with few attacks we couldn't ever lower our guard as there could well be more trouble on its way before dusk. Two Skyhawks were detected on radar at 15:46 way off to the Sound in the South direction. We were all now very tensed up and fully alert to these small groups of raids which could possibly be to keep us busy while a massive air strike was carried out on our Carriers by Exocet to commemorate their 25th Forces Day.

16:30 brought us to "Air Raid Warning RED". A lot of activity by enemy aircraft especially in the Sound and news also came in from our Operations room that our Sea Harriers were bombing Port Stanley Airfield. Another report also stated Pucara aircraft had taken off from Argentina and were on a heading of bearing 230°, 120 miles away. These could possibly have been heading towards the Carriers. The raid was now building up. A bearing 105° and now 80 miles to the West. The Combat Air Patrol (CAP) come in to intercept, flying from the West.

The order was given: "BRACE – BRACE – BRACE"

FUCK!! We were now under attack. The time is 18:18. Two Skyhawks were menacingly bearing down on us as our Bofor Gun Crew were throwing every shit they could at the incoming A4 Skyhawks. There was an almighty "BANG" that seemed come from Aft.

"SHIT was that a bomb or what? The ship has been hit!"

At 18:20 HMS Coventry opened fire all her guns and Sea Dart missiles. Somehow with absolutely the worst time possible the Sea Dart jammed on Coventry. These would have undoubtedly taken out one if not two of the aircraft, so it was left to the other defence systems to try and get these buggers before they got us. We were unable to fire Sea Wolf at this stage as Coventry was in our own sights but every other system was going full blazes at this time. I could clearly smell a strong acrid smell so I assumed the ship was on fire somewhere.

The First Aid Post I was now closed up in was fully set up in the Petty Officers' Mess with all the sterile stainless instrument containers and with the operating table fully secured to the deck. My prime task was to assist the Medical Officer or the Petty Officer Medical Assistant in any major surgery that had to be carried out. Daryl Poyzer was also with me and doing his utmost to help either the other First Aid Teams if he could get to them for assistance. Again the thought came to my mind and I looked directly at the Bulkhead and said, "Come on you bastard, if you're going to have me make it now and quick." If a bomb was to enter this Compartment at least I'd know little or nothing of it at all.

There was a lot of shouting and barking of orders along Two Deck as the damage, fire and repair parties were having to deal with the effects of the massive bang we heard earlier. The ship sustained a considerable amount of damage Aft, below the Flight Deck. This was caused by the first wave of attacks on us by two A4 Skyhawk aircrafts one of which fired a 1,000 pound bomb which entered the ship on our Starboard side Aft above the water line. The bomb careered through the ship destroying a good part of the Laundry then made its way up towards the Flight Deck where it punched through the Deck itself and because we had our Lynx helicopter secured on Deck in the centre, it severed it almost in half before bouncing over the Port side and miraculously, to everyone's astonishment, without going 'off' or exploding. The amount of damage it made in its path was unbelievable. The Chinese Laundry Man was completely in shock by his unwanted visitor and demanded to see the Captain to go to another ship as he thought this one was too noisy for him. To this day I don't really think that he fully understood that Britain was at war and thought this was just another normal ship's exercise until of course the 1,000 pound bomb wrecked his home.

There was a major fuel spillage on the Flight Deck and AFFF foam was used to stop the fuel igniting. Reports came through that we had a casualty forward of the ship on Deck 4c (two below me), in the Inflammable Storeroom. The Fwd First Aid Team were despatched to investigate. Five minutes only had passed and the time was 18:25. We had just been informed HMS Coventry had been hit by a bomb, which passed over us by inches. HMS Coventry had now received two direct hits by 1,000 pound bombs and both exploded. As I learned later although we received the bomb Aft it didn't cause a fire. The smell I previously detected must have been from the aftermath after it punched its way through and over the ship.

Full Combat Air Cover were now flying around us. The most difficult order any Captain will have to make will be to "Abandon Ship". This order was given by Captain Hart-Dyke Commanding Officer of the Type 42 Destroyer HMS Coventry at approximately 18:35hrs fifteen minutes after our first attack. Here you are in one of the most inhospitable climates around the globe fighting a war and then ordered to abandon ship as your home is about to be engulfed with sea water and lost forever beneath the waves. To hear this experience from previous Shipmates is bad enough and to know up to now we had lost Sheffield, Ardent and Antelope to be here to witness the sinking of one of our finest Destroyers was very soul destroying, not to mention the lives she would take down with her when she finally submerged and laid to rest. When "Abandon Ship" is ordered orange survival suits are worn by all the crew with life jackets worn around the waist. The majority of Coventry's crew had only minutes to get into their suits and jump over the side before the ship's drag would take them down as well when she finally went under. By this they had to swim as far away from the ship as possible and wait to be rescued. The water was freezing cold and it would only be a matter of minutes before more crew members would die from cold, hence it was essential all and every possible rescue team got to the Coventry's crew by the absolute quickest and fastest possible means and then bring them onboard HMS Broadsword for us to administer full medical support. To jump off a ship wearing a full survival kit at twenty to thirty feet up must have been a terrifying ordeal in itself with the knowledge you'd be jumping into freezing icy water but to add to this to survive you must at all costs swim away from the ship so as not to be dragged under with her once she went down.

The phone rang in the Petty Officers' Mess and I was informed by John (POMA) that the Coventry had abandoned ship and the main role now for all First Aid Teams was to attend to all the survivors which were being

HMS Ganges, The Mast – Erected in 1907 for boy entrant training purposes.

HMS Coventry on fire.

HMS Coventry sinking.

HMS Coventry keeling over to port.

HMS Coventry turning turtle.

HMS Coventry – the final moments before she sank.

HMS Antelope is hit.

HMS Ardent on fire.

HMS Ardent on fire.

HMS Sheffield on fire.

HMS Sheffield on fire.

The Lynx helicopter only slowed the bomb's progress.

Sea Kings at Ascension Island were very busy fetching extra stores, April 1982.

HMS Arrow.

HMS Hermes leaves Ascension Island for the Falklands April 1982.

brought onboard HMS Broadsword by all possible means of transportation: the small craft line; the ship's Cutters; Geminis (rubber dinghies) and the Sea King and Lynx helicopters. The air and sea were a swarm of activity of rescue teams. I found out later that it was four A4 Skyhawks that came in two waves of attack. Before this attack HMS Coventry had successfully knocked out two other aircraft with their Sea Dart missiles as they were coming out of San Carlos, so things were going well up to then. Pilot Officer Fuerza Aerea from the Argentinian Air Force set his sights on HMS Broadsword and with his camera running took the firing shots against our ship. These photos were then published in the Argentine national newspapers obviously to boost their nation's morale and no doubt for propaganda purposes.

Somehow a few weeks later a copy of the picture showing us under attack from the Argentine newspaper appeared onboard ship in the mail drop and one of the lads managed to get a copy for my diary for which I was very thankful.

This is where the 1,000 pound bomb "Bouncing" entered HMS Broadsword Starboard side AFT and went through the Laundry, up into the Flight, Deck destroying the Lynx helicopter before bouncing over the ship's side, hence the Broadsword's "Bouncing Bomb".

From now on every survivor would be treated for medical purposes in the Wardroom and Wardroom surrounding areas as this was now the Command Post for all our First Aid Teams. I now joined up with Surgeon Lieutenant Woodroof

Picture contributed by Emil Toppings ("Topsy").

(Senior Medical Officer), John Wicks, the Petty Officer
Medical Assistant, the Padre, a Petty Officer Cook, Leading

Steward Leading Cook, Caterer Daryl Poyzer and Stores' Accountant Kev Doidge with a couple of other First Aid Crew. We would be joined later by all First Aid Teams distributed around the ship once the threat of attack had ceased, which by now I think it had. The Argentine Pilots had now inflicted the worst possible damage to us and were now flying home back to their base.

Petty Officer Jerry Billinger and his fellow Stores' Accountants were now in full force to get all the Emergency Storerooms open and transfer as much of the extra clothing, blankets, boots, shoes, socks, overalls, medical suppliers, towels, life jackets, torches and basically everything he could get his hands on to assist us in the arrival of Coventry's survivors. The Catering Staff were also working flat out with the Supply Officer to help the Cooks onboard to prepare meals and hot drinks to everyone who came onboard. Of course we had to take into account what injuries we were likely to be dealing with as very serious injuries could be more harmed if the patient were to take in food and drink. This would have to be overseen by ourselves with the Senior Medical Officer. As I was waiting for all Stores to arrive from Jerry and his team I quickly went forward into the Wardroom Flat towards the foc'sle and opened the screen door to see when we would be expecting our first wave of casualties and survivors. The time was now 18:47 and right above me like a massive giant bird was a Wessex Helicopter hovering over the foc'sle and the Seamen Department assisting the arrival of our first men from Coventry. Before I dashed over to assist I couldn't help but notice the devastating sight I saw in front of me.

HMS Coventry with her bows facing to us was listing far over on her Port side, her masts precariously tilting towards the South Atlantic Sea. Smoke was pouring out from Bow to Stern and to my horror what I could see were the small rescue boots that were right beneath who seemed to be having tremendous difficulty getting away from the Destroyer as she was slowly bearing down on them. It seemed that at one point one of the boats carrying a full crew of survivors was doomed. It wasn't until later thankfully that Andy Coppell, an Able Seamen, who was the coxwain of his craft managed to get in and pull them away to safety and then on to us. Helicopters were coming in from all directions plucking off survivors as the ship was getting lower and lower in the water and seemed to be sinking at a considerable rate. At any time any one of the ship's magazines could have exploded and blown up the ship. But the courage of those boats' crews and pilots alike will be something I hold with great admiration and respect for the risk and danger they were prepared to go through for our fellow Shipmates.

Our first survivors were received at around 18:50 and by now we were ready to apply medical help. We knew what type of injuries to expect as the obvious were going to be severe burns, shock and especially hypothermia. It only takes minutes before this sets in and the person is in a coma and in those seas and weather conditions you didn't stand a chance.

My last glance at Coventry, before I brought on our first survivors from our Wessex, was to vividly see the sun setting as dusk was falling and seeing Coventry in a orange glow, not by fire, but by the sun setting. I thought in only a few minutes everything here will be gone and all that will be seen of this horrific moment will be the sun setting over a completely clear water where once a ship and lives had been taken.

As I rushed our casualties to the Wardroom Area I was glad to see that the only bath in the ship happened to be in the Wardroom Flat and that it had been filled with tepid water ready for the first serious cases of hypothermia. Tepid I say as it would be lethal to put a freezing temperature patient into a hot bath. Basically you would be doing the complete opposite to jumping into freezing water – the shock would have killed the patient. We were still waiting for the extra blankets from Jerry's team. A couple of the lads and I took the initiative as we were in the Officers' Wardroom Cabin Flat to strip all bunks of counterpanes, blankets, sheets, sleeping bags and any other bedding we could get our hands on until we could get the ones from Stores.

Jerry was doing his utmost to get those Stores to us but as we all knew that when a ship is fully closed down for war you essentially must go through the proper ship's control procedure. The first thing he would have to do is get the keys from HQ1 to the Storerooms, going through and down hatches en-route. Secondly he had to report to HQ1 every hatch he and his team opened and closed. Then he could get stores out, which when you are dealing with kidney-like hatches, which barely a full-grown man can just squeeze through, the task is quite enormous. Don't forget the ship was still at threat from aircraft and this procedure had to be adhered to at all times. If those hatches were fully opened and we received another full air strike the ship would flood in minutes if damaged and this would do no one any good.

Once Jerry's reports were made to HQ1 for the hatches to be opened and closed it was then reported to Command so at any one time the Captain knew exactly what hatches were open or closed, and because there were other tasks being carried out throughout the ship, for example the transfer of certain ammunition to the Gunnery positions, a strict control had to be made so only a certain amount of hatches were open at any one time. Again this was strictly monitored by HQ1 at my old Defence Station position. The Titanic unfortunately made the biggest error ever in not sealing off her Bulkheads properly, so when she hit the iceberg the water went from one compartment to the next then the next and so on until she sank – this applied here if we were to open the hatches. Even though we have a major emergency in saving lives the whole ship would be at risk of sinking if under attack. Anyhow the threat was lifted and no more aircraft were detected so we could relax the hatch routine slightly and it wasn't long before we saw the Emergency Stores in the Wardroom with Jerry and his merry men.

Although I wasn't aware of it until then but the day before the RFA ship Sir Galahad has been damaged by an unexploded bomb and was expected to be out of action for some days. Also the RFA Sir Lancelot had been damaged again by an unexploded bomb and the RFA Bedivere was slightly damaged by a glancing bomb. All three vessels were in San Carlos waters and were probably attacked by Skyhawks. Our own consolation for Monday the twenty-fourth for the Task Force was that seven Argentinian aircraft had been reported to have been destroyed, as ten were on the twenty-third of May, bringing seventeen aircraft down in two days.

Before I continue with the rescue of HMS Coventry this is the damage our ships had had so far in the last couple of days. HMS Glasgow had been moderately damaged off Port Stanley by an unexploded bomb dropped by an A4 Skyhawk. The bomb passed through her Hull and it took a few days to repair and she shortly returned to the UK. HMS Antrim had been very serious damaged on the twenty-first of May while patrolling in the Falklands Sound outside San Carlos waters, yet again by an unexploded bomb dropped by Dagger Aircraft. The UXB (unexploded bomb) was removed successfully. Again it took some days to repair.

My old ship F56, the Leander Class Frigate HMS Argonaut, was at first only slightly damaged on the twenty-first of May outside San Carlos water by rockets and cannon fire from Aermacchi MB 339A of CANA1 Esc, but then seriously damaged by two unexploded bombs dropped by A4 Skyhawks of FAA GRUPO 5. But after successfully removing the UXBs she also took a few days to repair and was declared operational but sent back to the UK.

HMS Brilliant had also been slightly damaged outside San Carlos water, again on the twenty-first of May by cannon fire from Daggers of GRUPO 6, but a different attack than we had on Broadsword and of course, as I've mentioned, HMS Ardent who was in Grantham Sound when she received her bomb hits and sank the following evening. We lost HMS Antelope on the twenty-third of May who received two unexploded bombs in San Carlos water but while being defused that evening, after her crew had been safely taken off, one of the bomb exploded killing one of the bomb team and she caught fire and sank the next day. Then there were the three RFAs with damage on the twenty-fourth. In all things were not going well at all for the British Task Force.

Back to just off Pebble Island where we were now in the full operation of trying to save as many lives as possible from HMS Coventry's crew. Two of our Harrier jets were hovering over the rescue area in case any more enemy fighter attacks came in which, thank god, they didn't. Although Coventry's Captain was one of the last to abandon his ship he arrived on board Broadsword in the second boat to be brought alongside. As expected we were having to deal with a vast majority of burns and shock from the survivors, but hypothermia was also a great concern for our First Aid Teams. We were working flat out to get their body temperatures up before their bodies lapsed into a critical state.

I went over to assist one of Coventry's crew members. whom I could see had suffered burns and greeted him by saying, "OK, Mate! I'll just take care of these burns." I helped as much as I could with the medical equipment I had for him. It was about ten to fifteen minutes later that I found out that this actually was the Captain of Coventry, a very tall Officer and like all the other survivors was wearing the orange survival suit.

The next patient I received after he had done the bath routine was Leading Steward Devine. I had known LSTD Devine years before when we both served on the Destroyer HMS Fife back in the seventies. He also was in the second batch of people to be brought onboard ship and incredibly he managed to avoid any burn injuries at all. He briefly gave me an account of the disaster from his point of view. Apparently the ship had gone to Action Stations when the enemy aircraft were picked up by radar and he also had closed up at his Action Station in the Forward First Aid Post when the bombs struck home. As he recalls he immediately had casualties himself to attend to and was doing his utmost best when within minutes the ship suddenly lurched over to Port. He thought maybe this was a zig-zag tactical course of action. Suddenly to his horror realised that the engines weren't running and the ship had actually keeled over on her side, so with him and the rest of his team he got as many people out of their present position and clambered up towards the Upper Deck to safety. The sheer panic of the ship going down and being trapped is a very, very horrifying experience for anyone. I would absolutely hate to think what the poor blighters felt who were four or five decks below with all the hatches securely shut tight which they all definitely would have been at this time. Leading Steward Devine continued by saying once he heard the order to abandon ship and after making sure the casualties in his care were OK he then had to pluck up courage by getting into the orange survival suit and jumping over the side as he could quite clearly tell the ship was going down FAST! He recalled to me it was one hell of a long jump and it seemed to take forever to hit the water and when he finally did it wasn't the shock of impact but the immense cold and contact with the sea that completely took his breath away. Once he knew he had survived all of this he frantically doggy-crawled over to the nearest life raft which at this stage already held 30 or so of his Shipmates. After successfully boarding his life-saving craft, which was a rubber dinghy, he vividly remembered having to plug a large gaping hole in the side by means of using his fist. But within minutes they were alongside Broadsword to be heaved in.

When Coventry finally lost her battle to stay afloat and silently slipped beneath the waves to be lost forever, the continuous search went on well into the evening, even as the sun had slipped away to put us into the night darkness. Broadsword successfully managed to receive 170 of the Coventry's crew and to give all immediate medical help as was needed. One experience of mine while attending to casualties with burns, shock and minor injuries, was that of a Chief Petty Officer with at least 70 per cent burns. After getting him on two of the four Wardroom tables to administer drips he lost consciousness. Along with the Medical Officer I thought we had lost him, but while bending over him to get a pulse and check his breathing he suddenly shot up from a lying position into a sitting position and looked at me straight in the eyes. The look of fear and horror I saw in those eyes will haunt me forever. After a couple of seconds he lost consciousness again but he still managed to live through the night until we could get him air-lifted to the Hospital Ship Uganda. Never, ever will I forget those eyes of fear in that man.

The Wardroom, acting as our First Aid Command Post, was a complete shambles with bandages, wrappings, drips, fluids, eye wash bottles, buckets of water, water bottles, blankets, sheets, sponges, stretchers, plastic cups and mugs along with injured bodies lying and sitting at every possible nook and cranny they could find. Obviously we had to overflow into the Wardroom Cabin Flat and use as many of the Officers' Cabins for our more seriously wounded. Everyone took their duties with absolute professionalism in all departments throughout the whole ship. Everyone, I mean everyone, played a major part in the safety and well being of the Coventry's crew members from one end of the ship to the other. Broadsword's crew members who were coming off watch were immediately at hand for the Coventry's Shipmates whoever they happened to be. Not once did I ever hear or see any rank, rate or order given throughout the whole ordeal. Basically everyone got on with their job in a good-hearted and high-spirited manner in the very sad and upsetting situation that the ships had endured in the last couple of hours. There's a true saying which goes: "Put Jack under immense pressure (Jack being slang for sailor) and he'll always come out on top with flying colours". How very true on this very day.

Once I had finished patching up my casualties and getting them comfortable around our Areas, I approached Captain Hart-Dyke and asked him if he would like to see our Captain, to which he replied he very much would. After briefly speaking to Surg Lt Woodroof the Coventry's Captain and I proceeded to the ladder from One Deck Wardroom Cabin Flat where I contacted HQ1 by phone to get permission to open the kidney hatch onto 01 Deck which is the Captain's Flat and where the Operations Rooms was. It was also where I knew our Captain would be controlling the whole of Broadsword and not on the Bridge where a lot of people might think a Captain would be.

Any major manoeuvres or tactics, either in war or peace, where a ship is likely to be under threat of attack is nowadays in the modern Royal Naval commanded in the Operations room. This becomes the Command Post until the threat is over. The Officer of the Watch (OOW) automatically takes responsibility for the Bridge Area with the Quartermaster at the wheel. Again on the Bridge are the Senior Yeomen (Signals) and possibly the Navigational Officer, all directly in contact with the Captain at all times.

After about five minutes, as I was at first refused due to other hatches already open throughout the ship, I was given the green light to proceed with Captain Hart-Dyke to 01 Deck and told then to report back to HQ1 once we had both entered through and secured the hatch behind us, which took us about a minute to do with all our kit strapped around us. I was still lumbered with carrying my life jacket, gas mask with spare filters, a full first aid bag with supplies of, for example, bandages, plasters, eye wash, scissors, tape and cotton wool and, in addition to this, all First Aiders must at all times carry not one water bottle container but two, so as you can imagine this is some weight to carry around the ship. But as we all knew this was absolutely essential equipment not only at the end of the day would it save your own life but could contribute to help save many others as well. So we were now in the Captain's Flat and the time if I remember was between 19:30 and 20:00hrs. I made the Coventry's Captain as comfortable as possible in Broadsword's Commanding Officer's Quarters, which I must add looked even more like a War Office than when I saw it last time. There seemed to be more maps and easels planted around the CO's Day Cabin with different coloured pins sticking into certain locations around the Falkland Island Areas. Before proceeding to the Operations Room I popped into my Pantry and dug out the kettle which had been stowed away for action, topped it up with water and clicked it on and also tried to find out where I'd hidden the cups and saucers. I never could remember where I put those things because everything just got stuffed in any where there was room when the ship went to action, but fortunately it only took a few seconds to locate those things along with the jugs, sugar bowls and spoons. The kettle was merrily purring away so I knew we had power in the socket so hopefully by the time I got back it should have been well into its bubbling hot water mode. My task now was to try and get hold of the Captain in the Operations Room who was still unaware that he had the Commanding Officer of Coventry in his Quarters, who understandingly was still very shaken and looking pale and tired. I honestly felt so sorry for the loss of Coventry and the burden that Captain Hart-Dyke and what was going through his mind then must have been unbearable. Even though he knew he had lost his ship nobody at this stage knew who and how many lives had been saved and how many we had lost. We knew for sure that we had managed to pick up or receive on Broadsword at least 170 personnel but had no idea of the numbers that were transferred or flown to other ships in the area. With the complement of the whole crew being from 265 to 275 we could only account for, at that stage, 170 members. That meant approximately 100 unaccounted for so far, until we started getting reports through from shore side and the other ships who had taken on the survivors. When the ship completely rolled over and on her final minutes afloat with her propellers clearly visible before she went under, men had reported banging on the ship's Hull with a heavy object. This is a terrible, terrible way to die and to think that the men who heard the last desperate cries for help, could not possibly do anything in their power to save them, will remain with them for the rest of their lives. It now became obvious that lives had been lost on the Coventry in her final moments of going under because of the men who heard cries for help, but were fortunate enough to get clear of the ship in time to save themselves.

Once I'd rooted out all the utensils and crockery in the Captain's Pantry I headed towards the Operations Room and slid open the door. Never have I witnessed being at the Command Post while war was in progress. This is where the battle was fought by the Captain and the Principal

Warfare Officer (PWO) as well as all the Technical Senior and Junior Ratings, each having a vital part to play on their numerous monitors, trackers, radar screens and firing positions dotted in every conceivable space in this area. Even during peacetime exercises I wouldn't be anywhere near here, as I would be closed up at my normal Action Stations two Decks below amidships. My first observation of the Area was that it looked like something from a 25th Century spaceship console panel with all the thousands of red, green, orange and white lights on the numerous displays and radar screens and with all the main lights off this was quite an impressive sight for the first time observer. The nickname the Navy has adopted for this Compartment throughout the Naval Fleet is called the "Gloom Room" but by the amount of activity going on at this present moment it was anything but a Gloom Room. There was a certain area or section that was solely for the purpose of the Command position where I would probably pinpoint our Captain, but glancing over to the far end where the charts were laid out it didn't take me long to spot him. I spoke, I think, to Petty Officer Chris Chapman and asked if I may speak to the Captain and soon the Captain was at my side somewhat bewildered as to why his POSTD should be in the OPs Room especially at this time. I quickly explained that the Captain of Coventry was in his Quarters and without any more explanation we were both heading towards his Day Cabin after he gave a quick brief to the Principal Warfare Officer (PWO). As soon as both Captains had settled I served tea, wearing full action gear. Both Captains were in full conversation when I exited the Day Cabin, closing the entrance dividing curtain as I left.

After about ten minutes I popped in to clear away the tea things and explained to Captain Canning that I'd get back to my First Aid Post to see if I could give any more assistance to the casualties, if only to be there for comfort. I rang HQ1 again to get permission to come down to the Wardroom Flat and opened the hatch to where I was. This time I was given the OK signal almost immediately and proceeded to the Wardroom where I met up again with LSTWD Devine. As he seemed to have lost all his footwear we both proceeded to another deck below to Two Deck Flat outside the Petty Officers' Mess where my Cabin was and as luck just had it I found a spare pair of plimsolls, which again luck had it, were his size. I of course gladly handed them over to him. The ship now had quietened down considerably and I took this opportunity to invite him into our Mess for a pint which many of ship's crew were doing in all other Messdecks before the transfer was to be arranged which would surely happen within the next few hours.

At war it is solely up to the Commanding Officer's discretion if all Messes and Messdecks throughout the ship are to cease issuing alcohol. If this order is given all bars have to be closed and locked. No such order was implemented on Broadsword by our Captain so it was a godsend especially under these circumstances to offer to our fellow Shipmates either a grog or a pint and in the Lads' Messes a couple of tinnies (beers) must have been greatly appreciated if only to lessen the pain, just for a few moments, of what they had all been through.

At around 20:00hrs the familiar sound of Sea Kings was with us to transfer all the very serious casualties on stretchers which would be airlifted on to the RFA Fort Austin. We were all briefed on how the transferring of the remaining Coventry's and survivors was going to be performed. At 01:00hrs Landing Crafts would be sent out to Broadsword for the beginning of three batches and then once boarded would continue to the RFA Fort Austin. The first of these transfers I would personally be involved in. We all congregated at approximately 00:30–00:45 inside the ship in 1 Mike Flat which is the AFT end of the ship forward of the ship's Hanger and Flight Deck. Once the order was given to proceed the route we were to take was on to the Upper Deck and head towards the Boat Deck where a scrambling net had been attached over the side of the ship. So after briefing everyone to hold on to the person in front of them by the lifebelt straps around their waist, as by now it was completely pitch black and under no circumstance were lights or torches to be used, everyone headed towards where the Landing Crafts would be. Firstly were all the casualties with injuries to arms and legs. These personnel obviously wouldn't be at all able to get onto, let alone climb down, a scrambling net so were hoisted by the ship's hoist onto the waiting crafts below. I said farewell to LSTD Devine and wished him good luck and was glad to see he was fit enough to be looking after a fellow Chief Petty Officer with another of his Shipmates. This all lasted for me for about one hour and at about 01:45 I popped down below, once this transfer had been completed, to see if I could help start to clean up, even if it was for a few minutes, as at 02:00hrs I was back at Defence Stations and would be until 08:00hrs that morning. Unfortunately HMS Coventry lost that fateful day twenty of her crew mates. As for the remaining crew who were on the Fort Austin, they were eventually transferred onto the Canberra which was acting as a Troop Carrier, as was the QE2 along with a few other large vessels, which I believe were the Nordland and the Assault Ship Intrepid, also there was another Troop Ship, I believe HMS Fearless..

By the way our number one Chinese Laundry Man from Hong Kong got his wish. He also was transferred with the Coventry's ship's company on the morning of the twenty-sixth of May. I can't really blame him as this was in fact our war and not his.

Only a few days before we had rendezvoused with the Cunard Roll-On-Roll-Off Container Ship the Atlantic Conveyor, commanded by Captain Ian North. She had only joined the Carrier Group six days previously to get supplies to our Troops. The ship itself weighed 15,000 tons and carried a crew of 160 men. Her cargo consisted of Sea Harriers, three Chinook helicopters, five Wessex helicopters and tons of essential stores for the Ground Troops. Fortunately before May the twenty-fifth all the Sea Harriers had been air lifted onto the two Task Group Carriers Hermes and Invincible, but because of the continuing air attacks in San Carlos waters it was impossible to get in to unload the essential helicopters and stores. On the fateful day of May twenty-fifth she was hit by an Exocet missile, the same type of missile that doomed HMS Sheffield. This had been fired by a Super Etendard aircraft. Originally the Pilot had fired at his first contact which was believed to be HMS Ambuscade, who responded immediately when the incoming missile was detected by Ambuscade's Radar Team. Chaff was fired which is a salvo (shell) that explodes away from the ship towards the attack which releases iron fillings or silver paper strips. This then deflected the missile away from Ambuscade and re-routed itself and locked onto, unfortunately, the Atlantic Conveyor. The missile exploded Aft of the ship directly under the Bridge and set off numerous raging fires. Eventually the fires were well out of control and the order to abandon ship was given. Captain North and eleven of his crew members were killed and after the ship had burnt itself out she sank on Thursday 26th May 1982.

That day thirty-two British Seamen lost their lives from the Merchant and Royal Navy. A sad day for all the country.

At 08:00hrs on the morning of the twenty-sixth the Captain addressed the ship's company to thank them all for the energy and effort that everyone put in for the rescue of HMS Coventry's crew and mentioned the tragic loss of the Destroyer itself and her twenty crew members who didn't make it. We were now to return to the Main Carrier Group to carry out repairs to the damage we had sustained under the protection of the Task Force. What was needed essentially were reinforced armour steel plates to be welded to where the bomb came through with a lot of work to be

Atlantic Conveyor.

done internally as well. Also the Flight Deck needed to be reinforced. This would be done by the repair ship Stena Seaspread once we got alongside her. Once this has been completed we would resume our normal goalkeeping role on HMS Hermes, the Flag Ship Carrier. Reports were still coming in that Skyhawk aircraft were attacking our ships in the Sound and it was reported that HMS Plymouth has managed to shoot down at least one aircraft. Apart from that there were no further incidents on the twenty-sixth.

Thursday twenty-eighth we carried out repairs all day to the ship. I managed to get onboard Stena Seaspread to meet some of the lads and see just what sort of stuff they carried on these types of ships. Although they tried to tell me how all this highly sophisticated equipment worked I still don't think I was any the wiser. Anyhow it was a good opportunity for a couple of hours to have a change of scenery. The Assault Ships HMS Fearless and Intrepid left the Sound to go to, I believe, the South Georgia areas.

As we had now lost our number one Laundry Man and probably wouldn't get a replacement until this conflict was over there was a growing concern about the build up of dirty laundry accumulating throughout the ship. Every sailor throughout the Naval Fleet be it Officer or Rating is taught in basic training how to wash, clean and iron his personal kit, but under the circumstances of war there was only so much to do for one's personal hygiene and then that must only be the basic cleanliness of one's self and kit. Who should come to the rescue but no other than our Petty Officers' Mess President, Petty Officer Electrician Dave Phelps with a team of two to three helpers who took over the laundry washing machines and steam pressures with no questions or complaints. The whole ship's company showed great admiration for Dave and his team, who were all volunteers for their new found and I might add additional task on HMS Broadsword.

"Thanks Dave and your Crew, good on yer mate".

The Flight Crew were busy stripping down two of the three Lynx helicopters we now had onboard to make one of them serviceable. As for our original Lynx which had its nose chopped off, would it (what's left of it) be given a float test (ditched over the side) or be flown off?

Throughout the day normal defence watch routines were carried out and at 12:30 a Sea King helicopter arrived on

Broadsword's Flight Deck to pick up our Captain who was to be flown to the Aircraft Carrier HMS Hermes to have lunch with the Task Group Commander, Rear Admiral Woodward, and to discuss the ship's programme. The Captain arrived back to the ship two hours later after being fed and watered.

The Navigator worked out that since leaving Plymouth on the 17th March 1982 we had sailed 9,727 nautical miles which is one third of the distance around the World. At around twenty minutes to eight we were to find out from the Captain what he and the Admiral had discussed. The Admiral thought that the next ten days could be very crucial for the recapture of the Falkland Islands and a lot of things were going to happen in the next few days. We were still to carry out our original role as goalkeeper to the Flag Ship and were to remain out there with the Main Carrier Group for sometime. Once the Troops had finally managed to recapture Port Stanley Airstrip they would then proceed to repair it ready for HMS Hermes to unload her Sea Harriers for the Royal Air Force to take them over. The Captain continued to say that HMS Brilliant had sailed to the repair docks area and once repaired she would then sail and join the Main Carrier Group where she would also take up her role as goalkeeper for the Aircraft Carrier HMS Invincible.

The Admiral at this stage was thinking seriously of a surface threat (ship to ship) to the Task Group, therefore had placed ships in a position accordingly for our Surface Attack Group (SAG). It was probably hoped when Hermes unloaded her Sea Harriers she would then make passage back to the UK, therefore would not require a goalkeeper. HMS Battleaxe and HMS Brazen, which are two Type 22 Frigates (like ourselves and HMS Brilliant), had already had orders to sail down and would be with us in the near future to relieve us. If all this went accordingly it would make our arrival back in the UK sometime in August or possibly early September. But as the Captain said anything could happen between now and then and we'd all just have to wait and see how things progressed from now.

News reached the ship at 20:40 that the 2nd Paratroopers had recaptured Darwin with casualties on both the British and Argentine Forces. It was thought that fifteen British soldiers died and four were injured and 108 Argentines were taken prisoners.

At nine o'clock in the evening Broadsword refuelled. Saturday the 29th May went without incident on the ship and our first report came from our Principal Warfare Officer (Aircraft) (PWO(A)). He explained at 15:35 over the main broadcast system that two Etendard aircraft carrying Exocet missiles had taken off from one of the Argentinian Airbases, therefore we were ordered in close to HMS Hermes for goalkeeping and Hermes had already made airborne her Combat Air Patrol (CAP) to add further protection to the Carrier Group. We were likely to go to Action Stations at a second's notice so as to be closed down fully within minutes.

Forty minutes later at 16:16 (with no incident) another report came through which made us all think that the lads shoreside were winning their war against the Argentine

Forces. It was reported that again the 2nd Paratroopers had successfully captured Goose Green and had taken a staggering 900 Argentine prisoners.

Looking out from the Bridge I was overwhelmed by the amount of activity going on around us. HMS Hermes on our Port side had four helicopters hovering around her. We had a Sea King right above us lowering NAAFI (Navy Army Air Force Institute) stores, most of it being nutty (sweets, confectionery, cold drinks etc), and about a mile in front of us I noticed HMS Invincible with about six Harriers flying around. Unfortunately though half an hour later, one of the Harriers on her landing approach on Invincible, slid over the side on touchdown. Thankfully the Pilot managed to free himself and was reported to be no worse for wear after his ordeal. The normal daily brief by the Captain confirmed the recapture of Darwin and Goose Green by the 2nd Paratroopers and the talking of the 900 prisoners. He also confirmed the Pilot was OK from the Harrier that went over the side from Invincible.

The next day, at three o'clock in the afternoon, Sea Harriers from both Carriers flew off for a major bombing run on Port Stanley. On their return one had to ditch, probably due to damage by anti-aircraft guns during the bombing raid but the Pilot was picked up safely. Sunday is supposed to be a day of rest: no such chance. We were to go to Action Stations twice before the day was out, but this time we came under attack in this Group by Exocet missiles. At 16:45 "Air Raid Warning RED" was piped and hands to Action Stations ordered; suspected Super Etendard were heading towards the Task Force Main Group (our direction). There was no contact by 17:35hrs so we reverted down to a lower scale, Air Raid YELLOW, and fell out of Action Stations to revert to our Defence Watches. No sooner had we all settled into Defence Stations, ten minutes to be precise and the ship was back to Air Raid Warning RED and back closed up to Action Stations. This was now for real as the Captain has ordered Chaff to be fired and enemy aircraft had been picked up on radar 48 miles to the South of us. Therefore an attack from Exocet was now absolutely imminent in the Task Group Sector. Two Harriers were already airborne to intercept the Super Entendard carrying deadly Exocet missiles and a report had come through from a Helicopter Pilot that he had detected clouds of smoke in the water which must mean a missile or missiles are heading our way. HMS Ambuscade (Type 21 Frigate) and HMS Glamorgan (Destroyer) had picked up Exocet on their radar screens but not as yet had any of our ships reported being damaged, so it was presumed that although they had been fired they completely missed their targets. Because the Super Etendard had a much higher speed than our Harriers it was not long before they were well out of range. At first it was believed either HMS Glamorgan's Sea Slug or HMS Exeter's Sea Dart could have possibly downed one of these Exocets and later it was confirmed that HMS Exeter's Sea Dart had done precisely that. We were back to Defence Watches with the 17:50 daily account from our Captain at 19:45hrs. Remarkably our Troops ashore were not only advancing but had captured yet another 500 prisoners; making up to now 1,400 Prisoners of

War. This must only mean one thing: the Ground Force Troops had broken the spirit of the enemy who as the reports we heard later were so badly equipped for the freezing weather conditions, I imagine they were only too pleased to become a Prisoner of War if only to get an extra layer of clothing and a hot meal. Reports were also coming through that a lot of Battery (shoreside) positions had now been commandeered by our Forces and thousands of rounds of ammunitions and fire arms had been seized from the Argentine Forces.

Broadsword refuelled yet again at 20:45 on Sunday evening (still 30th May). We were still refuelling at 22:20 when both ships were very, very vulnerable to air attacks and inevitably this was going to happen: one of the ships at some time was to have an air attack while in the middle of refuelling. "Air Raid Warning RED" was blasted over the main broadcast system followed by the pipe "Emergency Breakaway. Emergency Breakaway". This has got to be one of the most dangerous situations two Captains have to face while refuelling from ship to ship and under attack. Not only have you got the hazard of thousands of tons of fuel being transferred from the ships but you've got to sever the fuelling pipes connected and get away as fast as possible to a position to be in to make full use of your fire power against the incoming aircraft. Obviously during peacetime both ship's crew could have carried out this procedure dozens of times in exercises, should such a situation arise.

"Well by Fuck, it just has in a wartime state!"

Years ago I clearly remember doing this scenario during an exercise off Portland Bill in Dorset while we under close scrutiny by the Naval Flag Officers Sea Training Team (FOST). As I've mentioned previously the Royal Naval Fleet has a section made up of an Admiral and his Officers, Warrant Officers, Chiefs, Petty Officers, Leading Rate and Junior Rates, basically all ranks and rates, and their prime task is to put every ship in the fleet through every and anything we are likely to encounter, either during peacetime or war. This is a team who are Navy to test the Navy and make an overall assessment how the ship copes and reacts to what they throw at us, from the Captain right down to the most junior member of the ship's company. I again was serving on another Frigate at this time and during the weeks we were at Portland to go through the dozens upon dozens of different exercises we obviously, many a time, had to refuel at sea, although we all knew a Command by the Admiral's staff would come through at some stage on one of the refuelling evolutions. Nobody, not even the Captain, knew when the "Emergency Breakaway" would be put into practice.

On this particular ship one of my many roles apart from running a Wardroom Mess as their Mess Manager or looking after the Commanding Officer would be whenever we had a refuel at sea (RAS) my duty station would be to close up on the Bridge and take over the ship's wheel from the Quartermaster. He would then have another important position to go to until the ship was refuelled, usually the tiller flat for secondary steering. After obtaining permission from the Officer of the Watch (OOW) for which I reported,

"Permission, Sir. Petty Officer Steward to take over the wheel.." He would reply, "Yes please, PO."

Everything is done by the book and a tape recorder is usually running from start to finish of the refuelling in case anything was to go wrong so any mistakes would be in evidence if needed, should it come to an enquiry. Anyhow, after picking up the FOS Team by Seaboat at 06:00hrs, ("The Sea Riders" as it is best known to all Naval Personnel) we headed off to the open sea for more gruelling scenarios and exercises which these people would have panned really well in advance to put into practice. The whole ship knew that at approximately 10:30 we would be doing yet another refuelling procedure drill. Along with the other many drills we were to perform that day we all took it in our stride. At about ten o'clock Flying Stations was piped to receive an incoming Lynx helicopter which was to be met by the Captain once it had landed safely on Deck. The passenger was no less than the Flag Office Sea Training: "The Admiral". It really didn't take much to fathom out that to have the Admiral onboard must be to witness one of the drills the ship would have to perform during the day and that with the RAS only half an hour away. Before we were alongside the RFA there was a damn good chance that perhaps, only perhaps, could it be the "Emergency Breakaway" he was to be a witness to or was it something else? Nobody at this stage knew, except of course the Admiral and his team.

As we approached the refuelling ship and were being given numerous commands by the Captain, "Port Twenty,

Starboard Five, Amidships, Revolutions 30", I was more than aware I'd got the Admiral standing right behind me while I was sitting at the wheel control consul. As we made our approach to the RFA, I couldn't help thinking a bit jittery at this stage, as I could sense that some sort of a command was to be given at anytime. No sooner had the Line Firing Gun been fired to attach the main pipes to each ship than ("shit here we go"): "Emergency Breakaway", "Emergency Breakaway" was bellowed throughout the ship. I had never had to do an Emergency Breakaway on a ship before so it was no wonder I was crapping myself. What the bloody hell happens now? More than ever now I'd got to concentrate on everything the Captain ordered. Hell the whole ship's at my fingertips. I was more than ever conscious now of the Admiral behind me. I was sure I could feel him breathing down my neck. Now I made my biggest cock-up – either the Captain ordered Full Ahead or Full Astern both engines, I can't remember, but what I do know is whatever was ordered I completely fucked up and did the complete opposite. Shit, shit, shit. It only took seconds for the brain to clog into gear and realise the levers should be forward and not pushed back or was it they should have been pushed back and not forward? Bloody hell I was in a right pickle here, one mistake at the wheel and we were going crashing into the Tanker. Although it was a second or two at the most, to this day I'll always remember the horror of what could have happened if I didn't rectify this immediately. Talk about under pressure or what. Normally I'm OK under pressure but this just flipped me out. Anyhow, as I expected, it didn't at all go unnoticed by the

Admiral and I remember clearly thinking at the time any second now I'm going to get the bollocking of my life from the Admiral – I was just waiting for it. I could not believe my ears when he calmly came over smiled and said very, very quietly, "Bit bloody close that was, Petty Officer, but good to see you rectified it immediately. Well done." To my astonishment in the Assessment Report none of this was mentioned and the whole ship was assessed as "Good" for this particular drill. Phew, that was fucking close. I've always hated doing a RAS afterwards and dreaded the time when I had to report at my Station for this task, as it happens nothing ever drastically occurred on my remaining time onboard this particular ship.

Well, getting back to the absolute reality of the Emergency Breakaway. The air attack was definitely coming in. Petty Officer Ian Laurie took decisive action and cut the RAS line. A few minutes the ship fired Chaff. HMS Ambuscade, 27 miles away to the West, had an Etendard contact on radar and again two Harriers from Hermes went to intercept. The enemy aircraft were chased away and even though the fact we had an Emergency Breakaway the whole ship was reported to be closed up at Action Stations in less than four minutes. Not surprising, we'd done this enough times now to be able to do it with our eyes shut. It was also mentioned although we had to do a speedy getaway the ship managed to take on a full supply of fuel, therefore we were now carrying 100 per cent fuel in our tanks.

I'd just like to add that the story I mentioned with me being on the Bridge with the Admiral present and me taking control of the wheel and levers for the Engine Room isn't exactly quite true. I was in fact in control of the ship's levers but another member of the ship's crew actually was on the wheel. Usually this task is carried out by either the PTI (Physical Training Instructor) or the Leading Regulator and therefore I wasn't entirely on my own (I still cocked up though).

News was relayed to the ship at midnight that the Argentines had claimed to have seriously damaged the British Carrier Invincible with an Exocet missile. This would have obviously been due to our last encounter. In fact all the reports made were completely false and were solely published for propaganda purposes. The Aircraft Carrier Invincible suffered no damage whatsoever during the day.

HMS Invincible.

Night Gun Support (NGS) was carried out during the night and Lieutenant Commander Birch, who was our Principal Warfare Officer underwater (PWO (w)), confirmed that we did indeed come under attack by Exocet and a Sea Dart fired by HMS Exeter did indeed destroy one, or splashed it, as the Navy calls it. Still keeping to the 30th May it was announced that shelling continued as the British Troops advanced and the British 45 Commando secured Douglas settlement. I wondered if Simon Neill (person I was brought up with) was amongst them. I think Simon was a Corporal in the Royal Marines when all this flared up.

More intensive attacks now on and around the Falklands on Monday thiry-first saw bombing raids on Port Stanley Airstrip by Vulcan Aircraft at 08:52 and at 17:00 it was yet again bombed by six Harriers from Hermes. It was also reported that four enemy Etendard aircraft had landed around this airstrip. Our Flight Commander who was injured by shrapnel in one of the attacks to the ship was returned by Helicopter Delivery Service (HDS) at 17:20. He was lowered on to the foc'sle and headed his way to report to the Captain. Our Flight Deck was still being repaired and we'd just heard via the Flight Crew that when they were carrying out flight checks with our helo the welding apparently gave way underneath and the shoring collapsed completely.

"Try again, lads!"

HMS Argonaut had now been ordered out of "Bomb Alley" and was under repairs in our refit zone area. She managed to come out under her own steam although with very heavy damage to her foc'sle.

"Good for you, Argonaut."

This being the last day of May brought final news to us all that Mount Kent had been taken by the British Troops. It seemed to me everywhere was falling fast and furious to the British Commands and the Falkland's capital of Port Stanley was surrounded.

The first of June brought HMS Broadsword one month into the war from when we first had our Action Stations on the first of May. Up to then we had been at Action Stations twenty-four times. After yet another bombing raid on Port Stanley from Hermes Harrier, one Harrier had had to make an emergency landing due to being shot up. At 15:00 we rendezvoused with the Liner Canberra and sailed right alongside her for about fifteen minutes then took up position to guide her to land more of our Troops onto the Falkland Island. After the bombing raid at 18:00 one Harrier failed to return to Hermes. A rescue team was still searching to try and find the Pilot. Our Supply Officer was being transferred onto the Canberra at 22:00, he was then going to be transferred onto the Ferry Norland, another Troop carrying vessel to take charge as the Supply Officer for the Argentinian Prisoners of War onboard.

During the day it was reported that Britain had repeated its ceasefire terms to the Junta (Argentines' Military Forces). We also found out that morning the Gurkhas and the Royal Scots Guards had successfully landed ashore from Canberra. We were briefly called to Action Stations during the day but nothing came of it.

The Wednesday the second of June brought good news at 08:00 that the Harrier and Pilot thought to have been lost ditched at 18:00 that night. Fortunately the Pilot was found by a Sea King helicopter and pulled to safety from his life raft at 02:20.

The twenty-sixth Action Station alarm was sounded for us at 16:20 "Air Raid Warning RED", contact South West and again suspected to be a Super Etendard. CAP was immediately scrambled from HMS Hermes to investigate and we had a Hercules aircraft 60 miles to the North ready to do an air drop. Fifteen minutes later once the air threat was over we resumed back to the Defence Watch Station. A false alarm for Action Stations sounded at 17:25 but within five minutes we were back to normal Defence Watch Routine when the Captain spoke to the ship's company at 19:45. The whole ship's company morale was boosted to a high. Not only did we learn that because of the vast amount of activity surrounding the Falklands by our Troops but it was hopeful that we would retake the Island in or around a week's time, but more to the point the ship's crew hear is that on one of the Royal Fleet Auxiliary Ships (RFAs) were nine bags of mail for HMS Broadsword. Which RFA did we have to thank for holding our letters sent from our loved ones at home? What a terrific morale booster this was. The only drawback was that we couldn't receive it until at the very earliest the sixth of June. Well at least we all had a few days with something to look forward to.

"Roll on Sunday!"

At half past eight in the evening we refuelled the ship again and an hour and a half later we were fully topped up. Two Harriers had been flown down from the Ascension Island and it had taken eight In-Flight Refuelling Tanker aircraft to refuel them and another two Harriers were also expected to make the same journey shortly. The rest of the day was without incident.

At five o'clock that afternoon a Vulcan Bomber had to land in Brazil, being low on fuel. At 19:40, five minutes before the Captain's daily update, the First Lieutenant, Lieutenant Commander Molam announced to the ship's company that it had now been approved that we could send a message home by shipgram for free. One per fortnight.

"Hooray."

An account of events from a fellow Shipmate of the last few days and just before the eighth of June when disaster struck the Task Force.

On 29 May, 2 Para continued their advance towards the two settlements. During the heroic march they were attacked by six Pucaras but managed to shoot down four with the shoulder held Blowpipe missile but not without the loss of a Scout helicopter. The weather was unsuitable to launch the "Harriers from the Carriers" to support the troops so they battled on without air cover. The weather then improved and the GR 3s were again launched to support them, and bombed Goose

Green. The rest is well documented. Lieutenant Colonel H Jones led an attack on machine gun positions which were holding up the advance, and although he died in the attack it broke the defence of the Argentines and led to their surrender. 14 Paras died in the attack but they took 1400 prisoners in one of the bravest battalion actions ever. While the Paras were reaping in the results of their attack, the Royal Marines were quietly marching across a more Northern route and they took the strategic settlements of Douglas and Teal Inlet. The GR 3s continued their bombing runs this time attacking Port Stanley, Pebble Island and Mount Kent, and amongst all this excitement someone managed to shoot down a Mirage and a Skyhawk. All in all a very successful day where the ability of the British troops proved to be the ace in our hand.

Sunday 30th May saw the by no familiar retaliatory attack on the Task Force. Unable to gain success on land the Argentine Air Force seemed determined to avenge their losses ashore by dealing a crippling blow to a carrier. They launched a combined Etendard and Skyhawk attack on the Task Force but did not press it home with sufficient determination to hit a carrier. Launching on Exocet at the first contact that appeared on its radar screen the Etendard turned and ran for home while the Skyhawks attacked and bombed HMS AVENGER. The Exocet had been carelessly set at too low a height setting and had ditched harmlessly into the sea. All the bombs aimed at AVENGER missed and exeter's sea Dart splashed an escaping Skyhawk. The ships of the Task Force secured from Action Stations somwhat relieved and continued their efforts. It came as no surprise to receive outrageous news from Argentina that INVINCIBLE had been hit and seriously damaged in the attack. This was the third time she had been "hit". On the other occasions she had been sunk! The Harriers continued their bombardments of Port Stanley and Mount Challenger and one was hit by ground fire, ditching on the way home. The pilot was safely rescued. In the evening there was another call to Action Stations for an Etendard attack. This was something different – a night attack. "Chaff" was fired everywhere and at one stage the flare of a chaff rocket was mistaken for that of an Exocet and for one awful moment it was thought that a missile was heading for us. Nothing materialised and it was thought to have been an Etendard returning from Port Stanley to Argentina after the afternoon's abortive attack. More bombing runs on Port Stanley were carried out over the next two days and GLAMORGAN, AVENGER and ALACRITY continued overnight bombardments.

The Glorious First of June saw the land forces only 12 miles from Port Stanley. There was little air activity but one Harrier was shot down north of the Sound, the pilot being picked up later. On the day of the last Exocet attack, the BRITISH WYE a civilian support tanker had reported that she has been attacked by a Hercules aircraft and that bombs, which were kicked out of the aircraft's back door, had bounced off her forecastle without exploding. This was a new tactic because the BRITISH WYE, was stationed well to the east of the main group, and it appeared that the Argentines had opted for a desperate, unorthodox method of homing using the Hercules because it had a greater range than the jets. It was probably a tactic developed to attack the QE 2 together with the embarked 5 Infantry Brigade. However unknown to the enemy the QE 2 was allowed no nearer than South Georgia and she transferred her troops to other ships including the CANBERRA. They did attempt a second attack on the 1st June but fortunately a Harrier on a routine patrol saw the Hercules to the north of the Sound and attacked with Sidewinder and cannon, splashing the aircraft in a one-sided fight. NORLAND, the prison ship, left with prisoners taken at Darwin and Goose Green to head for Montivideo. Onboard was broadsword's supply Officer, Lieutenant Commander Alan JOHNSON who was seconded to help after "owning up" to having spent one year on the army staff course at Camberley. Meanwhile BROADSWORD headed east to rendezvous with the CANBERRA and then both ships turned west and after being joined by others headed for the islands to land the remaining troops. Napalm was discovered at Goose Green which angered everyone and ALACRITY voiced her feelings by shelling Fitzroy.

The next day saw two Harriers fly in from Ascension Island to help boost our depleted force and AVENGER, ACTIVE and AMBUSCADE shelled Pebble Island, Fitzroy and Diamond Mountain respectively.

The 3rd brought another two Harriers from Ascension and yet another unsuccessful Vulcan raid. This was made even worse by one Vulcan getting into difficulties near Brazil and having to make an emergency landing at Rio De Janeiro. Events were going so well ashore however that a Forward Operating Base for Harriers was now established at San Carlos. Here aircraft could refuel to increase their time on task over the islands. The following day saw Two Sea Harriers and 2 GR 3s sent permanently from the carriers to operate from this base. ARROW shelled Port Howard and CARDIFF, AVENGER and YARMOUTH bombarded Bluff Cove to support the Paras who had foot-slogged it overland from Goose Green. More shelling continued with CARDIFF, AMBUSCADE, ACTIVE and YARMOUTH all playing their part. CARDIFF also scored a spectacular hit with Sea Dart, shooting down a spying Learjet at 39,000 feet. Again this must have come as a great shock to the pilot who probably thought he was well out of range of surface launched missiles.

Progress was made swiftly over these days and although little is said here about the details of events ashore, suffice it to say that the troops were continuing to sweep up stray Argentine patrols as well as shooting down the odd marauding aircraft. All seemed to be going very well indeed until this changed on the 8th when the Task Force suffered its saddest day.

Getting back to Thursday 3rd June, after the 1st LT's broadcast the Captain addressed the ship's crew and as the Captain humorously put it, "While talking to you I am at present looking into my crystal ball." He went on to say, "The Argentines could be preparing a full scale attack on the Task Force between the fifth and ninth of June and they are definitely more than likely to now bring out their Surface Fleet Ships to use in combination with their Air Force, so we must be more than prepared for them. Even now political talks are still going ahead but they hold not much hopes on the Argentinian's negotiating personnel until all this is over once and for all." On a brighter note the Captain continued, "I have now received confirmation that mail will now be arriving hopefully tomorrow, flown in from the RFA Fort Grange and as expected nine bags will be delivered."

If a ship had been a couple of miles away in any direction they would have definitely heard the outburst of hooray from Broadsword's crew after the Captain's last comment. The crew were in utter excitement at the little joys that were going to be received by us all.

"Mail. From home at last!"

I thought the first announcement of receiving mail was jubilant enough but this was so overpowering because of the happiness on our ship. I bet a lot of us would have liked to ask the Admiral if we could do a stretch of goalkeeping on the Fort Grange for a while, until we received our mail.

"Only a thought though!"

I met up with my pal POMA John Wicks while on the Upper Deck as we were both up to get a bit of fresh air. Fresh air is an understatement as at 20:05 in the evening it was bloody freezing up there. It seemed John had been up there for some time, not only did he look like an iceberg but he informed me he had just done a count on the amount of holes we had received to the ship in the recent air attacks and up to now it stands (so he said) at 36 holes from Forward to AFT with the majority being at the Flight Deck Area and our Flag Deck Area close to the Bridge Wings.

Friday the fourth brought in another very cold, wet, freezing and now foggy day. Visibility was virtually nil. I thought I'd miss popping up for a breather – much warmer inside my cocoon. As expected the conditions were so bad, , mail would have to wait probably another day, as the First Lieutenant informed us. A few scares throughout the day but none serious enough to bring us to Action Stations.

Saturday (another weekend at sea) 5th June now makes it 80 days since we sailed from Plymouth on the seventeenth of March. Things seemed to have quietened down considerably. Now are we coming to the end of the conflict I wondered with only a few scares today by enemy aircraft and nothing came of it. Are we wise to relax a little? I don't think so you never know and it would be far too dangerous to think we were out of the woods yet.

As the Captain explained on the daily update broadcast HMS Hermes would be detaching from the Task Group for a few days to clean out her much needed boilers. When she came back HMS Invincible would then go into the refit area for essential work and once she rejoined the Task Group she would then relieve HMS Hermes who was to consequently sail back to the UK. So is it all over again we asked ourselves? There's no sign of their ships, not even a puff of smoke on the horizon to give away their position and the threat of air attacks seems less and less as the days go on.

Good news for Britain on the sixth of June as the Versailles summit supported the British position on Falklands. Hermes sails for the refit area, which is expected to be for at least eight days, to clean out her boiler completely.

HMS Brilliant still had radar problems involving the Sea Wolf Tracking System after the attack on the twenty-first of May but hopefully would be able to get it sorted out very quickly. As for our role now in the Task Group, as the Captain explained, it was probably while Hermes was away to be carrying out duties, for instance patrol or maybe acting as goalkeeper for the Invincible. We were all waiting for the Admiral's decision.

Although it seemed the war was winding down by no means was it over. The Falklands was still not taken and the Argentinians still had a griphold. The Task Group could not for a second drop their guard as we were still getting air threat attacks as things now started hotting up again at 12:20 on the Monday 7th June. HMS Exeter had fired her Sea Dart and shot down an enemy plane over Port Stanley which was at 39,000 feet. Aircraft not known at that stage but the concern was that of an Exocet carrying aircraft such as the Super Etendard. A lot of preparations were being made back home for the relief of the ships already out here. Who knew how long all this is going on for? But as the Captain explained there was still a lot of work to be done before we could even start to think of the prospects of going home yet.

At long last, there was the much awaited nine bags of mail delivered by the Helicopter Delivery Service (HDS).

The time was 17:00hrs, Monday 7th June. Better late than never as we all say. Thanks to all who helped get it to us 6,000 miles away. Cheers!

Argonaut, Alacrity, Glasgow and the RFA Fort Austin had now received their orders to leave the Task Group and were now on their way back to the UK. We all wished them a safe journey home and hoped to be joining them in the near future.

During the night HMS Cardiff and HMS Yarmouth carried out a Night Gun Support (NGS) with slight problems as we were to believe from Cardiff's guns. HMS Yarmouth let loose 200 rounds of ammunition from her 4.5 guns. I bet the barrels were red hot after that lot.

Tuesday the eighth of June started off with the normal routine of Defence Watch changes and the forenoon went smoothly with basic chores and cleaning that could be done in essential areas. It's quite remarkable that although the ship had been at war now for well over a month we could all muck in together and keep the ship in a reasonably high state of cleanliness. There's the Royal Navy for you, me hearties. Everything seemed peaceful enough and it seemed to me that we were in for another peaceful day – WRONG! At 17:00 everything was about to get very, very nasty for the ships in San Carlos water.

Throughout the whole Task Force all ships had gone to Action Stations. Time 17:00hrs exactly "Hands to Action Stations. Hands to Action Stations. Hands to Action Stations, Air Raid Warning RED. Air Raid Warning RED" blasted over the main broadcast system throughout the ship. Reports came in that a major air strike was in force at Port Pleasant, South of Bluff Cove. HMS Plymouth was hit Aft and dog fights could be seen in San Carlos waters. Plymouth was on fire Aft and Exeter also reported aircraft heading her way. Two Royal Fleet Auxiliary ships were in Bluff Cove ready to transfer hundreds of Troops, stores and ammunition shoreside when the air raid come in on the RFA Sir Galahad and the RFA Sir Tristram. Both these ships were full of men and equipment and the unloading had only just commenced when both ships were struck by bombs fired by A4B Skyhawks of GRUPO 6. The damage and casualties were enormous and the Sir Galahad had fires raging throughout the whole ship. How can anyone survive this onslaught? Men were screaming everywhere and a fleet of Rescue Vessels' aircraft were swarming over the area. The injuries, burns and dead were going to be exceptionally high from this attack.

It was also reported that four Mirage aircraft had joined the air strike against us. Plymouth apparently had managed to splash one and possibly two although she was mortally damaged herself. These air attacks against us only took minutes but the carnage they left behind when they hit their target was devastating. Later we were to learn the Plymouth received four direct hits from the Daggers of FAA GRUPO 6, but not one of these bombs exploded otherwise Plymouth would definitely not be with us now. The worst damage to a ship in this raid was to Sir Galahad. As I said, it was carrying hundreds of Troops waiting to be transferred shoreside. Sir Galahad was in Bluff Cove off Fitzroy and she was mortally damaged and fifty soldiers and sailors perished in this ship alone; some killed outright and others to die later with horrific burns and injuries. Sir Tristram was also very badly damaged and abandoned but later returned to the UK for extensive repairs. There were reports that we had lost another ship but was confirmed later to be false. Smoke was billowing out of Sir Galahad and the rescue went on well into the morning. Although I was not there to witness the destruction of Sir Galahad I can only imagine the horror at the scene with the Rescue and First Aid Teams doing their utmost to help the injured, wounded and the dying. The enormity of the lives lost will probably haunt them forever. Tuesday 8th May 1982 will probably be the worst or one of the blackest days during the Falklands War because of the amount of lives lost.

A saddened Captain spoke to his crew at 19:45 and confirmed those attacks. HMS Plymouth was now so badly damaged and was out of the war and so was ordered back to Plymouth, her home Port. There was some confusion as to what aircraft came in for this attack, either Skyhawks or Mirages, but no matter what the damage had been done and many lives had been lost.

While at my Defence Station in HQ1 at 01:00 on Wednesday morning a very unexpected report came through to the ship that a Civilian Tanker was thought to be under attack outside the Exclusion Zone. This was later confirmed at 02:10. The attack on the "as we now know" was on an Oil Tanker and had been fired upon by the Argentines' Hercules Bombers. The ship was a Libyan Tanker with an

Israeli crew, chartered apparently by the Americans. The attack had taken place 400 miles outside the Exclusion Zone and yet more reports came through she was under attack yet again. The ship was crippled and headed towards the Brazilian waters for safety. The Royal Navy sent one of the Hospital Ships (I believe HMS Hecla?) to assist.

The Hospital Ship HMS Hecla.

Five casualties were reported from HMS Plymouth. This report was replayed to us by LTCDR Birch from the Operations Room. Apparently one of the bombs that hit the Plymouth went through her Mortar Well, which is right Aft of the ship just below the Flight Deck. This area is also used by their number one Laundry Man or it was when I was onboard a Leander Class Frigate (HMS Aurora and HMS Argonaut). I hoped the Chinese man and ship's crew came out of it OK. The Sir Galahad was to burn out completely in

the next few days with the remaining crew and Troops
safely on shore and obviously to get off what they could
salvage for the Ground Forces. She was later, during June,
towed out to sea and sunk as a War Grave.

The rest of Wednesday the ninth was for reflection on
yesterday's loss to the British Nation. The ship's crew were
in a sombre mood as, I would imagine, were thousands of
other Soldiers, Sailors, Merchant Seaman and everyone else
involved in this war. Although Thursday the tenth was the
Duke of Edinburgh's birthday, I didn't think anyone here or
at home would be celebrating. How much more punishment
could our ships take? I thought we were supposed to be one
of the best equipped Military Forces in the World yet were
losing ships left, right and centre and still the Argentines'
Fleet hadn't shown any sign of coming out. This was purely
a fight from aircraft to ship. What if we start being attacked
by Submarines? The only consolation was that we had
managed to reduce their airforce by at least two-thirds. That
alone might save the war. I damn well hoped so, because I
seriously didn't think the Task Force could take much more
of this battering by their Pilots and our Pilots are working
round the clock to fend them off and doing a bloody grand
job as well, whether fighter pilots or helicopter pilots and
crew. I think everyone knew from the beginning that this
war would be fought primarily by the Argentine Air Force. I
know I certainly did on the way down from the Ascension
Island. Combat battle ship to ship wasn't my real concern
but definitely aircraft were. Sea Wolf, Sea Cat, Sea Dart,
Sea Slug can only do a certain amount of destroying but if
we have wave after wave of enemy aircraft there wasn't a

hope in hell of saving the ship. I felt this so strongly even before we were engaged in battle, and knew if ever there was a remote chance of us loosing this war it would definitely come from the air.

We were warned again by our Captain that there were strong indications that another large Air Raid was building up. This information had obviously come from Intelligence in shoreside monitoring around the Argentinian Airfields. This warning prompted at least a dozen Harriers constantly patrolling the air around the Task Group and the Falkland Islands. No more incidents that day, which now brings us to Friday 11th June.

Sadly that day brought us more news that the loss of life on the Sir Galahad was at least 40 of the Welsh Guard Regiment and the ship was reported to have at least 120 injured. Everyone was now fully aware that the attack to take back the Falkland Islands was very near.

Again mail was in the Task Group somewhere but who was carrying it was anybody's guess. Things were now getting very tense throughout the ship as the Final Assault to take back British Territory drew closer. Again and again we all kept asking ourselves how did this political crisis ever manage to get to this stage for war to have come about. Apart from all our families at home which there wasn't a second when we weren't thinking of them, our sincere admiration must go to all the Military and Civilian Personnel at home working flat out to back their Country and Troops. We knew every Dockyard in Plymouth, Portsmouth, Rosyth and others were doing their best to get the ships prepared for sea. It was clearly known by us that all the Dockyard Personnel and Civilian Staff had pulled out all the stops to back our lads up 6,000 miles away. We are truly thankful for all your support, thank you. The Royal Navy cannot operate without their Dockyards and Britons would not have their Country without the Navy – FACT!

At 16:30 we met up with the Atlantic Causeway, which is the sister ship to our lost ship, the Atlantic Conveyor and half an hour later a Sea King helicopter was hovering over the Flight Deck to collect the remains of our Lynx helicopter as shown in the photograph previously. Our Flight Crew had obviously salvaged and ripped out anything that was worth saving even just for the spare parts. The remains of the Lynx so I understood were being flown onto the Atlantic Causeway. "Bits" I think the Flight Crew call it. Heaven knows what they'd do with this hunk of metal. I supposed someone somewhere would make use of it for something.

The Captain's broadcast that evening confirmed things were really hotting up, as Royal Air Force GR3 (Group 3) and our Harriers had continuously bombed enemy positions throughout the day with no let up. It was now known that the final preparations were in full swing for the attack on Port Stanley the next morning. Vulcan Bombers would be sent in the morning between 08:00hrs and 10:00hrs so the next 72 hours would be very active in all positions shore and sea. Mail didn't arrive as expected. "Sorry," said the OOW, "but it will be here in a few days."

Unexpectedly the ship received mail in the late evening and amongst all the bags of mail were dozens upon dozens of backdated national newspapers from Britain. Although I'd received dozens of letter from my family and, I might add, from family I didn't know I had, I'd received a lot of well-wishes and good luck messages from family and friends. I personally haven't mentioned letters as it truly is personal, but I must mention one message that I'd just received from my Uncle Bob, Auntie Norma and my three cousins Richard, Mandy and Mark Fane (Mark joining the Royal Navy later on in life in the Fleet Air Arm). All the national papers were sending messages through their newspapers and mine came from the Daily Mail which was printed, believe it or not, on the day I was in the most danger of going down with the ship after loosing our Destroyer HMS Coventry and us receiving the bomb that didn't go off – how uncanny. Anyhow, the message read "Barrie Baked Bean (HMS Broadsword) Wish you were here!! Much love: The Gang of Five." This simple message from part of my family meant so much to me and we always have a laugh about the Baked Bean bit. Families make up such funny nicknames. I still don't know how it came to be Barrie Baked Bean yet – Ha, Ha!

As seen by another crew member: the events of Tuesday 8th June.

SIR GALAHAD and SIR TRISTRAM were unloading the last set of troops for the final assault on Port Stanley, the Welsh Guards, at Bluff Cove. Some of the troops were already ashore but others

Calling the Task Force

Taken from the Daily Mail 25/6/82.

were helping to unload ammunition when the overcast skies suddenly cleared and Mirages and Skyhawks bombed both ships. The bombs exploded setting alight the ammunition. Those who were not killed instantly were severely burned and soon the sea was full of soldiers trying to escape from the blazing ships. Over 50 Guardsmen were killed and many more injured. Several men of the RFA were also killed. A small landing craft was sunk with 6 killed. The Fleet Air Arm again became heroes out of the tragedy. Flying their helicopters in thick, blinding smoke they rescued many servicemen who would otherwise have died.

While the ships in Bluff Cove were being attacked, HMS PLYMOUTH was receiving similar treatment elsewhere around East Falkland. She was attacked with bombs, rocket and canon but despite being seriously damaged, she managed to bring down two enemy aircraft before limping back to the safety of the carrier group. Attacks were going on ashore but here the Argentines had little success and at the end of the day the Scots Guards had shot down four Skyhawks with machine gun fire, and two Harriers brought down two further aircraft, one each. The Argentines did not get everything their own way. Two more GR 3s flew in from Ascension and although one crash landed at the Forward Operating Base, our "air force" was slowly increasing.

By now most of the Navy's contribution, except the air operations and Naval Gunfire Support, was beginning to take a back seat as the troops prepared for the battle for Port Stanley – the one everybody had been waiting for, the one which would win the war and send the invader back where he came. The Argentines still persisted with their desperate tactics of bombing ships at sea, this time 400 miles north east of the islands. Unfortunately the Argentines were not too good at recognition and it was an American owned tanker flying the Liberian flag. None of the Italian crew was injured but it was subsequently found that an unexploded bomb had lodged inside the hull and the ship was ordered to leave Rio De Janeiro after she had limped there carrying a 6 degree list. We now know that she was taken out and sunk as being too dangerous to defuse.

Still now on Friday night the eleventh of June at 23:30 hours we heard from our Operations room that the General in charge of all the Argentine Ground Forces had been flown off the Falklands and was heading for Argentina, no doubt to brief Galtieri that they hadn't a hope in hell of coming out of all this with flying colours. The ships changeover watches at 02:00 on Wednesday twelfth which brought us all into another day of war.

Starboard watch had now resumed duty and Port watch had stood down for a few hours. The ships who had been allocated to carry out Naval Gun Support (NGS) that morning from 02:00hrs to approximately 06:00hrs were the Guided Missile Destroyer (GMD) HMS Glamorgan, two Type 21 Frigates HMS Arrow and HMS Avenger (I'd join Avenger in the fleet in a few years time) and the Type 12 Frigate, HMS Yarmouth. This NGS Group is apparently recorded as being the largest Naval Gun Support carried out in Naval history.

This continuous bombardment by our ships relentlessly against the batteries on shore was bound to involve some sort of retaliation and at approximately 06:00 HMS Glamorgan came under attack by an Exocet missile and was unable to shake off the incoming lethal missile. It struck her full force in her Engine Room causing massive fires to the Engine Room, surrounding Compartments in the after section of the ship and also the ship's Hanger and Flight Deck. It was not quite clear if the missile actually entered the Engine Rooms but reports came in that it had definitely caused death onboard the ship.

As we refuelled Broadsword an hour and three quarters later we learned that the Glamorgan had now managed to sail out of San Carlos Bay and was doing ten to eighteen knots heading for protection in the Main Task Group. We must have really been very low on fuel as we were still taken it on at 10:30. The Captain received a message passed on by our Navigating Officer that the Glamorgan received the missile through the Hanger and then it entered the Turbine Engine Room killing thirteen of its crew and injuring seventeen. All fires were believed to be under control. This was yet another blow to the British Navy with one of our Destroyers badly damaged. I think everyone was getting quite anxious now for the plans for the final assault to be put into force and it seemed every minute the Troops on land were getting every much closer to their goal.

Just before 11:00am Broadsword was fully topped up with fuel and we broke away from our RFA to continue with our patrol around the Falklands. 15:30 the same day brought our ship to its twenty-ninth Action Station alert since May the first, although this threat was classed as an Air Raid Warning Yellow it was decided to go to Action Stations as reports had come through from intelligence shoreside that two very, very fast aircraft had taken off from an Argentinian airstrip and were believed to be Mirage or Etendard. This was accompanied by a very slow moving aircraft which was thought to be one of their Hercules and possibly carrying either Paratroopers and Troops and Stores to relieve or back up their already existing forces shoreside. It had become common knowledge that the Hercules aircrafts were always escorted by two of their Fighter aircrafts. We learned early evening that Glamorgan had managed to re-join the Main Task Group after her missile attack and all fires were under control. Fortunately no further deaths had been reported and she would now no doubt go under repairs under the umbrella protection of the Main Task Group.

Shortly after hearing that we received information, again from intelligence on land, that a massive air raid was building up on the Argentinian airstrips and all ships were warned that it could be as soon as an hour or so away.

"God help us all".

You just could not help thinking with the ships we had lost or had been damaged that it was now that our own time was up. It got scarier and scarier every time now once we knew we were expecting a full-scale attack. By now we should have been well used to it but believe you me what you felt inside of yourself seemed to get worse. I know I kept thinking to myself, is this it? Is this going to be the day when we die? Then the next day came and the next and it got worse. You started to get paranoid that today, today I die. We've been lucky so far but surely it can't last? When and where is this bomb going to come from when – when –

when – today? Tomorrow? The day after? "Shit, Barrie, get your fucking act together." I told myself over and over again.

With all the hundreds of reports we had warning us of air attacks this one, our last report, had made me feel very, very uneasy. I consider myself as quite a strong-minded person and pride myself with the fact I can keep a cool head if under pressure. With all we'd been through so far why should that day of all days make me be more acutely aware of the fear I felt and feeling sick to the stomach due to the nervousness my body was enduring. I was physically sick. The only explanation I put it down to was that over the last few days there had been a tremendous amount of tension due to the build up of the final assault to retake the Falklands. We knew we were near to the final assault. This tension had now finally exploded in me and I couldn't help thinking that the next person they'd be flying off this ship on a stretcher, probably in a "straight jacket", would be me! Somehow that last damn report had really made me jittery and scared – why? "Chin up, Barrie. Come on, mate, do your fucking job," I said to myself. It passed thank fuck!

Nothing yet seemed to have come of this supposedly reported air raid and the ship seemed to have settled down by about five o'clock so we all reverted to our Defence Watch routine positions. CAP was continuously carrying out air cover and would do for sometime.

Good news for the survivors of the crew members of our lost ships HMS Ardent, HMS Antelope and HMS Coventry.

They had arrived back in Southampton, on the QE2 and by all accounts had received a tremendous home-coming welcome in Britain.

"We salute you all."

The attack on Port Stanley to recapture the Falklands had now started in the evening and was done in two stages (or phases). Phase One apparently was the previous night which was to take the high ground positions and was done successfully and Phase Two was to take the rest.

The threat by Exocet missiles now not only came from the Super Etendard aircraft but Firing Batteries and Launching Sites had been set up on land to fire these deadly missiles such as the one used to attack HMS Glamorgan. This obviously became much more of a threat to the Warships carrying out the night Gunnery Support Bombardments. With my previous shitty scary panic attack now over I still felt very acutely aware of how claustrophobic it is in a Warship once we went to Action Stations. Everything is locked down and secured and you are literally locked into your tin can. How I envied the crew members on the Upper Deck defending the ship. At least if they were to be zapped they would see it coming. Us poor sappers could only expect and hear our fate and this dreaded drowning fear once again returned to haunt me.

"Come on, get this bloody war over."

The British 3-Para mounted an assault on Mount Longdon. The Battle on this heavily defended position, which was supposed to last until dawn, proved much tougher and longer than expected. Mount Longdon and its surroundings were finally taken, after hand to hand and bayonet fighting with the Argentine Troops, position by position. The British casualties mounted to 23 men, one of which Sergeant Ian John McKay of 3-Para who was later awarded a posthumous Victoria Cross (VC). Forty-seven more British were wounded and six more British died shortly afterwards. The Argentines suffered over 50 dead and many more injured.

British 45 Commando took "Two Sisters" and 42 Commando took "Mount Harriet" with support from the guns of 29th Commando Regiment and Naval gunfire from Royal Naval Warships. The 2nd Scots Guards seized "Mount Tumbledown" in yet another bloody battle. Nine British and about forty Argentines lost their lives; another thirty-four Argentine soldiers surrendered and were taken prisoners. Thirty-two of the British Troops were wounded.

Before the day was out we knew Phase Two was definitely well under way. Changeover of Defence Watches at 02:00am brought us to the 13th June on a bitterly cold and wet Sunday morning. The day being as we all know a day of rest brought more of the ship's company together at the normal 10:00am church service held in the Junior Rates' Dining Hall (Eating Area for the majority of the crew).

Normally the church service was attended by most of the ship's officers and very few NCOs and even less of the rest of the ship's company but over the past few weeks attendance from the crew had gradually risen – we being one of the minority in attendance for this brief service conducted by the ship's Padre. If however the Padre wasn't onboard our ship at any time on a Sunday the Captain would always stand in and take the Service for the ship. The Lord must have been with us that day, as Action Stations were not sounded throughout the whole day.

Sunday indeed was a day of rest for us all onboard Broadsword. Needless to day this didn't mean the war stopped for the day, far from it. Sea Harriers on their regular Patrols around Port Stanley had spotted an Argentinian Fast Patrol Boat (FPB) anchored out of Stanley Harbour and without hesitation opened fire. Although damaged it failed to be sunk so before returning to their Carrier, either the Hermes or the Invincible, they contacted the nearest Royal Naval ship in the area which happened to be the Leander Class Frigate, HMS Penelope. Penelope immediately launched her Lynx helicopter and once in range fired her Sea Skewer missile and successfully sank it. Had it not been for the orange dinghy which was foolishly being towed behind the well camouflaged Patrol Boat the Sea Harriers would have been completely unaware it was there and it would have gone undetected. As it happens the boat's crew on the FPB might just as well have waved a banner stating, "Here I am, sink me", which of course we readily obliged.

What would this week bring HMS Broadsword on Monday 14th June? Ah yes, I knew there was something I had to do over the last couple of days but never got round to it. I was very conscious as the days went by that I was looking more like a ruddy sixties hippie with long uncared for hair. I desperately needed a hair cut as did a lot of our fellow crew mates but it was getting the time to get an appointment to see Chippy, who was our official Haircutter Chief. This job is completely a volunteer task for any of the ship's members who have some sort of qualification in haircutting and to make it an official source of income for the person carrying out the ship's barber bit it is agreed that a percentage of every sitting will got to the ship's charity. Not only by Naval Law does this now become official, once approved by the Captain of course, but everyone benefits and the remaining monies made given by each person paying for their haircut (usually about 50p) means that the person giving the haircut goes away with a profit for himself. Usually this person was in great demand especially as we had been at sea now for quite a few weeks and nobody knew how many more weeks we were likely to be so unfortunately we couldn't pop into one of our Seaboats and go and sail into the nearest town to call into the local barbers for a haircut. Anyhow I managed to get a slot in for four o'clock.

"Great that feels much better. I'm starting to look a bit more like a matelot again!" I don't know why I put this down in my diary, but it just seemed relevant at the time.

Two hours later we couldn't believe the news that is broadcast throughout the whole Task Force: "THE BRITISH ENSIGN IS NOW FLYING OVER PORT STANLEY"

Port Stanley had now been recaptured. The announcement was made from the ship's Operational

Rooms (Ops Rm) by our Principle Warfare Officer Air (PWO (A)) Lieutenant Commander Edmonds, as the Captain was in deep conversation with the Admiral in the Communications Room. Half an hour later we heard from our Captain and as he started off he said he has just finished speaking to Admiral Woodward the Falklands Task Group Commander. The Admiral in turn had spoken to all Commanding Officers on every Royal Naval ship and said that at that very moment negotiations were taking place (how many times had we heard this!) in Port Stanley for a truce. He then added once this has been established the British Forces would then start the task of cleaning up and repairing Port Stanley Airstrip for our Harriers and other British Military aircraft to land safely. The Admiral particularly stressed to all Commanding Officers that this was by no means the war over yet. He added that in the West Falklands, the Argentine Air Force and their Surface Fleet as far as they were concerned were still at war with Britain. So the only victory so far was the taking of the surrounding areas of Port Stanley and of course Port Stanley itself. His concern was deeply emphasised that all ships and Land Forces must still keep their guard up at all times as the Argentine Leaders of the Junta could unexpectedly throw a last ditch attempt to try and damage or destroy our defences. "BE ON GUARD" Although the Captain finished off by saying the flag was flying over Port Stanley, this surrender however had not yet been written down in documentary form and signed as stated by the Articles of War. The official announcement came on Tuesday the fifteenth by "World News Flash" at 06:00 and the statement that was broadcast was: "All Enemy Forces occupying the Falklands have now officially surrendered."

The ship continued to stay in Defence Watches until we ourselves were given the order to revert to normal sea watches, therefore all eyes were now on our Flagship. Apparently at 23:59 Monday 14th June 1982, a very historic occasion took place at Port Stanley. The large Argentine Garrison in Port Stanley was defeated, effectively ending the conflict. The Argentine Commander, General Mario Menendez, agreed to "An unnegotiated ceasefire with no other condition than the deletion of the word 'unconditional' from the surrender document", which he signed at 23:59. 9,800 Argentine Troops put down and surrendered their weapons. The signing of the Instrument of Surrender Document now made it official the war was over.

Tuesday 15th June brought us into absolutely foul weather conditions, literally the worst weather conditions I encountered since we arrived in the South Atlantic but with the jubilant news of the war now at is winding down stages who could have cared less. There were very high winds gusting over the crest of the waves with horrible black and somewhat threatening clouds overhead. To add to this as would be expected the high seas and heavy swells only added to our discomfort onboard.

More confirmation of the Signing of the Surrender Document came to us by the one o'clock "World News" radio programme which was relayed to all vessels worldwide and was transmitted directly from London. It amazed me more often than not that somehow the announcements made in the World News seemed to have more information on reports well before we did. Nevertheless it certainly kept us informed one way or another. What was announced on their early afternoon bulletin was that the Argentines were now ready to discuss the proposals of the Falklands now that they had surrendered and (obviously not) would not be flying against our Warships and Land Troops.

At three o'clock in the afternoon the British Prime Minister Margaret Thatcher addressed the House of Commons at the Houses of Parliament in London. She stated that the Instrument of Surrender Document was now officially signed and had of course received the authenticated version of this document and that 15,000 Argentine prisoners were at present being held at Port Stanley and all weapons had been laid down by the Argentine Forces.

The Argentinians shortly afterwards made their own announcement which came from the Argentinian Chief Air Marshall (who was attached to the Junta) who if somewhat quite brash stated in his own words that, "This may be one battle won by the British but by no means is this 'The Battle'." So there's another threat if ever there was one!

Although every formality of the Articles of War had been correctly executed at all the World National Levels this obviously didn't mean a damn thing as far as the Argentinian President was concerned: General Galtieri, head of the Junta (Armed Forces). The 11:00 news we heard that President Galtieri spoke to his people informing them that this was only a ceasefire (now Wednesday 16th) and they would be in repossession of the Falklands very soon. (Work that one out!)

Admiral Sandy Woodward, the British Task Force Commander, notified the British Government of his concern of the absolutely appalling conditions of the health and state of the Argentinian Troops on land. He continued to say it was almost impossible to save life at present as hypothermia and disease, for example typhoid, had set in too far and was spreading at an alarming pace. Unless the Argentinian Government reacted to their immediate needs they would be killing their own people through stupidity at this late stage.

Late afternoon on Wednesday 16th June brought bitter icy winds around the Falklands on land and at sea. It had been snowing on and off throughout the day. I can't imagine how terribly unpleasant it had been for Ground Forces fighting this war both on our side and the Argentines' side. It seemed to come to everyone's attention much more fully now how dreadfully badly equipped and clothed the enemy actually were. With the weather conditions deteriorating at an alarming pace daily this war would have only taken a few days to be over due to the extreme drop in temperature that was so quickly hitting those off-shore islands. The Argentinian Land Forces couldn't have withstood much more of this gruelling punishment for long without our own Forces coming at them from every side possible. It must have been a blessing to them when they finally had to surrender.

We had a few Helicopter Delivery Services (HDS) during the early part of the evening and topped up with fuel at half-sevenish. Hooray! Mail arrives very, very unexpectedly at half past ten the same evening and the mood in the ship and morale was boosting up by every second.

"Bloody hell, I don't half feel like a pint now. Perhaps tomorrow? Maybe!"

Shortly before midnight the Task Group received the Confirmation Signal from our Admiral throughout the Fleet and that was to go to Air Surface, Sub Surface, State WHITE, the lowest state for war threat.

Thursday morning as we still hadn't been given the green light to fall out of Defence Watch routines I dutifully went on watch at HQ1 at 02:00hrs – yawn, yawn! There couldn't be many more of these watches to do before the ship stood down from Defence Watches. I thought to myself of all the ships we had lost and more importantly of the complete waste of young lives that had been lost on both sides when perhaps none of this would have happened if only the negotiations had been more thorough before war was declared.

The order throughout the whole Task Force to fall out of Defence Watches was received onboard Broadsword at 08:00hrs on Friday 18th June. That in its own way meant that the conflict was well and truly over and it was time to pick up the pieces.

"Epilogue written by one of the lads from Broadsword"

The story of the fighting ends here but not the story of the Falklands. After the battle many things had to be repaired and some prisoners returned to Argentina. Many ships moved inshore to render assistance but not BROADSWORD as we were still required to protect HERMES well to the east. However we did provide a working party to help in Port Stanley.

Thinking we were destined to remain in the South Atlantic forever increased the boredom and this was only lifted at the beginning of July when we were ordered to go to Port Stanley with HERMES to put her air group ashore prior to going HOME. Delight rapidly spread throughout the ship and after a brief one day visit to the capital, both ships turned round and went full speed ahead for Ascension Island en route for UK.

Although everyone is happy to be heading home let us spare a thought for those who only made a one way journey and for their families. Let us remember that they made the supreme sacrifice for the freedom of others. While we live let us spare a thought to consider just how different it could have been...

The eight o'clock World Service News informed us that General Galtieri had been given the sack by his own Government in Argentina. His successor who was not well known at the time by his people was believed to be particularly hard on Economics.

Another of our Warships was ready to proceed back to the UK. HMS Arrow, one of our Type 21 Frigates, and the Aircraft Carrier HMS Invincible had sailed into calmer waters. HMS Arrow was expected to leave for the UK in the next eight to ten days. We were again berthed alongside the Royal Naval Repair Ship the Stena Seaspread, the ship was basically a floating Repair Dockyard Ship. We anchored in San Carlos Bay to carry out essential repairs to the ship and these repairs went on until Monday evening. Also alongside the Repair Ship was the Destroyer HMS Glamorgan. She sailed later that evening (Friday 19th) for Ascension Island which is in the middle of the Atlantic Sea and then proceeded on her way home to England. HMS Invincible headed North for her own repairs, which were expected to last for at least two weeks. When we rejoined the Carrier Group on Monday the Captain thought HMS Brilliant would also be sent home after the Invincible was back with the Carrier Group. HMS Hermes was due to sail for home soon afterwards and there was a strong possibility we also should be setting for home with her. This then made our passage home to be around August time when we should be alongside in good old Guzz (Plymouth, Devonport, England).

On Sunday 20th June the British re-occupied the South Sandwich Islands. Britain formally declared an end to hostilities and the 200-mile Exclusion Zone established around the Islands during the war was replaced by a

Falkland Islands Protection Zone (FIPZ) of 150 miles. As our ship's Padre was elsewhere in the Carrier Group our Captain led a very special Sunday morning Church Service at 10:00 in the Junior Rates' Dining Hall. This Service was especially for the Shipmates we had lost and all Land Military Personnel in the Army, Airforce, Royal Marines and all the other Regiments involved in this war.

CALL TO WORSHIP

God is our hope and strength; a very present help in trouble.

HYMN

FIGHT THE GOOD FIGHT WITH ALL THEY MIGHT:
CHRIST IS THEY STRENGTH AND CHRIST THEY RIGHT:
LAY HOLD ON LIFE AND IT SHALL BE
THEY JOY AND CROWN ETERNALLY.

CAST CARE ASIDE, LEAN ON THY GUIDE,
HIS BOUNDLESS MERCY WILL PROVIDE:
LEAN, AND THY TRUSTING SOUL SHALL PROVE,
CHRIST IS THY LIFE, AND CHRIST THY LOVE.

FAINT NOT, NOR FEAR, HIS ARM IS NEAR:
HE CHANGETH NOT, AND THOU ART DEAR,
ONLY BELIEVE AND THOU SHALT SEE,
THAT CHRIST IS ALL IN ALL TO THEE.

READING (Read by Captain Canning)

Then He entered the Temple and began to drive out the merchants from their stalls, saying to them, "The Scriptures declare, 'My Temple is a place of prayer; but you have turned it into a den of thieves.'" After that He taught daily in the Temple, but the Chief Priests and other religious leaders and the business community were trying to find some way of getting rid of Him. But they could think of nothing, for He was a hero to the people, they hung on every word He said.

THE CONDITIONS OF A JUST WAR

Jesus himself took a weapon, a whip, and applied sufficient force to achieve his objective when he found corruption in the Temple.

The practical expression of the Love of God in human activity is in the EXERCISE OF JUSTICE. In an attempt to humanise war and limit wanton slaughter the church formulated the PRINCIPLES OF A JUST WAR.

1. DECLARED AND ENGAGED IN BY PROPER AUTHORITY: Not an individuals whim, governments wage war against governments. We are not mercenaries but servants of our community through the government they elected.

2. ENGAGED IN FOR THE PROTECTION OF THE INNOCENT: and for the defense of the oppressed, not agreed or aggression.

3. FOUGHT ONLY WHEN PEACEFUL NEGOTIATIONS FAIL TO ATTAIN JUSTICE: As a last resort. We don't live by the sword but we are skilled in its use should all else fail.

4. THERE MUST BE A REALISTIC EXPECTATION OF SUCCESS: The just war is for the protection of the innocent not to sacrifice more lives unnecessarily.

5. IT MUST BE A JUSTLY WAGED WAR: Two wrongs don't make a right. Torture, wanton destruction and non-military targets cannot be justified.

ADDRESS

Just now, I would rather be in the Indian, than the Atlantic ocean, I would rather be in Cornwall than entering a War Zone BUT I have no moral qualms about being here and being part of this Task Force. I would like to think that if my part of the United Kingdom was invaded, someone would be prepared to do for my children what we may be asked to do for the Falklanders.

It is with this in mind that I invite you all, whatever you believe and in the name of all you hold dear, to share with me in the sentiment if not the conviction of the following prayers.

LET US PRAY

PRAYERS

Our Families - God, our Heavenly Father, look in love upon our families and friends. Protect them from harm, comfort them in loneliness and prosper them in all good things. Let no shadow come between them and use to divide our hearts and in your own good time bring us home to them again; through Jesus Christ our Lord. AMEN.

Before Action – O God, who sees that in this conflict we are seeking to serve you, and yet in the waging of it we must need to do many things that are an offence against your love; accept we pray you our imperfect offering, arm us with your spirit that our action may further the victory of your justice and truth; through Jesus Christ our Lord. AMEN.

Sir Francis Drake's Prayer – O Lord, when Thou givest to Thy servants to endeavor in any great matter, grant us also to know that it is not the beginning but the continuing of the same until it be thoroughly finished that yieldeth the true glory; through Him who for the finishing of Thy work laid down His life, Jesus Christ our Lord. AMEN.

NELSON'S PRAYER (Together) – MAY THE GREAT GOD WHOM I WORSHIP, GRANT UNTO MY COUNTRY, AND FOR THE BENEFIT OF FREEDOM IN GENERAL, A GREAT AND GLORIOUS VICTORY: MAY NO MISCONDUCT IN ANYONE TARNISH IT: AND MAY HUMANITY AFTER VICTORY BE THE PREDOMINANT FEATURE IN THE BRITISH FLEET. FOR MYSELF INDIVIDUALLY, I COMMIT MY LIFE TO HIM THAT MADE ME, AND MAY HIS BLESSING ALIGHT ON MY ENDEAVOURS FOR SERVING MY COUNTRY FAITHFULLY. TO HIM I RESIGN MYSELF AND THE JUST CAUSE WHICH IS ENTRUSTED ME TO DEFEND. AMEN. AMEN. AMEN.

The Service ended with the Naval Hymn.

The following pages are taken from extracts from members of the ship's crew on HMS Broadsword.

H Q 1

Working in HQ1 on the Incident Board at Action
Stations and being in contact with both Section
Bases, and the Ops. Room, I received the first
reports of imminent attacks and resultant damage.
When the voice at the other end of the line says,
"HQ1, After Section " (usually it's always Cook
Crooks that's first) "Explosion aft, patrols out",
you wait, wondering what sort of damage we've
got; is it bad? The MEO and DMEO start to plan
the ways to deal with floods and fires, and the
Watch in the SCC all seem to be looking at the
Incident Board. Then the reports come in. We have
a hole in the after Cleansing Station, through the
tailor" shop and through the Flight Deck. A bomb
has passed through us without exploding. We
breathe a little easier, but what other damage have
we got? SMEO nips off and does his on the spot
assessment and then all the reports come in, and
the picture on the Incident Board tells the story.
Looking at the Board and remembering what sort
of damage the ARDENT, ANTELOPE and
COVENTRY received and what happened to
them, I wonder what the Portland sea riders would
have to say. I know what I have to
say …"Somebody got it wrong and it wasn't US".

Everyone in the ship knows where HQ1 is and
what its function is. They now associate it either
with pipes such as "Do you hear there. This is

HQ1. Sitrep. We have received damage to the ship in the after section and this is being dealt with. All damage is under control", or with a certain Commander (E) suddenly leaping out on them with shouts of "Put on your anti flash", or "Don't you know you could be shot in war for leaving your Action Station".

For me though HQ1 at Action Stations, for real, even managed a number of amusing incidents. Such as closing up to find a Lieutenant and a Fleet Chief fighting as to who answers which phone and Commander (E) refereeing: or lying on the deck under attack and suddenly being asked "what kind of planes are they this time", or listening to MEO saying for the umpteenth time, "It's about time LMEM Barnes that this ruddy Seawolf got its act together" as the Bofors started banging away at a close range attack.

THE VIEW FROM THE FLIGHT DECK

The first encounter with the Argentine Air Force took place soon after lunch on Friday 21st May, when the Flight Commander and Second Observer had returned from a coastal search between Pebble Island and Cape Dolphin. Suddenly a Pucara counter insurgency aircraft appeared from ahead , screaming down the starboard side, dropping bombs well short of RFA FORT AUSTIN before

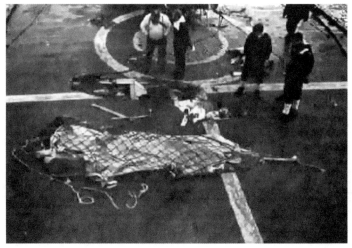

Jake and the Buffer discussing 'oles.

disappearing over the hill and into San Carlos Water itself, where it fired rockets at ARGONAUT, and escaped apparently unscathed to the south. Not long after that, wave after wave of Mirage fighter/bombers swept down on us – three separate attacks being directed at BROADSWORD herself. The first of these three came in from the starboard side. We had a GPMG and two LMGs back aft. The whole of the Flight's attention was drawn to these aircraft whistling past, clearing the top of the mast, and departing to the south west to return to base. Many rounds were pumped into the air in the general direction of the aircraft. It all seemed much like a Portland exercise. We may just as well have been firing blanks at incoming Hunters in a low level exercise. The next wave was to change all our minds.

AEM WEST and myself were following the path of two A4s, sweeping down the starboard side, clinging to the cliffs, well out of range. As I watched them turn, I noticed that WEST was crawling towards the hangar. Indeed, there was no sign of anyone around. Looking right behind me, over the port side, I could see why. Three Mirage were heading straight for us, the left hand one obviously heading for the flight deck and the exposed helicopter. There was only one sensible course of action but rather than head for the hangar, I ran up the starboard waist, collapsing on the deck. Picking myself up and counting the Mirages passing overhead, I ran to the hangar to see what, if any, damage we had sustained. In the hangar was a sight I had never before seen, nor ever wished to see again. Several of the team had been hit. Mercifully the injuries were not as serious as the amount of blood led one to believe.

The third and final attack that day was again pressed home by three Mirages, this time from the starboard side. We were few and far between on deck by this time. The Flight Commander was to my left, manning an LMG, whilst I remained closed up on the GPMG, but without a belt feed man. As the three aircraft closed, one conspicuously broke left, again aiming for the flight deck. Again the starboard battery let rip, only to see the aircraft 30mm cannon open up, and a bomb drop. That was enough for me – rapidly turning to my left, I launched myself under the hangar door. A few moments later, I poked my head out to see if all was well, but the Flight Commander had been hit in the fleshy part of his chin by a piece of shrapnel, and had to be rushed forward for attention. There had been no cover for any of us. It has been an almost futile gesture. Even so it was a help-so much so, that one Mirage was splashed by a combination of 40/60, GPMG, LMG and SLR fire.

The Saturday was much quieter. HMS COVENTRY and ourselves were deployed to the north of Pebble Island, to act as a Missile trap, with COVENTRY'S SEA Dart acting as an attack weapon.

On Sunday morning the 23rd, we found ourselves back in Bomb Alley, ready to take out any marauding Argentine aircraft. Once again, our Lynx departed on a coastal/surface search to the north, again finding nothing in the area. Having picked up two Fighter Controllers from FEARLESS (ex ANTRIM) the cab was tasked to investigate three contacts to the north of the AOA at about 50 miles, returning to land on ANTELOPE. That was when the fun started! Air raid warning red was piped minutes after they had shut down on ANTELOPE's deck. During several attacks by A4s, ANTELOPE was hit, port and starboard, by unexploded bombs, (one bomb hit the Air Conditioning Unit, allowing inert Freon gas to escape). This immediately caused a gas alarm. Our poor crew, minus anti-gas respirators, were in two minds whether or not to leap over the side and try to swim for it. The mere fact that they were standing talking about it of course meant there was no gas present, and they finally managed to leave for BROADSWORD; but not before having a good look at ANTELOPE's pole mast, which has been bent virtually double by an exploding A4, taken out by a combination of BROADSWORD and ANTELOPE'S Small arms fire.

Tactics again changed on the 24th; back to our original missile trap to the North of the Sound. We had very little activity, although the two FCs we had picked up earned their keep by controlling Sea Harriers into incoming raids, and successfully shooting down 7 aircraft.

This plot was repeated on Argentina's Revolution Day the 25th. We remained in defence watches until required to close up at Action Stations. Our first call being at 1234. Two aircraft had been detected 20 miles to the south, and closing. COVENTRY fired two Darts: lockouts sighted one parachute while the other aircraft was tracked by radar heading back over the land. Things then happened thick and fast, at 1800 – Air Raid Warning Red; 1805 – raid now west at 80 miles closing at 450 knots, CAP intercepting; 1820, and we are under attack; 1822, one UXB come inboard from the starboard quarter, exiting through the flight deck, taking with it the nose of XZ 729; 1825, COVENTRY has been hit and was listing to port.

The raids cleared, and we went to pick up survivors from the now capsizing COVENTRY. She lies on her side, a Wessex 5 resting his front wheels on her port side, winching men out of liferafts trapped by her Sea Dart launcher. There are a total of 10 helos dotted around the sky, picking up survivors who have drifted away in bright orange liferafts; checkiong pieces of flotsam to see if anyone maybe clinging onto them; more are heading in from the AOA.

The job of recovering the survivors continued on into the darkness. By last light the majority had been recovered, and were hustled below, stripped, showered/bathed to warm them up, and fed. It was not until nearly two o'clock in the morning that we finally saw the Ship's Company of HMS COVENTRY depart in an LCM to be taken to a holding vessel. I have never been so moved as when those men sat, huddled together against the chill winter's night, kitted out in borrowed clothes and shoes, with Pusser's towels and blankets, gave three cheers for "HMS BROADSWORD" not once but twice. Even as they pulled away into the darkness, those unfortunate souls were clapping and shouting their thanks to those of use left on deck.

HMS Coventry

I realised how close the enemy aircraft were when the Bofors opened fire. The next sounds to reach my ears were yells: "Take cover"… "Hit the deck." immediately followed by a series of sharp cracks. This was coupled with a sound which I can only describe as a handful of ball bearing landing in a tin bucket. Shrapnel is certainly no discriminator of metal or flesh as we quickly found out. Hearing a number of moans I tried to open the Magazine Door into the Hangar, but one of the Flight had fallen in front of the Door only allowing me to partially open it: just far enough to get my head out to see what was going on.

The sight before me then I will never forget. It appeared that everyone had been hit in some way, and it was obvious there were a lot of people in pain. I thought, "My God. They're all dead" . After informing HQ1 we had casualties in the Hangar 1 made my way to the Hangar via the Air lock and by this time everybody who hadn't been hit, and even some of those who had, were attending to the more seriously injured. I will always remember the calm and businesslike manner of everyone in the Hangar that day, including the casualties themselves. They behaved admirably: all doing a lot to help themselves and staying calm and collected, many still showing a sense of humour. Though being a "Fishhead" I was very proud to be closely involved with the "Waffoos" through that and other incidents on later days. Their support and sense of humour were invaluable.

And now we move between decks, firstly to the Operations Room from where, in semi-darkness the Command operates the ship's sensors and primary weapon systems. It is a "Star Wars" sort of place, computerized and luminous. This is how we prepared for war.

THE AFT SECTION BASE

"Hands to Action Stations" was a familiar pipe and one we all dreaded in the After Section of the Ship, but our first day at Action Stations was very quiet with no enemy action and we were all crimped out on the deck trying to snatch some

Z's We were all very confident about our ship's weapon system and had no worries about Argentinian Air attacks. But this was only the first day ...

21st May. As the morning came up we had a quick look at San Carlos Bay from the quarterdeck, but there wasn't much to see, just rambling hills and the odd sheep, which made me think of camping holidays in Wales. An hour passed quickly by, which gave way to another familiar pipe, "Air Raid Warning Red" and hearts were beating fast, people were going to the heads like it was going out of fashion: Seawolf was fired; there was a moment of silence and then tremendous cheering. Seawolf had made a kill.

Two minutes later we heard the Bofors open up, followed by the sound of small arms from the Flight Deck. We looked at each other ... suddenly the headset was alive with "Take cover", shouted to the rest of the Section, who hit the deck and then followed by the thudding of 30mm cannon shells ripping into the ship and planes passing overhead with a "Whoosh".

Then it was time to blanket search the after end. Damage was minor with holes everywhere, and then we discovered the dhoby had been hit, and that all the Flight along with the Leading Reg had suffered shrapnel wounds.

This was the first day: our initiation into the Bomb Alley "Suicide Squad". The days then moved slowly on. We had more attacks with no more damage and we had shot down several jets. It was on 25th May when we were all praying for darkness that Air Raid Warning Red was sounded and we were subsequently attacked with COVENTRY. A bomb passed through the ship shortly before COVENTRY was hit, causing damage to our hangar, helicopter and 2R passage and destroying the Tailor's shop. Everyone was surprisingly calm and men worked hard repairing our damage and tending to COVENTRY'S Survivors who were in very high spirits and who gave us all something to admire. We were very lucky the bomb didn't go off. That was one of our last days in Bomb Alley. We were tired but remained cheerful, and thankful we made it, though we will not forget those who didn't.

BOMB ALLEY

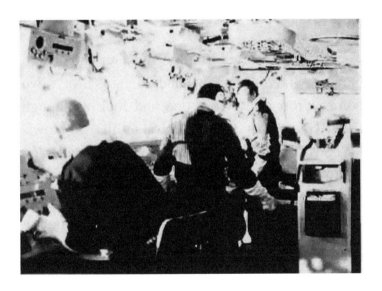

Looking through the Bridge windows it is a glorious sunny afternoon in the calm blue waters of San Carlos Harbour. Outside on the Bridge wings, chatting away but watchful, the Gunners and Marines, armed with rifles and machine guns look like a team out for a day's rough shooting.

Suddenly, out of a valley in the hillside a mile or so away across the smooth water, three Mirage aircraft appear and head straight towards us. The shout goes up, "Aircraft!" A line of tracer from the 40/60 Bofors gun shoots out towards one of the three although nothing will stop them. A line of water spouts race along the water from the aircraft, then there is a "Clang, clang, clang!" as their cannon shells hit the side of the ship. Now the three are close enough for the machine gunners and riflemen to engage. They bravely line up and open fire, "Pop, pop pop!" like a motor bike with no exhaust.

The three aircraft get nearer and nearer and nearer. Now they are only a few hundred yards away: two bombs drop away from one and look as though they will smash straight through the windows. "Whoosh!" the aircraft disappear overhead, and then "Bang, bang, bang!" as the 40/60 on the other side of the ship opens fire. The rough shooters run around the front of the bridge and start shooting again at the escaping aircraft. Left in the air, getting closer, are the two bombs.

They are dark green – shaped like giant Walls sausages with a spike in the end. They make little noise. One falls short: the other disappears from sight above the bridge roof … will it hit … or won't it ... it doesn't ... it splashes into the water, and a big plume of water shoots up as it explodes.

Bomb Alley ... here were are.

THE FOR'AD SECTION BASE

Although the For'ad Section did not receive much

damage during the air attacks such as the other ships of the Bomb Alley Group were blessed with, the 27 man crew plus the occasional visitor in the form of Midshipman Dubois or Thre If all gave vital assistance when needed in other sections of the ship. Even through the long hours of waiting for the attacks to come the team did not show any signs of fatigue; even the ones who had been up on the long 24 hours of night defence watches and daytime Action Stations. The maximum sleep which any member of the crew had over the six day period in Bomb Alley was 18 hours, split up over three six hour sessions.

During the air raids the whole section hit the deck, hands over heads and waiting for the Seawolf to shoot from the launcher above their heads. When this did not happen and the dull "Thud, thud, thud" of the Bofors was heard along with the sharper "Crack" of small arms fire everyone listened for the loud explosion to happen. During the air attack on COVENTRY two bombs went off under the ship and the force of these explosions lifted us all off the deck. While the Section was carrying out a search for damage the Gas Alarm went off over the broadcast, causing the blood to drain from nany faces. The alarm proved to be false, and looking back at the incident it was a funny sight to see everyone grabbing respirators, some with filters missing and some on upside down.

A sit rep from HQ1 gave us a rough estimate of damage to the ship and, most important of all the report that there were no casualties. The ship was then standing by to pick up survivors from COVENTRY. The men of the For'ad Section carried out their orders with great speed and discipline, which made the job of co-ordinating and directing from the Incident Board a much easier task. Great courage was shown by everyone that day, even when told that there was another attack on the way.

What started out as Just one more For'ad Section base, that took 20 minutes to close down to 1Z, changed to a very effective team in a very short time, managing to close the whole Section down within 3 minutes and able to cope with everything that was thrown its way.

PS. Thank you to the Chefs for all they did during the Campaign, Through thick and thin they always managed to come up with a "HOT" meal, and tea just when it was most needed.

That: postscript takes us on to the Supporting Services the Galley which appeared to run a special line in Porridge, and the First Aiders in their Crusader like red cross surcoats.

THE OPERATIONS ROOM

The ship joined HERMES and INVICIBLE a week after leaving Gibraltar; inevitably, being in company with the two carriers, the Gloom Room boys were working a two watch system much earlier than the rest of the Ship's Company.

The journey South was used to refine procedures and become familiar with the other ships in the Task Force. We set up the "War Office", the fount of all buzzes terrifying and true, frightening and false. SOO and SCO pinned up the charts, made their flags and markers and prepared for paper action.

A sunny respite was taken at Ascension when all that was black was painted grey and final touches were made to suntans. We estimated two weeks at Ascension awaiting the Amphibious forces; after a day we set off South again and within hours a periscope (?) was sighted and the realities of the situation were dawning on us.

No submarine was detected but Soviet and Argentine surveillance confined. The Russians used their large Bear aircraft and the Argentines employed Boeing 707; as they approached the carriers they were escorted off by Sea Harriers. But these were highlights in an otherwise monotonous routine – there were daily exercises but nothing to delay the plod into the ever increasing cold of the Southern Atlantic.

The Roaring Forties produced some rough weather; for the benefit of TV we closed HERMES and increased speed to generate some spray and to "take it Green". So much so that the First Lieutenant snapping away with his camera in the shelter of the Bridge Wing was drenched by a wave that came over the top of the Bridge! Much delight and amusement for those within the Bridge.

Helicopters were flying round the clock transferring stores and personnel from the RFAs and it was a sad incident involving a SeaKing 4 that, nonetheless, demonstrated the thoroughness of Portland Training. The aircraft had, unbeknown to any ship, flown into the sea just after dusk. The pilot sitting in his dinghy had released a red flare as we passed him about a mile away. "Red Flare Green 90" yells the OOW, ASWD deep in a long watch reverie comes to with a start "Take TCMs" he bellows. (Torpedo Counter Measures, in an ASW Exercise the firing of a torpedo by a submarine is signalled by a Green Flare).

We were involved in the search for the ditched helicopter and its crew for some time, eventually handing over to HMS YARMOUTH. Only the pilot was saved, nothing was found of his crewman, our first casualty of operation.

As we approached the 200 mile zone we received the great news that South Georgia had surrendered and the Submarine Santa Fe had been destroyed with no loss of life. "We'll wrap this up and be on our way to Singapore via Simons town in no time" thought the optimists.

May 1st and battle commenced, well for some; ships were despatched inshore for bombardment and to chase a possible submarine. We stayed in our usual station close by the HERMES. Some aircraft were shot down (Argentinian that is) and ships were attacked and slightly damaged and both sides withdrew to think about it. In the Ops Room we listened to fighter pilots and the bombardment ships some 100 miles away, it hardly seemed real; more like the games at DRYAD.

The warmongers amongst us were thirsting for action and the chance came on 9th May when we went inshore with HMS COVENTRY to lay a missile trap for Argentine aircraft and to bombard Stanley. The weather was cool and overcast with poor visibility and although COVENTRY fired 3 Sea Darts the results seemed inconclusive. Late in the day a helicopter was detected by the radars and was confirmed as an Argentinian Puma helicopter; we pointed this machine out to COVENTRY who destroyed it with a Sea Dart. We watched the event on the Seawolf TV system in Black and White, it all seemed so unreal.

We returned on the 11th but there were no aircraft the weather was awful and we rejoined the Carriers with nothing on the score sheet. It seemed to us then that we would spend the rest of the war following HERMES' bulk around, mainly in persistent fog. We followed her to Pebble Island and later we followed INVINCIBLE to Beauchene Island, and back.

20th May and we joined the Ships taking the troops to San Carlos; another eventful day, far more quiet than an exercise. By daybreak on 21st,

3 Commando Brigade were streaming ashore and the escorts were waiting for the expected air attacks. Never having been under air attack before nobody knew really what to expect; and then they arrived "Air Raid Warning Red, Aircraft in the Sound" became a familiar call. We operated in the Sound, in San Carlos Waterway, off the coast and towards the Western Islands. All the daylight hours were spent at Action Stations waiting for the aircraft; the weather was perfect for them we saw the ARDENT, ANTELOPE and COVENTRY go under and yet in the gloom pressing buttons watching it on radar and TV, listening to the radio circuits and the gunfire it hardly seemed possible. Even with COVENTRY's sad survivors littering the decks the truth of what was going on was hard to believe; even when the bombs were so close on the TV that they were out of focus and filled the screen and the dreaded words "Take Cover" we all ducked the wrong way. The TVs are on the starboard side but the bombs were coming from the port side, we all ducked to port away from the TV!

With COVENTRY sunk and a huge hole in the Flight Deck we were withdrawn back to follow HERMES, feeling guilty about leaving the others behind in San Carlos. But for all their success the Argentine Air Force seemed to have had enough, their attacks on the ships became very infrequent and were from high level – very inaccurate.

Perhaps we had all stood our ground long enough to make them back off and search for easier prey.

The rest of May passed, June and Surrender Day, we still followed HERMES. Then release from the Task Force and homeward bound, still following HERMES.

Each air raid seemed to be over in minutes. In fact we often closed up at Action Stations for several hours at a time and were amazed when it was all over that time had passed so quickly. The next account is of an airraid as heard in the Operations room.

The references to a multi threat environment points up the Ops. Room's involvement with threats above, on the surface, and underneath the sea. The next poem comes from the men concerned with the threat from under the sea:

THE REASON WHY

Within this small dit There is sadness and wit
It's about the TAS Division
Making their decision
Whether it is a submarine or whale
Or another bank of shale

Now the subs got away we think
But poor whale, he we did sink.
It was not for thirst of blood
For he could have been a sub.
Because of his size this innocent bystander
Is exactly the same as a Two-Oh-Niner.

The characteristics of his echo below
Show that of a submarine, you know,
So chances could not be taken;
The whale's life had to be foresaken.
By taking poor Moby's life away
BROADSWORD was sure to fight another day

THE AFT FIRST AID PARTY

The two dates, 21st and 25th May will stay in the ship's company's memories for a long time. Not least those of the After First Aid Party.

The First Aiders were split into two groups; one of four including the POMA John Wicks in the Sick Bay, and the second just the PO Writer and one up in 1M Flat. On the 21st we received reports of casualties and soon members of the Flight appeared from the Hangar, together with others from the Laundry and Tiller Flat. The 1M Team dealt with the more seriously hit Flight members, sending them along to the Wardroom for attention from the Doctor, and the Sick Bay party handled those casualties from 2 Deck and the lightly injured Flight members.

Luckily of course all our casualties were "relatively" light, and when we had done what was possible in the Sick Bay those not yet ready to return to Duty went down to the Petty Officers Mess which was in use as a holding area run by the Captain's PO Steward and a couple of men from the Action Messing Team. In all 16 casualties were treated from this raid.

By the 25th we were of course comparatively hardened fighters (!) but down aft we thought our final hour had come when with a loud bang that bomb entered the starboard side and exited through the Flight Deck doing a lot of damage on the way but fortunately causing no casualties. Our relief was cut short however when we heard that COVENTRY was sinking and that we were to pick up her survivors. There was a detailed plan to deal with this and all the preparations were put in hand.

The Flight Deck was of course unusable for helicopter casevacs and some changes had to be made but very soon survivors were pouring in from what seemed like every direction at once, but there were so many volunteers from our crew to do anything to help, that soon it was all sorted out, and things went swiftly and efficiently until all survivors were onboard and being looked after.

THE FOR'AD FIRST AID POST

The FFAP complement met in the Wardroom at Action Stations and consisted of Surgeon Lieutenant WOODRUFF, Jake (The Vicar) and four duty ambulances from the S&S. The Wardroom is easily transformed into its designated wartime role, equipped with nearly everything to do a heart transplant (well nearly!), to give you some idea of what the Wardroom is like, then imagine the austere surroundings of an NHS hospital – well that's like the Sick Bay; where we are as in fact more like a private clinic!

For most of the period we were closed up, some of our members were in total oblivion, in the Land of Nod. But for the days when HM Ships ARDENT and COVENTRY were sunk, in which our ship was involved, our motley team came together, and the First Aiders became the well oiled machine they were trained to be. Those few weeks showed that when it counted we were there, with our distinctive surcoats of white with red crosses, looking either like a target, or St George riding off after the next Dragon. We seemed always to be in the thick of the battles, giving rise to, " Ships may come, ships may go, but BROADSWORD lingers on forever". One small point to end on however. The Argentinians were always very inconsiderate, as their attacks always seemed to be either at the start of a meal, or whilst glancing at the attractive estates in the Wardroom's edition of "Country Life"…

AND IN SUMMARY

Our Doctor had joined in January for the Singapore deployment and in this as in so many other respects we were therefore well prepared for a long absence from UK. However extra medical stores were needed and these were delivered at Ascension, and from then on the Doctor and POMA were busy training first aid teams, preparing the Sick Bay and Wardroom as treatment areas, and making sure we were all in date for our jabs!

Our own casualties came from the two air attacks during our first day in Bomb Alley. Four of the ship's company were sent to a hospital ship, one returning after ten days and the others returning to the UK where they all made speedy recoveries.

The second call for the medical teams came during the rescue of COVENTRY'S people. All had reviving hot showers before being clothed and fed and then being looked after by the whole ship's company. The injured were all seen in the Wardroom with about 20 being flown on to the hospital ships. The remainder were later transferred with the rest of their shipmates to the RFA in San Carlos Water.

THE GDP

Anyone thinking about the things they might write for a Commissioning Book when we sailed from Gibraltar on 8th April is unlikely to have come close to the truth!

However, back to Thursday April 8th. We sailed from Gibraltar full of apprehension. What were the following weeks going to hold for us? One thing we did realise was that this was not going to be a training period; if something went wrong we knew we wouldn't be able to stop the serial and re-run it to get it right. We therefore had to try and visualize every tactical situation and practise it and get it right, first time. We exercised 40/60 shoots, 3" rocket re-loading (with great enthusiasm when we discovered that the Argies had the air launched Exocet) and small arms firings. Then we went on repeating it all, time and time, again so that by the time we reached the War Zone everyone knew everyone else's job.

Apart from all the training periods the passage down to Ascension was generally relaxed. The weather was good and everyone made the most of getting as much sun as possible.

After Ascension the sun lasted for a few more days and it didn't seem possible that it would soon be freezing cold and that we could be fighting for our lives. The News on the BBC World Service has probably never had so many listeners. Every hour, on the hour it would be tuned in, eveyone wanting to hear the same thing, that a political solution had been found. It was not to be. Before we knew where we were, we were inside the Total Exclusion Zone and everything was for real. The war was on.

Every day from now on we would be going to Action Stations at Air Raid Warning Red, and we had only three days to wait until the first fatality. On 3rd May HMS SHEFFIELD was hit by an air launched Exocet missile, and this disaster honed our alertness and reactions to every threat. However no more air attacks were to come into direct contact with the Carrier Battle Group again until 25th May when the ATLANTIC CONVEYOR was sunk.

After SHEFFIELD, BROADSWORD acted as anti missile escort either to one or other of the carriers or to naval gunfire support missions until the big day, Friday 21st May, the day on which we escorted the amphibious group to the beachhead in San Carlos Water.

On the following day our troops took the landing beaches. HMS BROADSWORD was subjected to wave upon of Argentinean fighter and bomber aircraft throughout daylight hours. To combat them we had the Seawolf missile; however the environment we were operating in did not let it perform to the best of its ability. To over come this gap in our defences we armed the GDP crew with small arms – more to give them something to do than anything else. After all, what chance have you with small arms against supersonic aircraft?

The first raid of the day came in. Seawolf, with the help of L/S BALL took the left hand target, which left two for the riflemen and 40/60 crew. The aircraft, flying at 15 feet above the sea, sent a trail of cannon fire snaking its way in splashes of water towards the ship. Undaunted the GDP crew stood its ground, matching fire with fire, putting up so much lead with 40/60, GPMG and SLR, that the planes would have to fly through it to reach us.

Only at the last minute did the brave gunners take cover, as the cannon fire raced its way up the ship's side and into the screens around the flag-deck. Once the planes had gone overhead, the team were on their feet again, recharging magazines, and checking all the gear. Those with shrapnel wounds were taken below; to come back minutes later, ready for more action.

And more action they were to have. More waves of aircraft were to attack during the long remaining hours of daylight, and yet the courage, spirit, and sheer staying power of those young men never faltered once, and were it not for the wall of lead that they bravely threw up into the sky, and through which the enemy had to fly, the pilots' aim would have been better, and their bombs might have found their mark. This was however only the beginning.

The next day we combined with HMS COVENTRY to act as a radar picket and anti aircraft missile trap to the north of the Falklands and the following day it was back to Bomb Alley to provide close AA protection for the ships at the Beachhead. Once again we came under heavy air attack, and once again the GDP crew did their job, quietly and efficiently, helping the ship combination to "splash" two A4s and five Mirage. The next two days were spent again with the COVENTRY on Air Picket duties and on the evening of the second day it happened. Four A4 attacked us, and two managed to get through our defences to hit the COVENTRY with the result that we know only too well. Having picked up the survivors, with the help of many brave helicopter pilots, we transferred them, and were then told to make our way back to the Carrier Group to "lick our wounds". We had also been hit by a bomb which fortunately did not explode and which miraculously injured no one onboard.

Many things will be written about this Operation, and many feats of herosim have been reported. The Canteen Manager of the ARDENT did a fine job and the world knows about it: the GDP crew of the BROADSWORD did a fine job, for five times longer. We are proud of them.

THE WE DEPARTMENT

I suppose the Department's work started at Ascension Island where we fully stored for war, with missiles and torpedos being put in all the places one should not put them! We even had a supply of the newly introduced Sea Skua, air to surface missiles to play with.

As soon as defence watches began the department was split three ways. The day work hands, watchkeepers, and our own local "councillor" loaned to the Town Hall Cleansing Department, as

"Starboard Watch Co-ordinator". How did the watchkeepers amuse themselves when not sleeping? You may well ask! Apart from RAS(L) and RAS(S), missile humping, and drying out trackers, they managed to find time to repair some 300 to 400 headsets, a dozen or so handsets, repair and rebuild three 15" signal projectors and numerous pairs of electronic ears for the Engineers … Some even had time to sit, and pass, their PPE.

At Action Stations the Department regrouped to help the ship repel boarders! The main body was the WART (Weapon Action Repair Team to you!), with the Torpedo prep team, Seawolf maintainers and the hands for the Damage Control parties who were spread around the ship. The WARTs were kept in the picture by the newly wired Command Open Line, and therefore had all the hot buzzes, such as "I think it's a Super E... or an A4... no it's not it's the CAP returning", and whenever Aircraft Warning Red was sounded a mysterious blue haze filled the Surveillance Office from numerous Benson and Hedges. (WEO never smoked his own!).

The department managed to survive without any serious damage. Only a few communications were severed: 3R Mess could no longer hear the dreaded pipe "Call the Hands", as their mess broadcast was cut off by a flying "visitor" who just happened to pass through the ship, and out again, giving the ship's Budgie a bloody nose on the way. SWEO had a cannon shell through his cabin but since it wasn't near his model ship he did not seem to worry. We were part of the ship's team and are proud of what was achieved

SEAWOLF

The Loading Crew used to sit/sleep outside the RU magazine in 02N Flat. When awake we used to discuss the probable entry point for an Exocet, and when a raid was reported we amused ourselves by playing poker dice. The only sound that broke the tension was the "clickety clack" of the bones on the metal deck. But nobody really belived that the Argies would get close enough to attack us, and certainly not to hit us. Another sound was added to the atmosphere all too frequently, that of the fault warning buzzer from the after tracker. Billy Whizz, or Bob MacGregor became blurrs as they tried to reset the faults before that cliche of cliches could be heard again on the Seawolf intercom, "radar, TV guidance fault cleared ... all green aft".

After the SHEFFIELD incident the off watch Ops. Room crew were moved down to join us, and then the off watch OOWs arrived with a Command Open Line. We were moved into the magazine, protesting at first, as I think Billy Whizz took some pleasure in clipping the door down and sealing the six of us in with six live missiles. The OOWs brought some yellow mats with them to lie on, but they some how found their way into the magazine, and L/S MUNN even found a blanket, and the magazine became a home from home. Of course inside we couldn't hear the Command Open Line or Main Broadcast very well, but we couldn't resist the temptation of making those outside think we could hear nothing at all!

Much amusement was found as a voice from outside shouted information that we already knew. It gave them something to do anyway! Looking back it's lucky that the ARGIES never had a missile that homed on us, because there were a lot of verbal missiles emitted from the after part of the ship.

Now we come to the fateful period May 21st-25th when the war really caught up with us. We had never bothered to wear tin hats before the air raid which strafed us with 30mm cannon. We had always thought that Exocet was the main threat and that Pusser had so far failed to develop an Exocet proof tin hat. We changed our minds when we saw the shrapnel that had been dug out of the after Seawolf launcher. If you looked in the magazine during the following raids all that you would have seen would have been 6 tin hats with feet as everyone tried to get as much protection as possible from them. After each raid Billy Whizz used to phone Jimmy Green in the forward Launcher Control room to see if he was OK. Jimmy was thought to be at the greatest risk when he crawled out from under his "Exocet proof rubber mat" to answer the 'phone. During the days in Bomb Alley a new pastime was developed that of predicting the time until dusk eg. "It will be dark in six hours" and after the next air raid, "It will be dark in 5 hours 45 minutes". A combination of a cold deck and tension caused everyone to have a frequent need to relieve themselves. We would have been great at putting out fires.

The time of the COVENTRY incident was the most harrowing, partly because we were hit ourselves. By this time we had managed to talk the sadists in 02N flat out of fastening all the clips on the magazine door. This was fortunate because when Billy Whizz's voice was heard shouting, "Evacuate aft. Everyone forward", we were in a certain amount of haste to split the scene. The remaining clips were thrown off the door and we were all out and down the hatches to 1 deck without touching the rungs of the ladders. It had been thought that there was still an unexploded bomb lodged in the after part of the ship. We found ourselves lying face down in the Wardroom flat when the chemical alarm was sounded. We were all wondering why we hadn't brought our AGRs with us! After the all clear we went on deck to assist with the recovery of COVENTRY survivors. That was the last of our action stations. The ready use mag never seemed the same after we had evacuated in such a hurry.

To our dismay the after launcher only fired one shot in anger. That was reported to have run true towards an out of range Argie plane that was about to bomb BRILLIANT. The missile scared the Argie into dropping his bombs too early (Phew).

Now we are heading home, having suffered no fatalities, our thoughts are with those who did not make it. IT COULD SO EASILY HAVE BEEN US …

A poem by one of the Deep Magazine crew;

THE WHITE FOREST

Sitting in the missile mag four decks down
Are Curly and Lou who wear a frown

Hatch battened up, all locked in
They sit and wonder, "Will we win?"

If we don't then how do we get out?
There's no one here to hear us shout.

After a while they stop wondering why;
Only to wonder will they die.

If that is to be, then how will they go?
Will it be quick, or painfully slow?

Looking around at the white sticks of death,
And with each bang, holding their breath.

"Listen", says one "It's the sound of a key"
Yes it's the one to set them free.

Up the ladder, up to the top,
Out of the hatch, two heads pop.

"What's been happening?" "Where's everyone gone?"

Guess it's over. Guess you've won.

B O M B   A L L E Y

Usually the scene of great activity during normal working days, the Main Galley coasts along, come the proverbial Hell or High Water cooking about 700 meals a day and rising to 900 during Defence Watches. Supervised by Petty Officer Cook Fudge (John) and manned by two Leading Hands and three Cooks, plus of course the Petty Officer Caterer Jim Goodwin and his dedicated organising team of Speed Feeders. During the recent turmoil, when we went to Action Stations nearly every day, the Galley produced a hot meal, on time, every time, even when the pipe "Hit the deck" was heard throughout the ship.

Pot mess immediately springs to everyone's mind but in fact the normal menu of three choices for each meal was adhered to as far as possible. The driving force to keep this machine running smoothly was not only supplied by the PO Cook but also by the Divisional Officer who frequently visited and sometimes even had his meal behind the counter, and by the boss, Lieutenant Commander A D Johnson, that mysterious person who always had a packet of Polos in his pocket (as well as an AGR full of fivers!) even when the NAAFI had been closed for hours.

The galley came in to its own when BROADSWORD played willing host to the survivors of COVENTRY, producing an extra hot meal for everyone, which goes to prove "always keep a little something in the fridge, as you never know just who might drop in to dinner!"

Due to the long period spent at sea, there were inevitable cut backs but the galley managed and even the ship's company didn't seem to mind that much, but "a sailor is never happy unless he is moaning"...

However, an outstanding discovery was made by the Chefs, courtesy of the Argentinians.

JACK CAN SURVIVE WITHOUT CHIPS !!!

Well done boys.

THE SPARKERS

The MCO staff form a very small part of the ship's company, two LRO(G)s and six R01(G)s. They are at the heart of every operation the ship does, providing the Ops Room with all their radio circuits so that they can have all the computer data they need, as well as Helo Control, AAWC, ASWAC and so on. However during the Operation our MCO had the workload of a much bigger ship meaning more than double the work usually experienced during an exercise, and of an intensity only briefly experienced at Portland! They had to change frequencies regularly of course, only to find our little friend, the Argy, already there "spoofing". All didn't go in vain however as we played the same game, monitoring Argie morse circuits to provide valuable Information for our intelligence sources ashore, and at sea.

THE GOLLIES

Much preparation was done to familiarise EW Operators with the Argentinian electronic Order of Battle before reaching the TEZ but the greater part of the knowledge gained remained unused as their Navy did not venture out beyond the 12 mile exclusion zone imposed by our Government. The usual problems of EW were compounded by the Argentinian equipment, most of which is European and some of it British. However it was EW which provided the first warning of numerous air raids and which alerted the Force as to the type of aircraft closing for attack.

One of the electronic countermeasures against Exocet (which was one of the enemy's main anti ship weapons) was the use of rocket launched "chaff" (of which more in the next piece) which was used successfully on at least one occasion.

However the reader may be amused to hear that the accidental firing of chaff on one occasion elicited a naturally rapid response from some members of the ship's company, who naturally assumed that we were suddenly under attack! The firer is still trying to live the incident down.

And now for BROADSWORD's secret weapon! One aspect of Electronic warfare is Chaff – an induced radar echo that looks like another ship to a distant enemy but is in fact only a cloud of shredded tinfoil. Chaff is usually fire by rocket, but … I thought to fire "chaff" from the funnel was impossible and when I was told that the funnel was going to be my "off watch" Action Station I thought it was all a big joke!

However my equipment for firing the "chaff" proved to be a wooden "U" shaped tube connected to an air hose and bottle. The idea was that I was to poke the tube through the funnel, turn on the air and then let the heat from the funnel gases take the "chaff" cloud into the air around the ship.

In fact I never actually had the chance to fire it! I'm not complaining but believe it or not being up in the funnel is actually quite frightening. The only way that I knew when to fire it was by a small light which was operated from the bridge, and I spent many hours waiting for the light to go on. I

had no means of communication with other positions so I was alone with no idea of what was going on around me.

My most memorable day, and which I'll never forget, although I won't forget any of my hours in the funnel, was on Thursday the 6 May. I was off watch, during the dogs when Action Stations were sounded at Air Raid Warning Red. After grabbing my AGR and life jacket etc I ran towards the funnel.

I was half way up the ladder when a "chaff" rocket was launched from below me. My heart missed a beat and I froze to the ladder. I had no idea what it was. I started to climb further up the ladder when another rocket was fired and again I stopped, perhaps in fear I don't know, and then after a few seconds I started climbing again to the top. It was only when I got my breath back and waited for the light to go on that I realised where I was and what had happened. Alone in the dark those rockets could have been anything. I was certainly glad when somebody came up to tell me Action Stations was over.

THE BUNTINS

During the days of Bomb Alley the intrepid team of Buntings carried on with their normal tasks of voice operating, flashing light, reporting signals to the OOW and keeping a lockout generally, as in peacetime. One of our men was closed up in the After Seawolf Launcher Control Room with his chalkboard, chalk, signal pad, pencils, aid is lamp, portable radio etc. ready to man the Emergency conning position if ever that was required; which thankfully was never the case! In addition the 3 Deck signal crew were armed with SLRs and assisted the GDP crew in the destruction and damage of four of the enemy's aircraft. That these aircraft meant us harm can be seen from the 30mm cannon shell hole in the Signalman's shelter (see picture); a hole punched in moreover just as Sgt Leslie was moving in front of the shelter … luckily he stumbled!

On the 25th May, after COVENTRY sank the buntings helped to bring survivor's aboard on the waists and boat deck, then manned lights and searchlights as darkness fell, as well as manning the seaboat to provide communications with the ship's bridge and helping to pull survivor's out of the sea.

We managed to establish direct voice communications on the Bridge with the hospital ship UGANDA and this radio circuit was used to pass vital medical information to and fro, and to give details of the helicopters which flew the 60 miles between us and the UGANDA.

AFTERMATH THOUGHTS OF REALITY

By: D J POYZER

As I look back for different ways
Of describing those frantic Bomb Alley days,
It's difficult to say how I really felt,
My thoughts disarrayed, the blows they've been dealt.
Sat down below with war up above,
The fight for our people, for the freedom they love.

Hours on end I dreamed and I thought,
First Aid and escape routes, the things I'd been taught.
Praying and hoping for luck without end,
Praying and hoping for the peace God will send.

Being chirpy and happy so I would not think,
of being stuck in a tomb, on a ship that might sink.

War was the reason, war is the word,
The lads from up top, their stories I heard,
Their injuries were true, they stood out a mile,
Their faces showed shock, yet they still raised a smile.
For me below deck, this is all that I saw,
For that is my place, my part in this war.

In action so tense, when is it my turn?
To float in the sea and watch my ship burn,
To lie in the passage, helpless with pain,
To take the full blast, see no life again.
My feelings confused, a tormented mind,
But soon when it's over, my senses I'll find.

And any day now, I'll be home on the train,
But forever my conscience will suffer with pain,
The stained reminiscence, the stories I'll tell,
Those bombs bringing terror, the missiles from hell.
The anger within me, I see families who cried,
For they were the sufferers, their loved ones have died.

So, as I look back for different ways
Of describing those frantic Bomb Alley days,
sit and I think, and ask myself why?
People should suffer and young men should die.

Countries must argue, why is this so?

Ask the politicians, they must know.

Our ship was guzzling up the fuel again so we refuelled at 11:30 on Tuesday twenty-second. The six o'clock World News stated that the Argentinian Government had completely collapsed. The Argentine Naval Senior Admiral and the Air Force Air Marshall refused to have anything to do with the Government if it was to be run by the Army.

At 12:00 approximately on Wednesday HMS Brilliant got the green light to make passage home (hopefully we would be next!)

The Flagship HMS Hermes informed us that she intended to sail into the Falklands Area at the weekend to show the ship's crew members what exactly they had been fighting for. We were asked to stand by to be escort.

Six bags of mail arrived onboard and the morale on the ship was extremely high. LT Connell and Leading Radio Hedge Hieghton had been selected to go to Port Stanley the next day to assist the Queen's Harbour Master and would be staying for about eight to ten days. When we did finally get the signal to steam home we would be calling in at Gibraltar via Ascension Island. At 14:00 the Captain went on HMS Hermes to have a late luncheon with the Task Force Admiral and arrived back on HMS Broadsword a couple of hours later.

The ship's company made full opportunity on Sunday afternoon while we were at anchor in San Carlos Sound to get a Liberty Boat from the ship as leave had been granted to all the ship's company who were not on duty to visit the local people on these Islands. I of course would never miss this opportunity as I thought I'd heard they have one pub on the Island. So after clearing it with the Captain to pop ashore for a few hours I linked up with a couple of my mates onboard ready to hit the local brew and probably get a souvenir (as it happens it ended up being a lump of Falklands' heather!) Jerry, John the Doc and I plus a couple of other shipmates managed to get on the third boat going ashore from the ship. As expected it was a bitterly cold day with strong icy winds from all directions and this was made more miserable by the freezing sea spray as we chug, chugged heading inland bouncing over the choppy sea waves in San Carlos Sound. I'd come fully prepared for this kind of weather and had put on two heavy Navy jumpers, foul weather jacket, woolly hat to cover my ears, two pairs of heavy woollen socks and a pair of hiking boots and, to finish off, two thick pairs of thermal trousers and gloves. I was so pleased that I dressed sensibly on this afternoon trip as the boat ride for the short journey ashore would have frozen even the most well insulated person from the cold climate. After trudging across some wasteland where we were dropped off we ended up on one of the main Falklands' roads. We guessed that the main Falklands' town would be about half a mile away and even though I was wearing about two stone of extra clothing I was still shivering with this bloody cold wind. It was freezing. I wondered if this really was worth all the bother but soon put this at the back of my mind as the pot of gold at the end of this was to get to this one and only "grog" house so as to down a few jars of ale and a few shots of grog! No sooner had these thoughts gone through my mind when this tremendous loud engine noise came rocketing down the road from behind us. As it got nearer it was discovered that the culprit was a large Army six-ton armoured lorry. We were, I suppose, in a group of about eight and no sooner had it spotted us than it gradually came to a halt. The driver and his passenger cheerfully shouted to us, "Come on lads, hop in, we'll give you a lift to Stanley." This was absolute music to my ears to be able to clamber onboard for at least some kind of shelter out of this wind. I must have managed to get probably the best possible spot in this truck because being a seven and a half stone nothing I ended up squeezed in right on top of the gear lever box cover and this was absolute bliss because it was throwing out so much heat it warmed my frozen bones up in seconds. When we arrived in Stanley ten minutes later not only did I have a bit of a glow on but I was as warm as toast. I'll never forget how much I really appreciated that very short journey by the Army giving us a lift. We certainly all very much appreciated them taking the trouble to help us get into town.

The mere fact we had been granted permission to have shore leave on the Falkland Islands at this stage was indeed an honour in itself as previously this was refused by the Land Forces Superiors as there was still so much confusion and disorder in the area and it was first thought that the last thing everyone wanted was hordes of British matelots tramping all over the place on a tourist trip. But this obstacle was soon put to one side and they backed down to our request as it would only be for a few hours if only just to stretch our legs to be on land for a while. As it turned out everything went fine and we weren't a hindrance to anyone.

There had been a very strong rumour or buzz on the ship that Port Stanley Post Office had a certain number of First Day Issue Covers of stamps to mark the twenty-first birthday of the Princess of Wales on July the first. (Princess Diana). Another issue also released was of the Prince and Princess of Wales leaving St Paul's Cathedral after their marriage, so the first priority before we frequented the grog house was to visit the local Post Office and chance getting hold of a set of these First Day Issues. As luck had it we all came out with a couple of stamps to commemorate this Issue as they had plenty in stock to sell. After bidding farewell to the Postmistress and Postmaster for the Falklands we decided to take a short (very short) tour of the Island to meet some of the local inhabitants. So armed with our cameras we headed out just to the outskirts of town but, more importantly, before we did the whereabouts of the local pub had to be established for our return, which was very soon sorted out by the first of the local community we came across, who were only too happy to point us in the right direction.

Two things I had in mind to achieve before I left these Islands and that was to bring back a little bit of the Falklands' heather for my diary and the other was to get a couple of photos of the very much talked about inhabitants: the penguins. Apparently these flightless birds are so noisy you don't have to go stalking them, they're more than likely to be stalking you just to find out who the hell you are on their Island. Needless to say it didn't take me long to get a couple of camera shots of these more than obliging seabirds scattered over the Island. The local people on the Island make most of their living in the Sheep Farming Industry with a small per cent in the local Fishery Trade. The Falklanders are a very friendly kind of people and although we might have just liberated the Island we were very conscious not to invade their privacy more than we had to. It was quite clear that only a few months ago this was a quiet running community minding their own business when suddenly hell lets loose and their life turned completely upside down with the invasion of thousands upon thousands of hostile Troops and equipment and their livelihood was immediately threatened. It must be and still must be very, very traumatic to say the least. This of course will never be the same again for them as to what their previous life was before and never will as from now on Britain will ensure a stronger military presence will be in occupation in the future on these Islands. So before heading back to the Island's main town with my pictures taken and the clump of heather carefully packed in my backpack, we merrily headed for the pub.

Although our First Day Issue Stamps should have been issued on the first of July we did manage to get them stamped or franked for that day. Although it was Sunday 27th June the Post Office was open and so we were very fortunate on both accounts.

Our Liberty Boat back to the ship was due to leave in two hours time at 18:00hrs. Ship's leave had been granted until

23:59hrs but for everyone to have a fair chance of setting foot on Falkland's soil it was only fitting for us to have only a few hours each so we could go back and let the other crew members have a chance to stretch their legs. So after a pint or twenty our party headed back to the berthing point where we were dropped off by Broadsword's ship's boats. It was an absolute pleasure not only to have the chance of getting ashore but it was so rewarding to have been able to talk and share stories with the Falklanders and to find out how things are done out in those very windy and cold islands we call the Falklands, six thousand miles from Britain in the South Atlantic.

With the whole ship's company now back onboard by midnight, we upped anchor shortly afterwards and on the first of July we were alongside the RFA Fort Grace to return the majority of live ammunition and to get more provisions and stores for the ship. The war may have been over as far as Britain was concerned but there was still a tremendous amount of work to be done both on sea and on land before we could think about being able to return to the UK. A few of the signals I'd managed to get from my fellow members of the ship's company came mainly from the Radio Operators in the Main Communications Office (MCO) who I'm sure would get into trouble if the Ship's Communications Officer (SCO) was to find out most of the duplicate signals were being passed under the Captain's Pantry Door solely for me to log into my day-to-day diary. Once the ship's company knew I was religiously doing this diary of events I had no end of information, snippets and pictures for me to make this into a proper exciting and enjoyable book. So really credit must go to the ship's company from every branch on board in the making of this book and of course not forgetting our Royal Marine Detachment, led by Bill Leslie their Sergeant, as they were and had been with the ship the whole time since we set sail in March from Plymouth.

"Up the Royals."

The threat may have been over for now but it was still vitally important we hold a strong military presence around the Falklands. We were to remain there for a couple more weeks and again when ready we would probably sail in company with HMS Hermes. At the time we were giving our full support to the Land Forces and to the civilians at Port Stanley and the surrounding islands. The only thing to do was to wait and be patient for the command for us to finally return home.

On the twenty-fifth of June (Friday) at 13:15hrs HMS Hermes anchored in Port Stanley alongside our Hospital Ship, the SS Uganda. An honorary fly past was performed by twelve Sea King helicopters and no less than fourteen Sea Harriers. On Sunday 27th June we sailed out of San Carlos waters and away from the Falkland Islands for the last time and headed out to sea to rejoin, once again, the Main Carrier Group.

We were at sea for at least one week and on the fourth of July the Captain was requested to lunch on the Guided Missile Destroyer HMS Bristol with the newly appointed

Admiral for Flag Officer Flotilla 3 who had now relieved Rear Admiral Sandy Woodward.

We received a signal for the first time from our new Admiral which read:

Signal: From C.T.G. (Commander Task Group 317.8 (F.O.F.3))

Message:

> HMS Broadsword take charge of HMS Hermes and proceed as previously directed (HOME).
>
> - : Admiral Flag Officer Flotilla 3
>
> - : END OF MESSAGE

Well, you can't get more of a clearer order than that – there's our green light to up sails and steam home.

THE SHIP NOW SETS A COURSE FOR HOME! AS ORDERED

Our first casualty of war in the Task Group.

History of the Falkland Islands

The **Falkland Islands**, also called *The Malvinas*, are an archipelago in the South Atlantic Ocean, located 300 miles (483 kilometres) from the coast of South America, 671 miles (1080 km) west of South Georgia's Shag Rocks, and 584 miles (940 km) north of Antarctica (Elephant Island).

They consist of two main islands, East Falkland and West Falkland, together with about 700 smaller islands. Stanley, on East Falkland, is the capital and largest city. The islands are a self-governing Overseas Territory of the United Kingdom, but have been the subject of a claim to sovereignty by Argentina since the early years of Argentina's independence from Spain.

In 1982 the islands were invaded by Argentina, precipitating the two-month-long undeclared Falklands War between Argentina and the United Kingdom, which resulted in the defeat and withdrawal of Argentine forces. Since the war there has been strong economic growth in both fisheries and tourism. The inhabitants of the islands, who are of mainly Scottish descent, are British citizens, and support British sovereignty.

The Falkland Islands have had a complex history since their discovery, with France, Britain, Spain and Argentina all claiming possession and establishing as well as abandoning settlements on the islands. The Spanish government's claim was continued by Argentina after the latter's independence in 1816 and the independence war in 1817, until 1833 when the United Kingdom took control of the islands by force, following the destruction of the Argentine settlement at Puerto Soledad by the American sloop USS Lexington (December 28, 1831). Argentina has continued to claim sovereignty over the islands, and the dispute was used by the military junta dictatorship as a reason to invade and briefly occupy the islands before being defeated in the two-month-long undeclared Falklands War in 1982 by a United Kingdom task force which returned the islands to British control.

The islands were uninhabited when they were first discovered by European explorers. There is disputed evidence of prior settlement by humans, based on the existence of the Falkland Island fox, or Warrah, on the islands, as well as a scattering of undated artifacts including arrowheads and the remains of a canoe. It is thought this canid was brought to the island by humans, although it may have reached the islands by itself via a land bridge during the last ice age.

The first European explorer widely credited with sighting the islands is Sebald de Weert, a Dutch sailor, in 1600. Although several English and Spanish historians maintain their own explorers discovered the islands earlier, some older maps, particularly Dutch ones, used the name "Sebald Islands', after de Weert. However, the islands appear on numerous Spanish and other maps beginning in the 1520s.

In January 1690, English sailor John Strong, captain of the *Welfare*, was heading for Puerto Deseado (in Argentina), but driven off course by contrary winds, he reached the Sebald Islands instead and landed at Bold Cove. He sailed between the two principal islands and called the passage "Falkland Channel" (now Falkland Sound), after Anthony Cary, 5th Viscount Falkland (1659–1694), who as Commissioner of the Admiralty had financed the expedition and who later became First Lord of the Admiralty. From this body of water the island group later took its collective English name.

The first settlement on the Falkland Islands, called Port Saint Louis, was founded by the French navigator and military commander Louis Antoine de Bougainville in 1764 on Berkeley Sound, in present-day Port Louis, East Falkland.

Unaware of the French presence, in January 1765, English captain John Byron explored and claimed Saunders Island, at the western end of the group, where he named the harbour of Port Egmont, and sailed near other islands, which he also claimed for King George III of Great Britain. A British settlement was built at Port Egmont in 1766. Also in 1766, Spain acquired the French colony, and after assuming effective control in 1767, placed the islands under a governor subordinate to Buenos Aires. Spain attacked Port Egmont, ending the British presence there in 1770, but Britain returned in 1771 and remained until 1774. Upon her withdrawal in 1774 Britain left behind a plaque asserting her claims, and in 1790, Britain officially ceded control of the islands to Spain, and renounced any and all colonial ambitions in South America, and its adjacent islands, as part of the Nootka Convention. In addition, the Nootka Convention provided for equal British, Spanish, and US rights to fish the surrounding waters of, as well as land on and erect temporary buildings to aid in such fishing operations, in any territory south of parts already occupied by Spain – the Falkland Islands being one of them since

1770. From then on Spain ruled the islands unchallenged under the name "Islas Malvinas", maintaining a settlement ruled from Buenos Aires under the control of the Viceroyalty of the Rio de la Plata until 1811. On leaving in 1811, Spain, too, left behind a plaque asserting her claims.

When Argentina declared its independence from Spain in 1816, it laid claim to the islands according to the *uti possidetis* principle, as they had been under the administrative jurisdiction of the Viceroyalty of the Rio de la Plata. Following a proclamation of annexation in 1820, actual occupation began in 1826 with the foundation of a settlement and a penal colony. The settlement was destroyed by a United States warship in 1831 after the Argentinian governor of the islands, Luis Vernet, seized U.S. seal hunting ships during a dispute over fishing rights. They left behind escaped prisoners and pirates. In November 1832, Argentina sent another governor who was killed in a mutiny. In January 1833, British forces returned, took control, repatriated the remainder of the Argentine settlement, and began to repopulate the islands with British citizens.

Demographics

The population is 2,967 (July 2003 estimate), the majority of which are of British descent (approximately 70%). The native-born inhabitants call themselves "Islanders". Outsiders often call Islanders "Kelpers", from the kelp which grows profusely around the islands, but the name is no longer used in the Islands. Those people from the United Kingdom who have obtained Falkland Island status, became what are known locally as "belongers', or to mean the islands belonged to Great Britain. The great majority of islanders are of Scottish and Ulster Scots descent, although are considered English. However, a few Islanders are of French, Portuguese and Scandinavian descent. Some are the descendants of whalers who reached the Islands during the last two centuries. Furthermore there is a small minority of South American, mainly Chilean origin, and in more recent times many people from Saint Helena have also come to work in the Islands. The Falkland Islands have been a centre of English language learning for South Americans.

The main religion is Christianity. The main denominations are Church of England, Roman Catholicism, United Free Church, Evangelist Church, Jehovah's Witnesses, Lutheranism, and Seventh-day Adventism. The extra-provincial Anglican parish of the Falkland Islands is under the direct jurisdiction of the Archbishop of Canterbury. The Falkland Islands form an Apostolic Prefecture of the Catholic Church. There is a small Greek Orthodox church in the Islands due to the presence of Greek fishermen.

Politics

Executive authority is vested in the Queen and is exercised by the Governor on her behalf. The Governor is also responsible for the administration of South Georgia and the

South Sandwich Islands, as these islands have no native inhabitants. Defence and Foreign Affairs are the responsibility of the United Kingdom. The current Governor is Alan Huckle, appointed July 2006.

Under the constitution, the latest version of which came into force in 1985, there is an Executive Council and a Legislative Council. The Executive Council, which advises the Governor, is also chaired by the Governor. It consists of the Chief Executive, Financial Secretary and three Legislative Councillors, who are elected by the other Legislative Councillors. The Legislative Council consists of the Chief Executive, Financial Secretary and the eight Legislative Councillors, of whom five are elected from Stanley and three from Camp, for four year terms. It is presided over by the Speaker, currently Darwin Lewis Clifton.

The loss of the war against Britain over control of the islands led to the collapse of the Argentine military dictatorship in 1983. Disputes over control of the islands continue. In 2001, British Prime Minister Tony Blair became the first to visit Argentina since the war. On the 22nd anniversary of the war, Argentina's President Néstor Kirchner gave a speech insisting that the islands would once again be part of Argentina. Kirchner, campaigning for president in 2003, regarded the islands a top priority. In June 2003 the issue was brought before a United Nations committee, and attempts have been made to open talks with Britain to resolve the issue of the islands. As far as the Falkland Islands Government and people are concerned there is no issue to resolve. The Falkland Islanders themselves are almost entirely British and maintain their allegiance to the United Kingdom. (See also Sovereignty of the Falkland Islands.)

Falkland Islanders were granted full British citizenship from 1 January 1983 under the British Nationality (Falkland Islands) Act 1983.

Geography

The Falkland Islands comprise two main islands, East Falkland and West Falkland and about 700 small islands. The total land area is 4,700 square miles (12 173 km²), approximately the same area as Connecticut or Northern Ireland, and a coastline estimated at 800 miles (1288 km).

Much of the land is part of the two main islands separated by the Falkland Sound: East Falkland, home to the capital of Stanley and the majority of the population, and West Falkland. Both islands have mountain ranges, rising to 2,313 feet (705 m) at Mount Usborne on East Falkland. There are also some boggy plains, most notably Lafonia, the southern half of East Falkland. Virtually the entire area of the islands is used as pasture for sheep.

Smaller islands surround the main two. They include Barren Island, Beaver Island, Bleaker Island, Carcass Island, George Island, Keppel Island, Lively Island, New Island, Pebble Island, Saunders Island, Sealion Island, Speedwell Island, Staats Island, Weddell Island, West Point

Island. The Jason Islands lie to the north west of the main archipelago, and Beauchene Island some distance to its south. Speedwell Island and George Island are split from East Falkland by Engle Passage.

The islands claim a territorial sea of 12 nautical miles (22 km) and an exclusive fishing zone of 200 nautical miles (370 km), which has been a source of disagreement with Argentina.

The Falkland Islands have a cold marine climate with strong westerly winds. It is generally cloudy and humid; rain occurs on more than half the days in a typical year. Snow is rare, but can occur at almost any time of year. Islanders themselves talk about two main areas of the islands, namely Stanley and the rest, which they call "the Camp", from the Spanish *campo* ("countryside").

Economy

Sheep farming was formerly the main source of income for the islands, and still plays an important part with high quality wool exports going to the UK, but efforts to diversify introduced in 1984 have made fishing the largest part of the economy and brought increasing income from tourism. The government sale of fishing licences to foreign countries has brought in more than £40 million a year in revenues, and local fishing boats are also in operation. More than 75% of the fish taken are squid, and most exports are to Spain. Tourism has shown rapid growth, with more than 30,000 visitors in 2001. The islands have become a regular port of call for the growing market of cruise ships. Attractions include the scenery and wildlife conservation with penguins, seabirds, seals and sealions, and visits to battlefields, golf, fishing and wreck diving.

An agreement with Argentina has set the terms for exploitation of offshore resources including large oil reserves, but climatic conditions of the southern seas mean that exploitation will be difficult task, though economically viable, and the continuing sovereignty dispute with Argentina is hampering progress. Defence is provided by the UK and British military expenditure makes a significant contribution to the economy. The islands are self sufficient except for defence, exports account for more than £125 million a year.

The largest company in the islands used to be the Falkland Islands Company (FIC), a publicly quoted company on the London Stock Exchange and was responsible for the majority of the economic activity on the islands, though its farms were sold in 1991 to the Falkland Islands Government. The FIC now operates several retail outlets in Stanley and is involved in port services and shipping operation.

The currency in use is the Falkland Pound, which remains in parity with Pounds Sterling–sterling, both notes and coins, circulate interchangeably with the local currency. The Falkland Islands also mint their own coins, and issue stamps which forms a source of revenue from overseas collectors.

After receiving the Admiral's orders to proceed back to the UK were now heading North. As the days went by the change in the weather was considerably noticeable for the better as we steamed towards the Equator. The time was absolutely right to stow away all our arctic clothing and winter woollies which the cold and stormy conditions in the South demanded us to don. It was heavenly to witness the slow but gradual appearance of sun mats, lilos, beach towels and any other basic and moderate sun bathing items that might be used by the ship's crew. Needless to say the morale boosted up every day as we got nearer to home. By the fourteenth of July it had been well over a week from leaving the Falklands and on Thursday fifteenth we would be, as every sailor is well aware of the tradition, "CROSSING THE LINE". This means to say we would have reached the Equator and the temperature was scorching hot but with absolutely no complaints from the ship's company. Arrangements for the crossing of the line ceremony had been well prepared days before and every craft, boat, ship, dinghy, tanker – basically anything that floated – will have gone through a similar ceremony on their vessel or craft for this occasion.

After such a fun and glorious day had by all we merrily steamed towards Ascension Island with HMS Hermes and just off Ascension Island as we had no Tanker to refuel, the ship re-fuelled with our Carrier.

We took the opportunity whilst passing Ascension Island to take on the minimal basic stores before our final passage home via Gibraltar; this time to unload any non-essential live ammunition before finally setting sail to England. I think it was on passage between Ascension and Gibraltar that we did a farewell steampast to HMS Hermes who would head on back to Portsmouth but I think the steampast may have been between Gibraltar and the UK, I'm not sure.

Now with us on our "Jack Jones" Gibraltar was our final port of call before home, which would be in only a matter of days.

As clearly seen the steel plate Aft below the Flight Deck where the 1,000 pound entered the ship and ripped our helicopter in half.

And bounced over the side, hence again the newspaper headlines back home: "HMS Broadsword and the Bouncing Bomb."

Where this taxi suddenly appeared from I haven't the faintest idea. Perhaps the ship's Engineers are knocking them out in their Workshops. Anyhow I think I'll ask Tony if he knows where the driver is.

"Er, Tony. Could you ask the driver how much the fare to Guzz is?"

"Okay, Mate! I'll just go and have a word with him. He's in our Mess having a grog at the bar."

"Oh well! Perhaps it's better to leave him there for a day or two. Thanks anyway."

Only a few more days sailing before we finally docked in Plymouth on Friday 23rd July, so it was a good time to gather one's thoughts about just what had happened in the past few months since we sailed in March. Before anyone settled down to a relaxing few days there was a most important requirement from every member of the ship's company.

To make sure that every member of the crew managed to get their families and friends in the Royal Naval Dockyard procedures of security still had to be maintained throughout the Dockyards. Therefore the ship's Master-at-Arms had supplied every Mess throughout the whole ship, from the Captain to the most Junior Member, a list of personnel that were expecting their families and friends on our arrival, so as to approve clearance when they arrived at HMS Drake. There they would be looked after by a very organised and professional team specifically tasked to do just that for every ship's arrival from the Falklands. The Captain had already sent ahead a Liaison Team from our ship to team up with the shoreside team at HMS Drake in Plymouth. The message from our 1st LT via Daily Ship's Orders was made very clear that there would be absolutely no restrictions whatsoever on the amount of people that would be allowed into the Dockyards, but we must still submit all names for clearance. So when we finally got the list we had to append the names.

In the Petty Officers' Mess.

As there were no restrictions on the amount of guests we could invite along to see the ship come alongside my list was reaching to at least twenty-one. My list started with Ray and Pippa, my foster parents until I joined the Royal Navy at the age of fourteen/fifteen and their children, Debbie and Caroline but not unfortunately Simon who was still out in the Falklands with the Royal Marines. I hoped to meet up with Si later. Debbie's husband Robin and their children; then there's Ray's second wife Ann with Ann's daughter Helen; Caroline's husband Phil and Ray's brother Jack and his wife Sylvia and their son Malcolm, who was to keep my war anti-flash as a souvenir once we got alongside; then Bob and Norma my auntie and uncle, who travelled all the way from Saffron Walden in Essex with my three cousins Richard, Mandy and Mark. As I mentioned Mark was to join the Naval Fleet Air Arm a few years later. Mum (Hazel Ashley) came down from London with a friend and finally Tim and his wife Jill (Tim and I grew up together) and their children Suzanne and Emma Louise. So my party alone was going to mean for me a fantastic reunion. I knew each and every one I have just mentioned were all praying for my safe return and I love and respect them all.

The atmosphere and high spirits were at their highest possible level as you would expect on any Warship but very rarely would you get the morale this high in any other circumstances and it went up another notch as every day drew nearer.

While we still have a couple of days to go I just would like to reflect on two ships that come to my mind when I first joined the Royal Navy on the fifteenth of September

1969. Firstly a brief note and a few pictures of my first ship and shore base training establishment, HMS Ganges at Harwich.

My boy training started off in wooden huts and after about eight weeks we moved over to the main establishment where the real training took place for a further eight months (thirty bob a week was our initial payment – £1.50)

A bit before my time.

Royal Navy Training Establishment HMS Ganges.

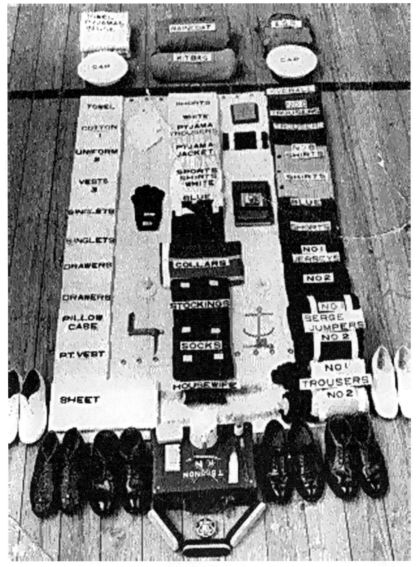

Kit Inspection.

My period of time entertaing the Royal Navy Mess Decks

Sunday afternoon was our only time away from the shouting and bullying from all our aggressive instructors. I

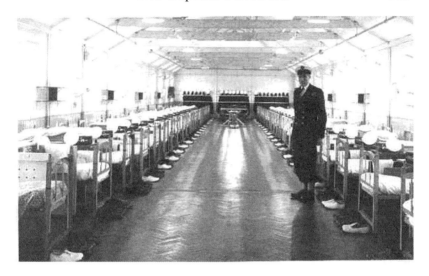

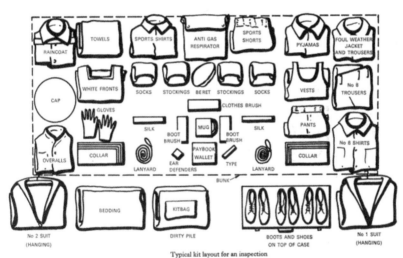

Kit layout from 1975 ratings manual.

suppose even their vocal cords needed a rest from the yelling and shouting they administered to us all – thankfully. Anyhow, whoever made the statement that the best time to test your courage and strength is in your early teens definitely wants his bloody head examined. As it turns out the Main Ganges Mast fascinated me as a challenge, so

one Sunday afternoon after sports I told a couple of classmates I was going to have a go for the top. About a dozen of them dutifully turned out to witness my challenge. I must have got about three-quarters of the way up this never-ending obstacle before I chickened out, obviously to the disgust of not only to my classmates but me especially. The next Sunday (only two observers this time) took me as far as half-way up to the top of the pole. Shaking like a leaf I came down again to the disappointment of my only two observers. I thought if I could get as far as this it will only take that little extra determination to reach my goal and get to the button at the top. When you climb this mast you are only allowed to be in sports gear and wearing plimsolls. The tradition every year, the manning of the mast, is done for the passing out ceremony and a button boy is always nominated to finally ascend to the top. Approach to the 11¾ standing disc at the tip while all the other members of the display man the rest of the rigging (lucky for them). This is all done in military precision to music. Although it had never been my intention to be in the forefront on the passing out parade as button boy I was absolutely determined to crack this challenge before I left training at HMS Ganges.

It must have been at least three weeks before I made another attempt, this time my audience was one. Again I reached the last haul to the twenty-foot pole at the top. You have to shin up with no supports whatsoever and if you were to fall at this stage basically that's your lot; you'd probably bounce off the nets and land twenty miles away in some field and never to be able to take up the challenge again. I reached the point of where I got last time and was determined more than ever to crack this bastard once and for all. My body was uncontrollably shaking more than I've ever, ever known but with my plimsolls firmly gripped around the pole and my sweating, trembling hands I went up another few agonising inches. "Come on, Barrie mate." I was saying to myself. "Just show these buggers down below you can do it." Another few inches literally put me in reaching distance of my final target. There was no question now of backing out of this – absolutely not.

I don't know what made me think of this at this crucial time but my thoughts went to the story we were all told weeks before and that was that apparently years ago some Leading Regulator (Naval Policeman) whose job was to run the shore establishment's Post Office came back off shore as drunk as a skunk late in the evening. Well we all know what drink does: of course it makes you more of a daredevil than ever. As the story goes the Leading Regulator decided what a hell of a good idea to show these raw recruits just how damn easy it is to climb a few poles with ropes attached. Give him his due he must have got a fair way up before he lost his balance and fell onto the safety nets dozens of feet below, then was catapulted into the air, probably higher than he had just fallen, where he was promptly killed outright, going through the roof of his own Post Office. Well at least he would have been at work on time if only in body and not in soul. I'm sure to gain access to your own place of work would have been easier by using the front door rather than crashing through the roof.

I was now scrambling onto the eleven and three-quarter inch steel white disc at the top in the middle of the button which I was completely unaware is a thin hooked thin metal bar. This is obviously to hold between your legs while you carry out the traditional act of saluting the four corners of Ganges. Although I'd now gripped this metal bar and managed to crawl on the button and was in a bent down position shaking like mad all over I finally managed to stand upright and slowly – very, very slowly – to turn myself to the four corners of Ganges, saluting every corner before I moved around on the button to the next corner. At the very top of this mast there is only one jackstay (fibre rope) which will take you all the way to the ground. Stretching out once my mission had been accomplished I grabbed the jackstay and wrapped my feet over the rope cross-legged and gracefully made my way to the bottom to be applauded by a dozen or so of my Shipmates who were hurriedly told that this time Barrie is going for it. I was as pleased as punch; I had finally made it on the third attempt. My foster parents, Mr John Vestey and his wife Winnie, who sad to say are now both deceased, said before I joined the Navy that there would be many bridges to cross in life, that is challenges and I of course thought the first would be here at Ganges. So this attempt of the mast was the first challenge at a mere fifteen years old, which put me in great stead for my future career. This definitely taught me my own strength and willpower of mind.

Uncle John and Auntie Winnie (as I always called them as foster parents) had always brought me up to be strong minded. Not only do I thank them for my childhood but I thank them for the life they gave me along with Pippa and Ray who took over the fostering responsibilities from when I was nine to when I joined the Navy. John and Win used to manage a children's home in Horsham near Reigate, Surrey in the fifties and early sixties; a place called "Kingesley Manor". Unfortunately it had to be closed down due to financial difficulties but when they moved on to Okley in Surrey, Tim, Trudy, Anne and I were fortunate enough to be in their charge. Trudy and Anne moved on to private schools and Tim and I started our primary days schooling in the early sixties. To this day I admire Ray and Pip for taking on the burden of us two as if they didn't have enough to do with four children of their own to bring up; Debbie, Caroline, Simon and then later Michael. We all still keep in touch, and I love them all.

I think out of the twenty-six people in our whole division only about four of us took up the challenge of actually reaching the very top. The picture of this mast is very deceiving as on the last twenty feet at the top, when you have to shin up the pole like a monkey, there are no supports whatsoever for you to grab hold of. Should you make a mistake it's the pole and you, nothing else for the twenty feet haul. That's actually where the challenge and willpower lies – there and there only. Mind you after I had saluted the four corners at Ganges it was a bit nerve-racking to pluck up the courage again to get hold of the jackstay and come down this one rope which when looking down, the ground seemed miles away – mission accomplished.

After leaving HMS Ganges I had a short training period in HMS Pembroke, the Stewards School in Chatham, Kent, then moved on to the Royal Naval Air Station in Portland, Dorset, HMS Osprey, when I was a Steward to a Captain and Mrs Morrison. From there I joined my first ever ship in the Navy and it wasn't a Warship it was "The Royal Yacht Britannia".

I remember joining the Royal Yacht Britannia in 1971 laden with my heavy long brown Naval issue sausage kitbag and my pussers' green suitcase. It was like walking the plank to get to her as you had to walk along about a dozen pontoons at Whale Island where she was moored, which is near the Gunnery School, HMS Excellent. This was a task in itself to get to the gangway; anyhow after being absolutely knackered I finally boarded her and settled in. After being used to a nice comfortable bed to sleep in shoreside it came as quite a shock to me, believe it or not, that I had for the first time ever to make up a hammock for a bed. This was never taught to me in Training and even though it was the Royal Yacht, in the early seventies very much still in use were hammocks for the Junior Crew Members and being sixteen you couldn't get much more Junior than me. It took me ages to work out how to string up this canvas bag of shit so it would hang and swing properly. Thankfully a few of the experienced crew members gave me a helping hand. A completely pitiful performance, but what a hell of a lot of aggro you have to put up with just to get your head down and if that wasn't bad enough I got an even bigger shock after being out on the town for the first time in Pompey with my new found Messmates. We had downed a grog or twenty which was great until 07:00hrs at "call the hands" and being turfed out of this swinging canvas bag of whatever with strings all over the place and told promptly by the Leading Hand to get it lashed up and stowed. This was a nightmare in itself, but to get this done, have a wash and shave, grab a bit of breakfast and then get into the proper dress of the day was virtually impossible. Obviously and not at all surprisingly I didn't make a very good impression when I had to report to the Chief Steward in the Wardroom half an hour late (not a good start!). As days passed on it wasn't hard to understand that it was much easier to put up the hammock before proceeding ashore than it was to stow it or, should I say, lash up and stow it the next morning. Anyhow, after about three weeks I got the hang (excuse the pun) of it.

Although I only stayed on the Royal Yacht Britannia for a few months I was itching to join a Royal Navy Warship and a few weeks later the orders came through for me to join the

Leander Class Frigate (F10) HMS Aurora. At the time this ship had become part of the Standing Naval Force North Atlantic Squadron (Stanaforlant) and the Commodore was no less than Commodore John Fieldhouse who later, ironically, became the Commander-in-Chief overseeing the Falklands conflict as our Top Admiral – Admiral Sir John Fieldhouse.

It still makes me laugh that when Commodore Fieldhouse visited my ship two years later on HMS Argonaut. He by this time had been promoted to Admiral in 1974 and I had been rated to Leading Steward to the Captain of Argonaut and as the Officers were all lined up in the Captain's and Officer's Flat ready to meet the Admiral, who came straight over to me and bellowed, "Well done, Fieldgate."

"Sorry, Sir?" was merely my reply. Again he bellowed, "Well done, looks like we've both been promoted."

A gesture like that one never forgets.

Finally what we'd all been waiting for was to be in the Plymouth Sound. It was nine thirty on Friday 23rd July and everyone was busily getting changed into their best uniform before we went alongside in Devonport, Plymouth to meet all our families. I don't think I need to elaborate on how the ship's company were feeling as we sailed up the Sound. There was talk we all might get a gong (medal) for this. Ah well if we do, it could keep my solitary one company; the one I have for long service. It can become its oppo rather than have me bouncing it up and down on my chest alone

Goalkeeping – Wessex Helicopter on scout patrol.

and when I clean them both in silver dip I might treat them occasionally and dip them in rum; that should keep "em merry.

It was so great to meet all my family and friends and everyone turned up that I mentioned previously. We had a great reunion together as did everyone else; it was a day to remember.

This is what is meant by goalkeeping, basically making sure no balls – sorry no bombs or missiles – get through the net to hit the Carrier.

Starboard Bofor practice shot, Mal Palin plugs his ears. Contributed by Sunset from the bridge of HMS Glamorgan outside San Carlos.
Emil Topping.

Bofor crew, San Carlos water, May 1982. Cpl Al Wimpenny in firing position, loader AB(M) Mac McArthur. Contributed by Darby Allen.

RAS with HMS Hermes. Contributed by Emil Topping.

Sunset from the bridge of HMS Glamorgan outside San Carlos.

Captain below decks with some of the crew members.

Our chiefs. Senior rates mess taken on the way back from the Falklands.

Members of the Supply Department. That's me in the front row and by the looks of it someone is doing his best to finish me off before we get to the Falklands!

Sgt W. J. Lesley.

*Back row: 'Jan' Yeo, 'Scobie' Beasley, Lt Cdr Bray, Chief Yeoman Barrie.
Middle row: Brian Halliwell, Darby Allen. Front row: Sam Morton, Tom
Newell, Keith Marsey, 'Hedge' Heighton. Photo Contributed by Darby Allen.*

The guns crew. Front MNE M. A. Elstow, MNE G. W. Morris (Mo).

Smile.

1st Lt Lt/Cdr Mowlam on the Bridge.

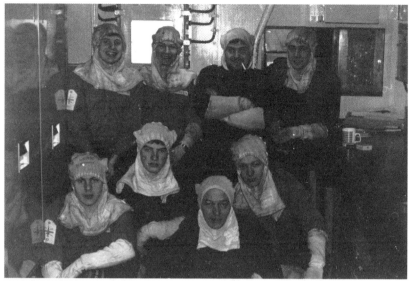

WEM(O) M. R. Palin (Mal), WEM(R) D. Webster (Spider), ?, WEA/A Davies (Nat), WEM(O) A. Bentham (George), WEM(O) A. W. Knight (Tony), ?, WEM(R) S. Hicks (Steve).

Taff Whitehouse and Droopy alias Kim Sadler. Contributed by Emil Topping.

Front: WEM(R) S. A. Caddick (Steve), WEA/A J. A. Foster (Foz) reading book, WEM(O) I. F. Forbes (Jock) hand on floor, WEM(O) M. R. Palin (Mal) waving.

WEM(R) D. Webster (Spider) – In action mode.

WEM(R) D. Webster (Spider) – Out of action mode.

WEM(O) Mal Palin.

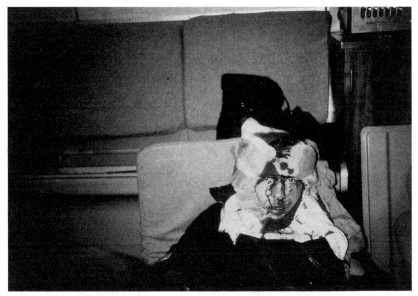

Our first casualty on HMS Broadsword. AEM(R) Chris Bill with a nasty looking head wound after the flight deck was hit. Photo courtesy of Chris Bill.

RO(T) Sam Morton next to 30mm shell hole in signalman's shelter. San Carlos water, May 1982. Contributed by Darby Allen.

*RP's Division, Chris Chapman and his merry men. Contributed by Emil
Topping.*

HMS Broadsword now in another Navy.

MEM(M) K. Lyon (Kev) front left.

Photo contributed by Emil Topping.

We're there somewhere! She can just be seen catching the sun as she comes round the corner.

White spray can be seen from the water cannons of the dockyard boats.

Heading for No. 3 wharfe.

Nearly there.

By now family and friends could be seen on the jetty.

Reverse a little. The patched up bomb hole can be seen here.

Guard rails down ready to receive the gangway.

We overshot by a few feet.

A few words from the Captain before everyone reunites.

Ship's company flow onto the jetty to meet family.

A tearful moment.

Chris Bill home at last. Contributed by Chris Bill.

Some damage down aft patched up. Picture courtesy Bill Oddy.

Bomb entry point picture taken alongside in Plymouth. Picture courtesy Bill Oddy.

Bomb exit point. Picture courtesy Bill Oddy.

Bullet holes aft under the flight deck. Picture courtesy Bill Oddy.

Epilogue

The human race somehow will always be at war with each other wherever in the World. They may start from a very trivial domestic disagreement and then escalate into a full scale war even World War. However it starts unfortunately there is always loss of life. The Falklands Disagreement had been going on since 1600 as the Chronicles of the Falklands show.

And finally just a brief note from our Commanding Officer whose comments on past Broadsword issues I've used.

In the Royal Navy there is one accolade for a ship which is prized by those who serve in her more than any other, that is that she is a happy ship. Throughout my time onboard this has applied to HMS BROADSWORD. Wherever we have been, whoever has visited us, the reaction has been the same; the ship's welcome has been warm and friendly, and there is an obvious team spirit.

It was this spirit that more than any other quality showed itself during Operation Corporate. Each worked for the other and together we worked for the common good of the Task Force. We have every right to be well satisfied and proud of what was achieved and our part in it.

Bill Canning

(Royal Navy Retd) Captain Bill Canning DSO MBE DL
Commanding Officer HMS Broadsword

Naval Terminology, Jargon and Slang

A

A4 Skyhawks	Argentinian aircraft
Abaft	Further aft, as "Abaft the beam".
Abeam	On a relative bearing of 90 degrees (abeam to starboard) or 270 degrees (abeam to port).
Aboard	In or on a ship. Extended to use ashore, as aboard a naval station.
Accommodation Ladder	A ladder suspended down the side of a ship to facilitate boarding the ship from boats.
Admiral	Derived its pronunciation from the term for a Moorish chief. A Moorish chief is an Emir, and chief of all chiefs is the EMIR-AL, from which we get our English word "Admiral".
Aermacchi	Argentinian aircraft
AFFF	Aquerous Film Forming Foam. A fire-fighting agent which is mixed

with water and sprayed on flammable liquid fires. Pronounced "A triple-F". Aka "Light Water" for the foam's ability to float on oil or gasoline. Replaced protein foam. Unlike blood-based protein foam, AFFF is self-healing, in that holes in the foam blanket will close by themselves, preventing reflash.

Aft

In, near or towards the stern of the ship

After

That which is farthest aft.

Afternoon Watch

The 12:00 to 16:00 watch.

AGR

Anti-Gas Respirator.

Ahoy

Ahoy or demand for attention as "Boat ahoy". This old traditional greeting for hailing other boats was originally a Viking battle-cry.

All Fast

Tied or lashed down as necessary.

Allotment

Assignment of part of military pay directly to a person or bank.

Aloft

Generally speaking, any area above the highest deck.

Alongside

Beside a pier, wharf or ship.

Amidships

An indefinite area midway between

the bow and the stern. Rudder amidships means that the rudder is in line with the ship's centreline.

Anti-Flash	Protective Gloves and Hood (White). Made of cotton.
Artificer	(RN) Engineering Technician.
ASAP	As soon as possible.
Astern	Directly behind a ship.
At Loggerheads	A serious difference of opinion. A Loggerhead is two iron balls attached by an iron rod, which was heated and used for melting pitch. Sailors sometimes used them as weapons to settle a grudge so that when fighting they were "at loggerheads".
Athwartships	Moving or placed from side to side aboard ship, or straddling a particular position. At right angles to the ship's centreline.

B

Ballast	Weight (solid or liquid) loaded into a ship to increase stability.
Banyan	A barbecue or party on the flight

deck, usually with steaks and beer. The term is derived from "banian", a garment worn by an East Indian sect which neither kills nor eats meat ("Banyan" is a species of tree). In the 18th century, the British navy denied its sailors meat on Mondays, Wednesdays, and Fridays; these days were known as "banian (or banyan) days". The term has now come to mean just the opposite.

Barge

An admiral's boat. A type of motor boat assigned for the personal use of a flag officer.

Barnacle

Small marine animal that attaches itself to hulls and pilings.

Batten

(1) A long strip of steel or wood that is wedged against the edge of tarpaulins or a hatch to make the hatch watertight; (2) removable wood or steel members used in a ship's holds to keep cargo from shifting.

Batten Down

The act of applying battens to a hatch; extended to mean the closing of any watertight fixture.

Beam	(1) The extreme breadth of a vessel; (2) a transverse frame supporting a deck.
Bearing	The direction of an object from an observer, measuring in degrees clockwise form a reference point. True bearing is the angular difference between lines drawn from the observer to true north and to the object; magnetic bearing is the direction of the object measured on a magnetic compass; relative bearing is the angle between the ship's head and the object.
Belay	To cancel an order; stop.
Bell-Bottom Trousers	A phrase that described the pants of sailors. Of all the reasons given for the extreme width of sailor's trousers at the bottoms, the obvious and practical one remains the best: they were easy to roll to the knees when the owner was swabbing decks.
Below	Below decks; below main deck.
Berth	Space assigned ship for anchoring or mooring.
Big-Wigs	This slang term for men in high

positions gathers its meaning from the fact that senior officers in the old British Navy, actually did wear huge wigs.

Bilge	(1) Bottom of the hull near the keel; (2) to fail an examination; (3) bilge water is foul water, so to apply the term to oral or written statements implies that the statement is worthless.
Billet	An allotted sleeping space; an individual's position in the ship's organisation.
Binnacle	A pedestal which supports a compass. Typically found next to or in front of the ship's wheel.
Board	(1) The act of going aboard a vessel; (2) a group of persons meeting for a specific purpose, as an investigation board.
Boat	A small craft capable of being carried aboard a ship. Or the common terminology for a submarine.
Boat Hook	A staff having a hook at one end. Used for feeding a boat off; hooking a line, and so on.

Boatswain	Pronounced "bosun", refers to the mate, warrant officer, or petty officer in charge of boats, rigging, and ground tackle aboard ship.
Boatswain's Chair	A seat attached to a gantline for hoisting a person aloft.
Boatswain's Locker	A compartment, usually forward, where line and other equipment used by the deck force are stowed.
Bofors	Guns
Bollard	A squat cylindrical fixture attached to a pier or quay, with small horizontal horns, which are used for tying off lines. Used to secure lines, such as mooring lines.
Boom	A spar used for hoisting loads; usually movable.
Bosun	The phonetic spelling of "boatswain".
Bo'sun's Pipe	A whistle used for passing orders on a ship, also called a Boatswain's Call before the 1900s. It can be traced back to the day of the Crusades, 1248 AD – whistle!
Bow	Front of ship (the pointed end).

Bravo Zulu	Phonetic pronunciation of "BZ" from the NATO signals codes. Signifies "Good job" or "Well Done".
Breakaway	The act of disconnecting from an UNREP ship and manoeuvring clear. Can be either a normal or emergency evolution, the difference being simply how quickly the various actions are accomplished.
Bridge	Platform or area from which ship is steered, navigated and conned; usually located in forward part of ship. Area in the superstructure from which a ship is operated.
Bronzy Bronzy	Sunbathe.
Brow	The proper term for what is often called the "gangway", the temporary bridge connecting the ship's quarterdeck to the pier.
Buffer	(UK) The senior rate responsible for seamanship evolutions, typically a Chief Boatswain's Mate.
Bulkhead	A naval wall.
Bullshit Artist	A glib person, or one who lies.
Bunting	Flags

Bulkhead	A vertical partition in a ship; never called a wall.
Bulwark	Solid barrier along the edge of weather decks.
Buoy	An anchored float used as an aid to navigation or to mark the location of an object.

C

CAP	Combat Air Patrol
CBM	Chief Bosun's Mate
CO	Commanding Officer.
Crusher	(RN) A member of the Regulating Branch, i.e. Naval
CORRO	Correspondence Officer
COST	Continuation of Sea Training
CPL	Corporal.
CPO	Abbreviation for Chief Petty Officer.
CTG	Commander Task Group
CTP	Cocktail Party (Drinks etc).
Cabin	Living compartment of a ship's commanding officer.

Cable	A line, wire, or chain that connects a ship to its anchor.
Call The Hands	Morning call for ship's crew.
Captain's Table	(RN) A disciplinary hearing or requestmen.
Chart	Nautical counterpart of a road-map, showing land configuration, water depths, and for navigation.
Chippy	Shipwright (carpenter etc).
Chits	The name "chit" for a note or voucher, was introduced into our language in the days of the East Indian Company.
Chuffed	(UK) Extremely pleased.
Civvies	Civilian Clothes.
Club Swinger	Physical Training Instructor (PTI).
Colours	National ensign; distinguishing flag flown to indicate a ship's nationality. Naval ceremonies are performed when national flag is hoisted at eight o'clock in the morning and hauled down at sunset.
Commission	To activate a ship or station; written order given to an officer rank or authority.

Commission Pennant	A long, narrow, striped pennant flown only aboard a commissioned ship.
Commissioning Ceremonies	Ceremonies during which a new ship is placed in service. It is customary to invite friends of officers and others interested to attend the ceremony, along with the sponsor who christened the ship.
Commodore	The officer rank above a Captain. This title arose from a practiced economy of the old Dutch Admiralty. In her war with England, Holland found herself short of admirals and distressingly short of cash. She solved her difficulty by creating a brand new rank of "Commodore" which carried with it all the responsibilities of an admiral, but only half his pay.
Companionway	Deck opening giving access to a ladder (includes the ladder).
Compartment	Interior space (room) of a ship. Spaced enclosed by bulkheads, deck and overhead, same as a room in a building.
Course	A ship's direction of travel, not to be

confused with healing, which is the direction in which the bow is pointed at any given instant.

Court-Martial — Military court for trial of serious offences (summary, special, and general court-martial).

Crossing The Line — The traditional ritual, now introducing the greenhorn to King Neptune in fun and merriment; originally was a very serious procedure among the Vikings, and was practiced with all kinds of severe tests to see if the novice could really stand the hardships of the ocean.

D

DC — Damage Control.

DMEO — Deputy Marine Engineering Officer.

DOs — Divisional Officers.

DPO — Duty Petty Officer.

DSO — Deputy Supply Officer.

DWEO — Deploy Weapons Electrical Officer.

Daggers — Argentinian aircraft.

Darken Ship	To turn off all external lights and close all openings through which lights could be seen from the outside of the ship.
Dead Ahead	Directly ahead; a relative bearing of 000 degrees. Dead astern is 180 degrees relative.
Dead Reckoning	This navigation term was originally spelled "ded" (the abbreviation for deduced) reckoning. An unscholarly British shipmaster thought the "a" had been omitted, so he inserted it. Ever since then, even the officially printed forms spell it "dead" reckoning.
Deadlight	A glass window set in the deck or bulkhead.
Deck	What the civilian calls a floor.
Deckhead	Roof.
Deploy	Tactical term used for dispersal of troops; also disposition of ships in battle formations. Also in peacetime for a ship to go on deployment.
Dhobi	Laundry.
Dhobi Dust	Washing Powder.

Dinghy

This name for a ship's smallest boat, usually made of rubber.

Distance Line

A line stretched between two ships engaged in replenished or transfer operation underway. The line is marked at twenty foot intervals to aid the conning officer in maintaining station.

Division

In the organisation of ship or plane groups, the unit between sections and squadrons; in shipboard organisations, sailors and officers grouped together for command purposes; a component group of a department.

Dog Watch

This name for the split watch between the hours of four to six, and six to eight p.m., was originally "Dodge Watch", as it allowed seamen to escape (or dodge) standing the same watch every day of the voyage. As time went on, the names gradually corrupted to the present "Dog Watch". (16.00hrs to 18.00hrs – 18.00hrs to 20.00hrs

Dog Watches

The 16:00 to 18:00 to 20:00 watches.

Double Up	To double mooring lines for extra strength.
Draft	The vertical distance from the keel to the waterline.
Drip	(RN) Complain.
Drunkex	Any evolution characterised more by the amount of alcohol consumption than by accomplishment of any goals (other than getting toasted, of course).
Drydock	A dock from which the water may be removed for the purpose of inspecting or working on a ship's bottom; it may be either floating or built into a shore.
Dusty	(RN) Stores rating, especially one concerned with food. More fully "Jack Dusty". "Jack o' the Dust". In its original usage, the "Dusty" was a sailor (Jack, in British naval terminology) assigned responsibility for the bread room, where flour was stowed.

E

EOT	Emergency Operating Theatre.

ETA	Estimated Time of Arrival.
ETD	Estimated Time of Departure.
Ease	To relax; to slack.
Eight Bells	This measure of time originated in the days when a half-hour glass was used to tell off the four-hour watches. Each time the sand ran out, the ship's boy, whose job it was to reverse the glass, struck a bell to show he was attending to his business. Thus, eight times he turned the glass, and eight times struck the bell.
Embark	To go aboard ship preparatory to sailing.
Engine Order Telegraph	Electromechanical device that transmits orders to the engine room concerning desired direction of turn and general speed of the engines.
Ensign	(1) The national flag; (2) the lowest grade of a commissioned officer.
Executive Officer (XO)	Regardless of rank, the officer second in command of a ship, squadron or shore activity. In early days, such an officer was the first Lieutenant.

Exocet	Missile.

F

FC	Flight Commander.
FOG	Flag Officer Gibraltar.
FOST	Flag Officer Sea Training.
FWD	Forward of ship.
Fanny	(UK) A Mess tin. Named for Fanny Adams, a girl who was murdered and dismembered about the same time that tinned meat was introduced into the Royal Navy.
Fender	A cushioning device hung over the side of a ship to prevent contact between ship and a pier or another ship.
Firemain	Piping systems to which fire hydrants are connected.
First Watch	The 20:00 to 24:00 watch (also evening watch).
Flag	An Admiral, aka "Flag Officer" because such officers are entitled to fly a flag denoting their rank.
Flag At Half-Mast	Begun in times of mourning in old

sailing days, indicated that grief was so great it was impossible to keep things shipshape. Half-masting of colours is the survival from days when slack appearance characterised mourning on shipboard.

Flag Officer — Rear Admiral, Lower Half; Rear Admiral, Upper Half; Vice Admiral, Admiral, and Fleet Admiral are flag officers.

Flagstaff — Vertical staff at the stern to which the ensign is hoisted when moored or at anchor.

Fleet — An organisation of ships, aircrafts, marine forces, and shore based fleet activities, all under one commander, for the purpose of conducting major operations.

Flight Deck — Deck of ship on which planes land and take off.

Flood — (1) To fill a space with water; (2) a rising tide.

Flotsam — Floating wreckage released from a sunken ship.

Flunky — Steward.

Foc'sle — Forecastle (Front of ship).

Fore	Forward.
Fore and Aft	The entire length of a ship, as in "Sweep down fore and aft".
Foremast	First mast aft from the bow.
Forenoon Watch	The 08:00 to 12:00 watch.
Foul	(1) Entangled, as "The lines are foul of each other"; (2) stormy weather.
Four-ringer	(RN) Captain.
Fox Oscar	Fuck Off.

G

GDP	Gunnery Direction Post.
GIB	Gibraltar.
GO	Gunnery Officer.
GPMG	General Purpose Machine Gun.
Galley	Space where food is prepared. Never called a kitchen.
	The most logical explanation for ship's kitchens being called galleys, is the one which maintains the word is corruption of "galley". Ancient

mariners cooked their simple meals on a brick or stone galley laid amidships.

Gangway	(1) The opening in a bulwark or lifeline to provide access to a brow or accommodation ladder; today, more properly called a "brow", the temporary bridge connecting the ship's quarterdeck to the pier. (2) given as an order, it means "Clear the way". Originated as a call for junior personnel to give precedence to a senior while crossing the gangway.
Gash	Garbage or rubbish. Also used to refer to any unwanted items.
Gemini	Rubber Motor Dingy.
Goffa	Any non-alcoholic drink (why bother?).
Goffer	A large wave. Usually shouted as a warning.
Gong	Medal.
Gopping	(RN) Awful, horrible.
Granny Knot	A bungled square knot.

Greenie	(RN) (1) Electrician. (2) Weapons Electrical Branch.
Grog (Now we're talking!)	(UK) Pusser's rum mixed with two parts water. So called from the name of the officer that regularised the issue of watered rum aboard British .ships. Admiral Vernon was referred to as "Old Grog" for his habit of wearing overcoats of a material called grogram.

H

HQ1	Headquarters.
Hammock	Canvas Bed
Hand	A ship's crew member.
Hatch	A square or rectangular access in a deck.
Hatch	An opening in the deck, and its closure. Sometimes (incorrectly) used to mean a watertight door, which is mounted vertically in a bulkhead.
Haul	To pull on or heave on a line by hand.
Heads	Toilets.

Heave In	Take in line or cable.
Heave To	In a sailing ship, to come into the wind and essentially stop, with minimum sail area exposed. Used to wait out a squall or storm.
Heaving Line	A line with a weight at one end, heaved across an intervening space for the purpose of passing over a heavier line.
Helm	Mechanical device used to turn the rudder; usually a wheel aboard ship, a lever in boats.
Hooky	(RN) Leading rate. So called from the fouled anchor rate badge.
Hot Rack (or Rack)	Sharing of beds due to a lack of living space aboard ship.

I

Illuminated Round	Star shell.
Inboard	Toward the centreline.
Inlet	A narrow strip of sea extending into the land.

J

Jack	Starred blue flag (representing the union of the ensign) flown at the jackstay of a commissioned ship not underway.
Jack	(UK) (1) General nickname for Royal Navy sailors, (obsolete from "Jack Tar"). (2) The Union Jack, a small flag flown from the jackstaff on the bow of naval warships.
Jack Dusty	Storeman.
Jack Tar	International nickname for government sailors, because of the custom among old Navy men of giving their work clothes a light coating of tar to waterproof them.
Jackstaff	Vertical spar at the stem on which the jack is hoisted.
Jackstay	Any horizontal line or wire.
Jacob's Ladder	A portable rope or wire ladder.
Jetty	A structure built out from shore to influence water current or to protect a harbour or pier.

Jimmy, Jimmy the
  One
(RN) First Lieutenant of a ship.

Jolly Roger
Banner showing skull and crossbones, the royal standard of His Imperial Majesty Neptunis Rex.

Joss, Jossman
(RN) Master at Arms. The "Fleet Joss" was the Fleet Chief Petty Officer Master at Arms.

Jump Ship
The act of deserting a ship.

Junta
Argentinian Military Regime.

K

Keel
The lowermost longitudinal strength members from which the frames and plating rise.

Keelhaul
Ancient form of punishment from the days of sail, in which a sailor was thrown overboard and dragged under the ship to the order side with a line. Usually fatal, and if not, then causing serious injury due to the barnacles and other hard objects encrusting the hull.

Keel-hauling was a brutal punishment inflicted on seamen

guilty of mutiny or some other high crime in the "good old days" of sail. It practically amounted to a death sentence, for the chances of recovery after the ordeal were slight. The culprit was fastened to a line which had been passed beneath the vessel's keel. He was then dragged under the water on the starboard side of the ships, hauled along the barnacle-encrusted bottom and hoisted up onto the deck on the port side. If the barnacles didn't cut him to pieces, and if he hadn't been drowned in the process or the operations, he was considered to have paid for his crime and was free.

Killick

(RN) Leading rate. Often used with the branch name or nickname.

King Neptune

The mythological God of the Sea. He always presides, with his court, at the line-crossing ceremony.

Knock Off

Cease what is being done; stop working. Quit working.

Knot

(1) A Method of forming an eye in a line, or of typing the line to or around something; (2) a speed term that means nautical miles per hour.

A measure of speed, equating to one nautical mile per hour. "Knots per hour" is incorrect usage.

Measure of speed of ships and aircraft as "the destroyer was making 30 knots" or "top speed of the plant is 400 knots". To ascertain the speed of his vessel, a British commander had knots tied at regular intervals in a coil of rope. The rope was then tied onto a log and the log heaved overboard. With an hour-glass, he timed each knot as it disappeared over the taffrail thus originating the custom of telling a ship's speed by knots instead of miles.

L

LHOM	Leading Hand in Charge of Messroom.
Ladder	Stairs aboard ship. Found in a "ladderwell" (stairwell).
Landing Craft	Vessel especially designed for landing troops and equipment directly on a beach.
Lanyard	(1) Any short line used as a handle

or as a means for operating some piece of equipment; (2) a line used to attach an article to the person, as a pistol lanyard.

Lash

To secure an object by turns of line, wire, or chain.

Lash Down

Tie all moving objects and secure.

Lashing

Line, wire, or chain used to lash an article.

Launch

(1) To float a vessel off the ways in a building yard; (2) a powerboat, usually over 30 feet long.

Liberty

Authorised absence of individual from place of duty, not chargeable as leave. No period of liberty shall exceed four days.

Liberty Boat

Various small craft used to shuttle personnel ashore and back aboard when the ship is anchored out rather than moored alongside. May be operated by a civilian contractor or by ship's personnel.

Limey

Because it was practically impossible to carry fresh fruits and vegetables on long voyages years ago, British Parliament decreed that

	each sailor must drink a pint of lime juice daily as a preventative against scurvy. Thus came the nickname for British ships, and Britishers in general, hence the word Limey
Log	(1) A ship's speedometer; (2) the act of a ship in making certain speed, as "The ship logged 20 knots"; (3) book or ledger in which data or events that occurred during a watch are recorded.
Log Book	As early ship's records were inscribed on shingles (cut from logs) and hinged so that they opened like a book, the name "Log-book" was logical and lasts to this day.
Look Alive	Admonishment meaning be alert or move fast.
Lookout	Person stationed topside as a formal watch. Reports all objects sighted and sound heard to the OOW.
	Seaman assigned to watch and report any objects of interest; lookouts are "the eyes of the ship".
Lower Deck Lawyer	(UK) A know-it-all sailor.

M

MAA	Master at Arms.
MEO	Marine Engineering Officer.
MNE (RM)	Royal Marine. (Royals)
Magazine	Compartment used for the stowage of ammunition.
Main Control	The engineering space from which the operations of the engineering spaces are controlled. Watchstation of the EOOW (Engineering Officer of the Watch).
Main Deck	The uppermost complete deck.
Main Drag	Main passageway.
Main Space	Engine room or fire room or, collectively, both/all.
Mainmast	Second mast aft form the deck.
Make and Mend	Originally, a half-day off from normal ship's work to make and/or mend clothing.
Make Fast	To tie off (a line) securely.
Make Way	(1) From the Rules of the Nautical Road, when a ship is making way she is proceeding under her own power, whether by engine or sail (or

oars, for that matter). Often confused with UNDER WAY (q.v.); a ship which is adrift (not under power or sail) is under way, but not making way, even though she may be moving with respect to the seabed due to wind and current effects. (2) A command to get out of the way.

Master at Arms   A member of the ship's naval police force. Usually the senior NCO)

Masthead Light   A twenty point white running light located in the fore part of the ship. May or may not be on the foremast.

Mate   A shipmate, another sailor.

Matelot   (RN) A sailor. Actually, the word is French and means, literally, sailor. The reason sailors are referred to as matelots. Pronounced to rhyme with "glow".

Mayday   Distress call via radio, anglicised from the French *M'aidez* (help me).

Memo   Memorandum.

Mess   (1) Meal; (2) place where meals are eaten, as, mess hall; (3) a group that takes meals together, as the officer's mess.

Mess Cooks	Persons for the day to clean Messdeck.
Messdecks	Crew's eating area.
Midwatch	The watch that begins at 00:00 and ends at 04:00.
Midwatch	A watch stood from midnight 24:00 until 04:00. Aka "Midbitch", "Midshitter", "Balls to Four".
MOD	Ministry of Defence.
Mooring Line	Lines used to tie the ship to the pier or to another ship. Mooring lines are numbered from forward aft; the direction they tend (lead) is also sometimes given. 'Number one mooring line' typically is made fast at the bow, and tends straight across to the pier or other ship. Spring lines tend forward or aft of their attachment point.
Morning Watch	The 04:00 to 08:00 watch.
Muster	To assemble crew.

N

NAAFI	(RN) Navy, Army, and Air Force Institute. Provides canteens, shops,

	and other services to the armed forces ashore and afloat.
NAS	Naval Air Station.
NBC Warfare	Nuclear/Biological/Chemical Warfare.
NCO	Non Commissioned Officer.
NGS	Night Gun Support.
NO	Navigating Officer.
Navigator	Officer responsible, under the captain, for safe navigation of the ship.
Neptune	King Neptune, Neptunis Rex.
No Joy	No radio contact, or no visual contact. Sometimes used to say "it didn't work".
Number 8s	(RN) Action working dress.
Nutty	Sweets, chocolate, etc.

O

OOD	Officer of the day.
2nd OOD	Second Officer of the day.
OOW	Officer of the watch.

2nd OOW	Second Officer of the watch.
Ops Rm	Operations Room.
Oak Leaves	Oak leaves are used in insignia as a tribute to the memory of the staunch ships of oak in the good old days of sail.
Offshore	Some distance off the shore, as contrasted to inshore.
Oilskins	Garments made from cloth which has been made water-resistant by impregnating it with linseed oil.
Old Man	Seaman's term for captain of a ship.
Oppo	(RN) Friend.
Opposite Number	(RN) (1) Anyone carrying out comparable or equivalent duties on another watch.
Oscar	(1) The dummy used for man overboard drills. (2) The international signal flag hoisted for "man overboard". (3) Phonetic alphabet for "O".
Overboard	Over the side.
Overhaul	(1) To repair or recondition; (2) to overtake another vessel.

Overhead	The underside of a deck forms the overhead of the compartment next below. Never called a ceiling.
Overheads	Ceilings.

P

PO	Petty Officer.
PTI	Physical Training Instructor.
PWO	Principle Warfare Officer.
Party	A group having a common temporary assignment or purpose, as working party, line handling party, liberty party.
Passageway	A hallway aboard ship.
Passageway	A corridor used for interior horizontal movement aboard ship. A hallway on ship.
Pay Out	To feed out, or lengthen, a line.
Pier	Structure extending from land out into the water to provide a mooring for vessels.
Pilot	(RN) The navigating officer.

Pinkers	(UK) Gin or gin and water/tonic to which has been added angostura bitters.
Pipe	The act of sounding a particular call on the boatswain's pipe.
Pipe Down	Originally, a call on a boatswain's whistle sending the crew below. It has come to mean "be quiet". Lights out.
Piping Aboard	A ceremony where the arrival of a senior officer is signified by the blowing of a bosun's whistle.
Piping Hot	Originally, meals were announced aboard ship by piping (blowing a call on the boatswain's pipe). If a meal is piping hot, it has just been served and is therefore hot.
Pongo	(RN) Soldier. May be mistakenly used to refer to a Royal Marine.
Poop Deck	A ship's afterdeck received its name from the old Roman custom of carrying Pupi (small images of their gods) in the stern of their ships for luck.
Port	To the left of the centreline when facing forward.

| Port and Starboard | (1) Watch schedule where one stands six (or four to eight) hours on, the same amount of time off watch, then back on watch. Aka "Port and Stupid". (2) Before ships had rudders they were steered by an oar which was positioned on the quarter. This side was known as the "steer board side" which, over time, was corrupted in "starboard side". For a long time, the other side of a ship was known as the "larboard" side, even into the 1700s. This led to confusion and difficulty in giving orders during storms, etc., where it might be easily confused between starboard and larboard. Since the larboard side was also the side of the vessel which was placed against a pier or dock, it become known as the "port" side, i.e. when you went into port, that side of the ship was against the pier. |
| Portholes | Port holes were originally gun ports. In early days, no provision whatever was made for admitting air or light into the crew's quarters, which remained foul and gloomy until recent times. |

Pot Mess	Stew.
Pusser, pussers	(RN) (1) Supply Officer. (2) Anyone who goes "by the book". (3) Of or belonging to the Royal Navy. The term is a corruption of "Purser".

Q

Quarter	Area between dead astern and either beam.
Quarterdeck	Deck area designated by the commanding officer as the place to carry out official functions; station of the OOD in port.
	Part of the main (or other) deck reserved for honours and ceremonies and the station of the OOD. The quarter-deck received its name in the days when decks were in tiers. The "half-deck" was half the length of the ship, and the "quarter-deck" was half the length of the half-deck.

R

RAS	Refuel at Sea.
RFA	Royal Fleet Auxiliary.

RPO	(RN) Regulating Petty Officer.
Rabbits	(RN) Souvenirs.
Radar	A device that used reflected radio waves for detection of objects.
Range	(1) The device that uses an object from an observer; (2) an aid to navigator consisting of two objects in line; (3) a water area designated for a particular purpose, as a gunnery range.
Rank	Grade or official standing of commissioned and warrant officers.
Rattle (in the)	(RN) In official trouble, or report.
Rear Admiral	The title of Rear Admiral was first given to divisional commanders of reserve fleets hence, the inference of being in Reserve, or "In the Rear".
Reef	An underwater ledge rising abruptly from the ocean's floor.
Reflash	The re-ignition of a fire, generally due to hot spots.
Relief	Person assigned to assume the duties of another.
Relieve	(1) To take the place of another; (2) to ease the strain on a line.

Riser	A pipe leading from the fireman to fireplugs on upper deck levels.
Rock Apes	Gibraltar Monkeys.
Rogue's Gun (or salute)	(UK) The single gun salute fired at the commencement of a court martial.
Roll	Dynamic movement of a ship or aircraft about the lateral axis, i.e. a tilting of the deck from side to side.
Rope	General term applied to both fibre and wire rope. Fibre rope usually is referred to as line; wire rope, wire rope or just wire.
	Natural or synthetic, woven, braided or twisted (or some combination), it is called "rope" as long as it is on the spool. As soon as you unroll a piece and cut it off, it becomes "line".
Royal Marine	(RN) British Marine. "Her Majesty's Royal Marines".
Royals	Royal Marines.
Run Ashore	Leave the ship for a night out.

S

SA80	Self Automatic Riffle.

SAS	Special Air Service.
SBS	Special Boat Service.
SCO	Ship's Communications Officer.
SGT	Sergeant.
SMEO	Squadron Marine Engineering Officer.
SMG	Sub Machine Gun.
SNO	Squadron Navigating Officer.
SO	Supply Officer.
SOP	Standard Operating Procedure.
SSO	Squadron Supply Officer.
SWEO	Squadron Weapons Electrical Officer.
SWO	Surface Warfare Officer.
Sack	Bunk.
Salvo	One or more guns fired together, or the shells which have been fired.
Salty	One whose level of experience is extreme. One who is "in the know" regarding matters maritime.
Scrambled Egg	The gold braid found on the cap brim of a senior officer.

Scran	Food, meals, etc.
Scribes	Writer.
Scupper	The waterway along the gunwales.
Scuttle	(1) Round, watertight opening in a hatch; (2) the act of deliberately sinking a vessel; (3) To punch a hole in something.
Sea Anchor	A device streamed from the bow of a vessel for the purpose of holding the vessel in the sea.
Sea Daddy	Someone who takes a less-experienced crewmember under his or her wing.
Sea Story	A tale of nautical or airborne derring-do. Differs from a fairy tale only in that while a fairy tale begins "Once upon a time", a sea story begins either "There I was", (aviation version) or "This is no shit", (Seaborne version).
Sea Wolf	Missile.
Seaworthy	A vessel capable of withstanding normal heavy weather.
Shake A Leg	An admonishment to move faster.
Shellback	A worthy person who has crossed

the equator and survived the punishment given by King Neptune court for the offence of being a pollywog.

Ship's Company	Refers to the officers and men assigned to the ship.
Shipshape	Neat, clean, taut, in fine shape.
Shit In It	(UK) Leave it alone.
Shitfaced	Drunk.
Shitting	Lying to, or attempting to con, someone. "Are you shitting me?"
Shoal	Similar to a reef, but more gradual in its rise from the floor of the ocean.
Shore	The land in general, but usually refers to that part adjacent to the sea.
Show a Leg	The traditional call made at reveille, it originated in the days of sail when women were let aboard ship. At reveille, a woman in her hammock would display a leg thereby was not required to turn out.
	Slang term for ordering men to turn out, originated in King George III's time, when women were allowed to accompany sailors on long voyages.

It was customary when ordering seamen from their bunks, for the bos'un to demand, "show a leg". If the leg was covered by a stocking, he knew it belonged to a woman; otherwise the skulker would promptly be routed from his bunk.

Sick Bay — Ship's hospital or dispensary. Ship's hospitals were originally known as "Sick Berths", but as they were generally located in the rounded sterns of the old battle-wagons, their contours suggested a "bay", and the latter name was given them.

Sippers — (RN) Drinks, usually containing alcohol.

Sitrep — Situation Report.

Skate — One who avoids work.

Skipper — Commanding Officer. Apparently from the Dutch "Schipper", which means, essentially "he who ships".

Skivvies — Navy slang for men's underwear.

Skua — Missile.

Skylarking — First coined to express the fun enjoyed by robust young seamen who would scramble to the fighting-tops of ships and descend to the decks by sliding down the backstays. Now used to describe someone who is goofing off.

To engage on irresponsible horseplay.

Slosher	(RN) The cook, or the cook's helper.
Slush Fund	The money accumulated by the ship's cook through the sale of slush, the salty fat which collected during the boiling of salt meat abroad ship. The sailors used the slush on their biscuits, and the cook got to keep the money.
Smart	Snappy, seamanlike, shipshape.
Smoking Lamp	From the square-rigger days, a lamp from which personnel could light their pipes or cigars. In contemporary usage, signifies whether smoking is permitted or not. If the smoking lamp is out, no smoking is permitted.
Snorkers	(RN) Sausages.
Sod's Opera	(UK) An impromptu variety show put on by the ship's company, usually of a bawdy nature.

Son of a Gun	Traditionally, a male child born (or conceived) afloat. An archaic term from the days of sail, when crewmen were typically not let ashore for fear or desertion. Women were let aboard (the regulation said "wives", but this was immediately and widely ignored, or at least winked at), and even carried at sea at times.
	This term dates back to when men of certain ratings, including gunners and gunners mates, were allowed to take their wives along to sea with them. If a boy was born on the voyage, he was half-humorously, half-contemptuously referred to as a "son of a gun".
Spanner	(RN) Wrench.
Sparker, Sparks	(RN) Radio Operator.
Speed Feed	Fast food applied at war.
Splash	Signifies the kill of an aircraft.
Splice	The act of making an eye, or of joining lines or wires together, by intertwining strands; the joint so made.

Splice the Main Brace	Have a drink. Originated in the days of the sailing navies.
Squadron	Two or more divisions of ships or aircrafts.
Square Away	Put in proper order; make things shipshape. Meaning everything in its proper place or order. A phrase which described a square-rigged ship bracing her yards to run away before the wind.
Stanchions	Vertical posts used for supporting decks; smaller, similar posts used for supporting lifelines, awnings, and so on.
Stand By	To prepare for or make ready to.
Starboard	Direction of the right or the centreline of boat or ship as one faces forward.
Starboard Side	Because the Vikings shipped their star (steering) oar on the right hand side of their vessels, and called the side of a ship its "board", the right hand side of vessels has ever since been designated as the "starboard" side.
Station Card	A chit granting permission for a

	junior enlisted sailor to go on leave. Usually implies that all his assigned work is done and he is not in trouble at the moment.
Stern	Back of ship.
Stern Light	White navigation light that can been seen only from astern to six points on either quarter (total of twelve points, or 135 degrees).
Stoker, Stokes	(RN) Marine Engineering Mechanical, Technician or Artificer.
Stores	(1) (service of Supply) Almost anything which is handled or consumed aboard ship, e.g. food, spare parts, etc. (2) (Aviation) Weapons or other devices which can be carried by an aircraft.
Stow	To put gear in its proper place. To store or pack articles or cargo in a space.
Stow	Put away.
Stripey	(RN) Able rate with two or three good conduct badges.
Super Etendard	Argentinian aircraft.
Swain	(RN) Ship's Coxswain.

T

TACTAS	Tactical Towed Array Sonar.
T.Z	Total Exclusion Zone.
Tactical Diameter	The diameter of the circle first described by a ship's turn. Tactical diameter is larger than final diameter due to the momentum of the ship, which derives the ship outside of the arc of its turn at first.
Tail	Towed sonar array.
Tarpaulin	Canvas used as a cover.
Thwart	Plank set athwartships just below the gunwales in an open boat; act as a set and provides support to the sides.
Tilly	Crew bus or other transport.
Tinnies	Tinned beer.
Toasts	In the British Empire, toasts were drunk at dinner to the reigning monarch (also known as "the loyal toast"). The Navy eventually received special permission to drink the loyal toast while seated (due to the lack of headroom common to ships of the day). In addition,

traditional toasts were drunk on specific days of the week. They were:

Monday – "Our ships at sea".

Tuesday – "Our native land".

Wednesday – "Ourselves and no one like us".

Thursday – "A bloody war or a sickly season" (and therefore more rapid promotion).

A variant was "A bloody war and quick promotion".

Friday – "A willing foe and searoom".

Saturday – "Sweethearts and wives". (someone would usually pipe up "and may they never meet!")

Sunday – "Absent friends".

Topside	General term referring to weather decks.
Tot	Measure of Rum.
	(RN) A half-gill measure of Pusser's Rum (approximately two fluid ounces). Used to be daily issue,

served neat to Chiefs and Petty Officers; mixed with two parts water for other rates.

Turn In   Retire to bed.

Turn Out   Get out of bed.

Turn To   An order to begin work. Starting work.

Two-and-a-half ringer (RN) Lieutenant Commander.

U

UXB   Unexploded bomb.

Upper Deck   Compartments outside ship.

V

VertRep   Vertical Replenishment. (Bringing stores aboard ship by use of a helicopter.)

Victuals   Food.

Volumetric measure:-

4 gills make a pint

2 pints a quart

2 quarts a pottle

2 pottles a gallon

8 gallons a firkin

2 firkin a kilderkin

2 kilderkin a barrel

2 barrels a hogshead

2 hogsheads a pipe

2 pipe or three punchoens a tun

In brief, then, a gill is a quarter of a pint, where a pint is twenty fluid ounces.

W

WEO	Weapons Electrical Officer.
WO	Warrant Officer.
Waffos	Fleet Air Arm.
Wafoo, Wafu	(RN) Naval aviator; Fleet Air Arm personnel.
Waist	The amidships section of the main deck.
Wardroom	(1) A compartment aboard ship near officers' stateroom used as officers' mess room. The wardroom originally was known as the

Wardrobe Room, being the place where officers kept their spare wearing apparel and also any loot they won while on service. It was not until years later that it served its present purpose and became the officers' mess room. May also be used for meetings, briefings, etc; (2) The complement of officers aboard ship.

Officers' messing compartment.

Warning (Red, Yellow, White)

Reports the threat status. "Red" signifies attack imminent, or ongoing. "Yellow" means attack is likely. "White" signifies attack unlikely.

Watch

The standing of duty shifts, follows:

00:00 – 04:00 – Midwatch

04:00 – 08:00 – Morning Watch

08:00 – 12:00 – Forenoon Watch

12:00 – 16:00 – Afternoon Watch

16:00 – 18:00 – First Dogwatch

18:00 – 20:00 – Second Dogwatch

20:00 – 24:00 – Evening Watch

	The purpose of the dogwatches is to permit the watchstanders to eat the evening meal. These watches are said to be "dogged".
Wets	(RN) Drinks.
Whinge	(UK) To whine with extreme overtones of self-pity.
Winger	Mate, buddy, or pal.

X

XO	Executive Officer. Second-in-command of a vessel.

Y

Yardarm	The port or starboard half of a yard is the port or starboard yardarm.
Yeomen	Senior Rate Signals.

Z

ZULU Time	Greenwich Mean Time (GMT). Used in radio traffic when the origin of a dispatch is expressed in GMT, i.e. "17:00 ZULU".

Zs   – Sleep, or snoring "Let's go bag some Zs".

"The Book Ends on this Note"

Great Britain has never been short of National Heroes from our men and women over the centuries, be it on land, sea or air in their achievements to defend our Country in battle or a quest for a personal challenge in normal everyday life. So going back to the 16th Century to our present 21st Century here are just a very few achievements and quests from the very people of our land in the past and present.

1552 – 1618

Sir Walter Raleigh – Navigator Author and Poet

1588 – June

Sir Francis Drake – Defeat of the Spanish Armada

1697 – 1762

Admiral Sir George Anson – Navigator

1728 – 1779

Captain James Cook (Royal Navy) – Famous Explorer,

Navigator and Maritime Pioneer. Died in Hawaii after a local brawl. He also was in Command of HMS Resolution at the time of his death.

1805 – 21st October

Admiral Lord Nelson – Battle of Trafalger.

1815 – 18th June

The Duke of Wellington – Battle of Waterloo.

1846 – 1848

Rear Admiral Sir John Franklin – Discoverer at the North West Passage and an Explorer of the Arctic. Died on June 11th 1847 near King William Islands on this disastrous voyage due to being locked in pack ice for two years.

1841 – 1920

Admiral Sir John Fisher – 1st Baron

Captain Robert Scott (Royal Navy). Expedition to the Arctic on HMS Discovery. Unfortunately this ended in failure trying to get to the North Pole.

1859 – 1935

Admiral of the Fleet Sir John Rushworth Jellicoe (1st Earl Jellicoe) Famous for the 1916 Jutland War.

Admiral Sir David Beatty – Again famous for the Jutland War.

1934 – 1945

Sir Winston Churchill – British Prime Minister in the

Second World War. It is also famously known during the Blitz of London when King George VI and Queen Elizabeth were advised to leave London, Queen Elizabeth reply was quite frank as she is known to have said "The King is not prepared to leave London, so therefore neither am I and if I'm not prepared to leave without our King nor will my children (Elizabeth II our present Queen and Princess Margaret).

Field Marshall Bernard Montgomery (1887 – 1976) – Famous in the Second World War and who was also the Highest Ranking Officer in the field at the time.

Sir Edmund Hillary – First attempted to climb Mount Everest.

Sir Francis Chichester – Sailed around the World single handed on Gypsy Moth IV completed the voyage on the 28th May 1967.

Sir Chay Blyth – Sailed around the World non-stop in his 59ft Ketch "British Steel" single handed.

Admiral Sir Sandy Woodward – Task Force Commander for the Falklands War.

Admiral Sir Alan West – Now our First Sea Lord who was the Commanding Officer on HMS Ardent in the Falklands War. Unfortunately the ship was lost with many lives due to the Argentinian Air Strikes.

Ellen MacArthur – Record time holder for the single handed sailing around the World of 27,354 miles in 71 days and 14hrs 18min + 33secs. Beating the previous record holder Francis Joyon who completed it in 72 days 22hrs 54mins and 22secs therefore she beat the record by one day 8hrs 35mins and 49secs.

1970 – Sun 9th Nov

Barrie Fieldgate conquers the climbing of the famous HMS Ganges main mast after three attempts to reach the top. The remarkable achievement was witnessed by one of his Messmates who watched from the ground. Although this was nerve-racking experience, minute by minute he edges towards the summit. The last twenty feet prove to be the most daunting as there are no wire or rope supports to reach out to while going up the pole. Finally he clambers on to the tiny button at the very top and, with very shaky legs, he manages to put the narrow metal bar, which is in the middle of button (metal disc), between his legs. Then, as Naval Tradition states, he salutes the four corners of HMS Ganges, before making a hasty retreat down by the use of the main jackstay at the top, and slides down this to reach the ground. (Sorry! But I couldn't resist adding this to the list of achievements!)

THE END

Falklands Medal and Rosette, 1982.

Long Service and Good Conduct Medals.

Admiral Horatio Nelson.